Industrial Revolution 4.0, Tech Giants, and Digitized Societies

Tai Wei Lim

Industrial Revolution 4.0, Tech Giants, and Digitized Societies

palgrave
macmillan

Tai Wei Lim
Singapore University of Social Sciences
Singapore, Singapore

ISBN 978-981-13-7469-2   ISBN 978-981-13-7470-8   (eBook)
https://doi.org/10.1007/978-981-13-7470-8

Cover illustration: Haiyin Wang/Alamy Stock Photo

This Palgrave Macmillan imprint is published by the registered company Springer Nature
Singapore Pte Ltd.
The registered company address is: 152 Beach Road, #21-01/04 Gateway East, Singapore
189721, Singapore

CONTENTS

PART I

Section on Industrial Revolution 4.0, Tech Giants, and Digitized Societies

Tech Giants, Digitized Workplaces and Societies: Comparative Area Studies Analyses of North American and East Asian Responses to Industrial Revolution 4.0

INTRODUCTION AND LITERATURE SURVEY

An example of digital systems in its tangible form is a hardware product like computers and they are binary systems. They use a series of 1s and 0s to create instructions to run a programme. This lies at the heart of all digital devices and hardware. Digital electronic reader devices like Compact Disc (CD) players, hard discs, digital cameras and video recorders also read instructions that consist of 1s and 0s. Sounds are only one form of data that can be stored in an analogue or a digital format. In the field of music, for example, cassette tape recorders, LP record players, video recorders (including VCRs) are all examples of analogue machines that read off magnetic tapes. No binary systems are involved. An LP player has a pin that reads information off the uneven skid lines of the machine and converts them into sounds.

Analogue technologies record the exact sounds but digital technologies try to approximate sounds sound waves using 1s and 0s when the machine is an audio device. Computers can only work with binary systems (digital systems) and therefore analogue sounds have to be converted to digital bits so that sound waves and music can be edited and manipulated with special effects. Digital information is intangible and their integrity does not decrease with time, unlike analogue media for recording sounds. The same feature of permanence in data storage applies to other forms of data as well. Starting from 2002, devices across the world started storing data in digital platforms more than analogue platforms and, since then, human progress towards total digitization of data has not let up.[1] Digital technologies and the data they store

---

[1] Leontiou, Andrea, "World's Shift from Analog to Digital Is Nearly Complete" dated 2 October 2011 in NBCNews.com [downloaded on 1 January 2017], available at http://www.nbcnews.com/id/41516959/ns/technology_and_science-innovation/t/worlds-shift-analog-digital-nearly-complete/#.WulhlqSFOUk.

© The Author(s) 2019
T. W. Lim, *Industrial Revolution 4.0, Tech Giants, and Digitized Societies*,
https://doi.org/10.1007/978-981-13-7470-8_1

are the basis and foundation of the current digital revolution. The ongoing digital and robotics revolutions form the core subject of analysis in this publication.

This writing was conceptualized as a monograph that can also be used as a textbook for readers who are interested to look at the digital revolution in multifaceted and multidisciplinary perspectives. Due to the complexity of the subject matter, including the impact of digital technologies on human lives, jobs and societies, the author selected an area studies approach to look at the subject matter. Area studies have the advantage of being multidisciplinary and so, embedded in this writing, one can find arguments, points, observations and analyses related to the emergence of the digital world. The lens and elements of political science, political economy, public policy analyses, international relations, cultural studies, technology studies, sociology/anthropology, contemporary China studies (Sinology) and history are utilized in this area studies approach to understanding the emergence of the digital economy, tech giants and the virtually interconnected world. The multidisciplinary area studies approach also does justice to the complexity of the subject matter. It does not pretend to be comprehensive but provides a survey into some of the major issues confronted in Industrial Revolution 4.0, especially in the East Asian context.

Another reason for utilizing area studies is most tech companies at the forefront of Industrial Revolution 4.0 originate either from the US or China and this is indicated in almost all major rankings of digital tech multinationals in the world. Outside the two countries, there are a small number of companies from the European Union (EU) and from East Asia (e.g. South Korea) in the same rankings, which are otherwise dominated mainly by American and Chinese companies. The headquarters of major tech giants in the world are now found in US's Silicon Valley or Shenzhen/Zhongguancun/Haidian/Shanghai in China. Interestingly, the largest tech companies in the US and China are mirror images of each other. Baidu is China's foremost search engine as Google is for the US and the rest of the world. Alibaba.com is China's answer to US's Amazon.com. WeChat is the Chinese counterpart to Silicon Valley's Facebook. Thus, for the first time in human history, there are two parallel universes in the virtual world headed respectively by two great economic powers.

Given that Chinese tech companies operate in half of this digital space, an area studies approach is utilized to understand China's positionality in this digital revolution. These dominant digital multinationals in the US and China are often collectively known as tech "giants" or tech "titans" in the popular media, trade professional books and academic writings. Some have even compared them with the colonial empires of yore or monopolistic trading companies like the British or Dutch East Indies Company (V.O.C in the Dutch case) of the eighteenth and nineteenth centuries. Their dominance (and the historical/sociopolitical events leading up to their dominance) as well as support and resistance to their continued powerful positions by equally powerful domestic, regional and international organizations, states and individuals will be examined in the volume.

There is a political-economic element to this, especially in the case of China or US companies in the EU. The commercial and economic dominance of tech giant/titans have attracted the attention of the powerful Chinese state (currently run by a strongman regime at the point of this writing) and the supranational state entity of the EU. The dominance of tech giants has provoked responses from powerful entities to curtail some activities of these tech giants/titans. Some of these tech giant companies were fined for unfair practices in the EU while others were cited for privacy concerns. Some tech giants/titans were also accused by the EU and other stakeholders of hoarding IT human resources talents within a closed circle or restrict the mobility of these individuals through tacit agreements. Besides the EU, the anti-monopoly and antitrust instincts in the US is also agitating to break up monopolies and titans if they are proven to practise unfair competition. American suspicions of any excessively large business entity stimulate public opinion, media commentaries and legal enforcement against those companies. There is an anti-monopoly instinct in American capitalism which is counterbalanced by an equally powerful instinct to recognize and reward innovative companies.

State regulators are watching the activities of the tech giants closely. Some activities of these tech giants have not gone unnoticed. Tech giants are also so large that they buy over innovative small companies when they pose a threat to the giants' technologies, or if they spot a good deal to purchase an innovative company. An example often cited by existing literatures is Facebook's takeover of WhatsApp for a perceived exorbitant price. For some detractors of the tech giants, they argue that users of the digital products are actually not end customers but suppliers since their personal data is sold to a third party Socially, dependence on smartphone, digital apps and online software have also resulted in the reduction of face-to-face (F2F) interactions and personalized communication between humans. Resistance and punitive measures by states and super-states as well as the social consequences of overdependence on digital tech giants and their products will be examined in this writing.

This writing will also examine the perspectives of users who benefit from using the products and services of tech companies. Not everyone is against the dominance of the tech giants or/and the effective and attractive products they offer. Some of these products like Facebook are free of charge. Tech giants are nimble and reactive to the market. They are also efficient in cutting down costs due to efficient logistics, digitization of information that can be communicated instantaneously for rapid decision-making and reduction of red tape, fast to accept innovative products and implement new technologies and unburdened by old school approaches that are swept away by strong charismatic leadership. These are the usual characteristics of successful tech giants. Many also try to upgrade their public image by engaging in charitable, philanthropic and ethically conscious community work. This is a deliberate effort to ratchet up the companies' image through Corporate Social Responsibility (CSR). Therefore, their supporters argue they are more ethically conscious than old school industrial giants. Supporters of the tech giants argue that they should not be penalized for being successful in cornering market shares and that free market should be allowed to determine their successes and failures in the future.

In this sense, the publication recognizes and highlights the political implications of the rise and emergence of tech giants and the benefits and challenges they bring about. The tech giants themselves defend their record as job generators in that it works with a large number of suppliers and contractors in logistics, product supply, R&D, deliveries, construction work for its facilities, etc. These suppliers, subcontractors can handle certain niche assignments more nimbly and efficiently than the tech giants. Because of these suppliers and subcontractors, tech giants argue they are net jobs creators and not destroyers. They support a whole ecology of workers, entrepreneurs, employees and part-timers through the companies they deal with. In this way, the tech giants behave like the industrial giants before them, except nimbler and with more efficient logistical chains. Therefore, they should not be treated any differently from other industrial giants. In the Chinese case, the tech giants are supported by the state, thus, they are even more complementary with state requirements. It also makes the tech giants more dependent on the authorities. Thus, punitive actions can be swift if there was dissonance between state interests and tech giants' business activities. Authoritarian governments can ban, fine or publicly criticize tech giants if they fall out of line using their trump card which is an access to a profitable consumer market.

This monograph examines the digital revolution from a new perspective in that the latest digital and innovative developments are not only influencing Asia and especially China, but these changes are not only taking place in the Western world alone. It shows that influential factors such as consumers, history and political science have been neglected in the past and play a major role in innovation development as well as in modern economies. A more holistic approach in presenting business processes to students is very important and has been neglected in the past. In this way, this writing is at the vanguard of a new way of writing the Industrial Revolution 4.0 and its impact on developed societies. This can be divided into 4 major parts. First, this project traces the history of industrial revolutions 4.0 (Industry 4.0) in different regions such as Japan, the EU, US, Singapore, ASEAN (Association of Southeast Asian Nations), Chinese Taipei/Taiwan, Hong Kong Special Administration Region (SAR) and mainland China (People's Republic of China). Second, it further explores the specific case study of China. Section A in particular allows us to understand the discursive development of China's latest tech "giants" such as Alibaba, Huawei, WeChat etc. Third, it discusses the drawbacks of the Industrial Revolution 4.0 by highlighting the long-term implications of the rise and emergence of these tech giants. Lastly, this publication contemplates how the younger generation can equip themselves to face challenges in the future workforce brought about by the technological disruptions.

Most textbooks however only look at these topics from a very particular perspective. The book is trying to help students understand that the impact on digital technologies goes beyond business processes. Technology management and innovation are topics that need to be more prominent in business studies and business schools. On top of this, this writing embeds the topic in other areas (such as history, international business, consumer behaviour) as well which are equally relevant and interesting and has not be done so far in existing literatures. This perspective can help readers understand the interactions—not only between different scientific disciplines—but between different players and nations in the world economy. In terms of its textbook features, this writing is useful for university learners in picking up the subject of the fourth industrial revolution in broadly understood terms. It examines this subject by looking at the first three industrial revolutions and their effects on society giving particular attention to the job market. It then spends the bulk of the book examining the Fourth Industrial Revolution—the role of globalization and technology in impacting work—giving especial attention to American and Chinese companies. The textbook feature also comes with a number of cases studies, exercises and answer banks.

Existing Literatures

Several books were examined for this writing. The first publication is *What to Do When Machines Do Everything: How to Get Ahead in a World of AI, Algorithms, Bots, and Big Data* written by Malcolm Frank/Paul Roehrig/Ben Pring published by Wiley. This important publication paints the scenario of cutting-edge technologies like Artificial Intelligence (A.I.) and robots going mainstream and featuring in a major way in the lives of human workplaces and homes. The author comes up with some strategies to cope with this automated digital world. It construes the digital revolution in binary terms, either evolve or be left behind and that is the main message of the authors. Malcolm Frank, Paul Roehrig and Ben Pring's publication provides good insights into tech developments in the near future and some ideas about coping mechanism. Like many publications in the English language, it does not differentiate or highlight the very different political-economic and sociopolitical contexts of the US and China, accounting for differences between the developments of tech giants/titans in both countries. This writing value-adds to the Wiley publication by discussing this aspect and situating the discussion in East Asia. Another contribution made by this writing to Frank, Roehrig and Pring's co-authored book is its multidisciplinary analysis. While the Wiley publication is oriented towards business-centred trade professional readers, this writing is mainly embedded in social scientific discussions. The analyses in this writing are also country-specific following area studies format. It seeks to understand, for example, Chinese ideas about digital developments through its sociopolitical and socioeconomic lens. Very often, business imperatives alone cannot fully explain Chinese policy decisions and/or implementation. Contemporary Sinology helps to decode the complexities in this area.

This writing also taps into trade professional publications as the subject matter is still very new and trade professional publications offer a popular understanding of ongoing changes brought about by digital technologies. A good example of this genre is Duncan Clark's *Alibaba: The House That Jack Ma Built* published by Ecco in 2016. This book was written from the perspective of someone who knew Ma personally as an early advisor to the company and a long-time acquaintance of the founder himself. In this manner, Clark uses the advantage of a standpoint view to articulate the insights behind the emergence of a powerful Chinese company in the digital world. Such publications value-add to books published by academic presses that tend to be stronger on theoretical ideas. It articulates real world thinking and reflects practical experience in the digital industry.

Porter Erisman is another author (of *Alibaba's World: How a Remarkable Chinese Company Is Changing the Face of Global Business*) who has personal experience in running the company as Alibaba's Vice President and worked on past projects related to the rise of Alibaba and Jack Ma. He is also well-versed in emerging markets and his book serves as another updated resource on the Chinese tech world, again from a trade professional perspective. Clark and Erisman's narratives corroborate each other. It also shows the contrast between running the company as an advisor and an executive who is highly involved in the daily decisions of the company. Taken together, both perspectives can provide a more complete picture of the company and its founder. This writing's contribution to the abovementioned two books is to situate the same subject matter in a broader comparative context, comparing and contrasting the US and Chinese visions and worldviews for the digital universes of the present and the future workplaces and societies. This writing's multidisciplinary approach can better integrate Erisman and Clark's insightful empirical details into the contents to analyze the digital economy's overall development and contextualize them in the framework of general changes taking place in human spaces. It can also be contextualized against the backdrop of rising economic competition between US and Chinese companies in capturing their respective domestic market shares as well as lure the world's internet users.

Mike Hoefflinger's *Becoming Facebook: The 10 Challenges That Defined the Company That's Disrupting the World* published by AMACOM in 2017 is the US counterpart to the two books above on Alibaba. Hoefflinger wrote his book from an insider perspective as a computer engineer and marketing innovator who served alongside COO Sheryl Sandberg. Like Clark and Erisman's book, Hoefflinger also writes from a standpoint perspective and integrates real practical experience into his publication. It is a contemporary historical account of the company, including its trials and tribulations, as well as successes. The gradual maturity of Facebook as a tech giant is also articulated in the publication. Contrasting the developmental histories of Facebook and Alibaba distills the political-economic and environmental conditions from which these tech giants emerged.

The books mentioned above with historical narratives of US or Chinese tech giants are the newest publications on the subject matter at the time of this writing and are only a sample of publications whose insights are integrated, corroborated or examined in this writing. But, they are not the only resources consulted for this project. This writing also taps into numerous media resources, company reports, government white papers, policy papers/ briefs, think tank papers and other secondary sources useful for interpretive work. These materials were curated by the author for interpretive work. In addition to interpretive work, the author will also draw insights from conversations with experts on the subject matter, academic conferences/seminars with relevant themes, intellectual exchanges and site visits to the workplaces transformed by digital technologies. The author's work in the private sector's non-governmental organizations (NGOs) provides a practical insight into the needs of a digital economy from the enterprise perspective in addition to his academic work.

Situated in ASEAN, a regional organization often characterized as occupying the driver's seat in regionalism in East Asia, the author has the unique perspective of viewing the development of digital economies and capabilities of two great economic superpowers from afar, through objective eyes and sufficient distance from the two leading drivers of digital developments. At the same time, ASEAN is an old friend of the US and its East Asian alliance network as well as a partner with China's Belt and Road Initiative (BRI) which also has a digital/cyberspace element. ASEAN under the advocacy of its 2018 Chair Singapore is trying to construct a network of smart cities and may welcome technologies from the West, China and India for this mega-project. US's digital products are used almost universally in the region and needs no further elaboration. In the popular cultural realm, Facebook (FB) has attracted users from the region and is part of youth culture as they curate and record their daily lives. Young Southeast Asians are also increasingly using social media apps to interact and chat with each other. Smartphones installed with Android, Apple operating system (OS) or Microsoft OS have proliferated all over the region. US is the universal benchmark for what's cool and its soft cultural power in this aspect is very strong. Southeast Asian consume US digital products and services enthusiastically.

China is also building communication networks and infrastructure under the Belt and Road Initiative (BRI, formerly known as One Belt One Road or OBOR), and the main participants in such projects are the state-owned construction and telecommunications companies (or SOEs, State-Owned Enterprises). Thailand and Pakistan have already signed up for integration into the Beidou satellite (global positioning) project. When these countries' infrastructures are gradually built up and their logistics improved, China can start selling their goods to them. Chinese mobile phones built by Huawei is a popular item in Southeast Asia. Southeast Asians also use WeChat to communicate with their friends in China or use the WeChat app in the smartphone to pay for shopping items when they are touring China. Simultaneous engagement with the US and China gives ASEAN societies a unique perspective on digital developments (including cooperation and rivalries). ASEAN is perhaps described aptly as an island in the great ocean watching two large ships (US and China) passing by in two different directions. Its perspective is grounded on an unmoving island object (symbolizing neutrality and objectivity) while the crew on both ships are watching each other as their ships navigate past each other (symbolizing a subjective view of the event, depending on which ship one is aboard).

HISTORICAL BACKGROUND

Historically, the advent of technology has helped to improve productivity and moved humans to achieve higher value-added work outputs. In the first industrial revolution, looms replaced manual labour in manufacturing textiles. During this revolution, women were the unsung heroes of the era as their nimble fingers and dexterity in operating loom machines saw them hired in large numbers in the factories that produced the textiles. As the first industrial revolution progresses, brute strength of beasts and human labour were gradually substituted by mechanical machines operated on human-generated forms of energies. In the latter half of the first industrial revolution, steam engines created the energy output necessary to operate the mechanical machines that were previously powered and limited by brute strength of domesticated animals. This greatly increased the effectiveness of work output and, at the same time, it started the process of globalization that would make the world smaller through the maritime route. Steam engines made it possible for humankind to travel against weather patterns. In the maritime silk route from Europe through the horn of Africa, Arabian Seas, Indian Ocean and Straits of Malacca for example, a route that was plied by the Arabs, Persians, Sung (also spelt as Song) Chinese and then the Portuguese and Dutch in that order, sailing boats travelled according to the monsoon patterns, dependent on the seasonal direction of the wind. The Portuguese efforts at mercantile trade, resource exploitation and eventually colonization paved the way for the decline of the historical overland Silk Road.

But, with the invention of the steam engine, British merchant and naval ships were able to ply the seas at will without restrictions from wind directions. It also made the British a world naval power. Globalization 1.0 would henceforth continue unabated with the steam engine powering locomotives penetrating into the hinterlands of great continents, the first trans-Atlantic flight, invention of high-speed rail (HSR), invention of jet engines and subsequently the commercial airliners flying the friendly skies. Air travel proliferated with the onset of budget airlines, making travel extremely convenient and affordable for many tourists. Meanwhile, in terms of manufacturing aspects, the early twentieth-century stages of the first industrial revolution enters a productivity hike phase with Taylorism and Fordism. Taylorism utilized stop motion techniques to standardize and reduce the number of steps needed to manufacture a product. It made the conveyor belt format of production possible. Fordism went a step ahead and made the products affordable for the workers who manufactured them. This effectively creates a new phase of mass production, one that would create a large middle class as Industrial Revolution 1.0 and Globalization 1.0 benefits a large swath of the world, a process that continues with some major interruptions (e.g. the Great Depression, World Wars I/II, etc.) into the booming post-war 1960s.

In the 1960s and 1970s, the world would experience Industrial Revolution 2.0 with the advent of electronic transistors manufacturing, home consumer electronics and the world's first mainframe and then personal computers. This revolution created three very much sought-after "jewels" in the household: washing machine, television and refrigerator. This was later accompanied by the proliferation of the microwave oven, based on technologies originally designed for the military. Some of the first industrial robots also appeared in this era in the US (Detroit, Michigan to be specific) car manufacturing industry for applying paint jobs as paint pigment/fumes was toxic and hazardous to human health. In Japan, due to rising labour costs and surging demand during its economic high growth period in the 1960s, industrial robots were utilized in the manufacturing sector to meet heightened demand for its consumer products. This was especially the case in its economic boom decades that lasted from the late 1970s to the 1980s and robots may eventually replace some aspects of human labour to cope with manpower shortage arising from an ageing population in that country. (Refer to Chapter 6 [Case Study 1 on Japan's Future Robot Replacement] for more details.)

Industrial Revolution 2.0 displaced human jobs as robots, automation and mechanical machines became the workhorses of mass manufacturing industries. While human jobs were displaced, robots were still prohibitively expensive, represented long-term investments and their installation faced the wrath of trade unions so their numbers were mitigated and curtailed based on the price factor and social conditions. Moreover, the machines still needed human operators, maintenance crew and quality control supervisors. Thus, Industrial Revolution 2.0 prescribed a continued role for humankind. During this phase of Industrial Revolution, robots were also programmed by humans and were incapable making autonomous decisions, nor were they self-thinking and most did not have self-learning capabilities that can emulate and clone human actions or decisions. Most did not have A.I. capabilities, the robots did exactly what they were programmed to do. If an error was made by a robot, it was considered a programming error made by a human programmer.

Industrial Revolution 3.0 began to assume a weightless form as it started to venture out into cyberspace. It was also the beachhead for Globalization 2.0 as Information and Communication Technologies (ICT) shrunk the world even faster, much more so than even the fastest transportation technologies, including jet engines that can now fly faster than the speed of sound. Communication and interactions became instantaneous in this era. Message boards, emails, chatrooms and BBS emerged for people to communicate with each other globally. These developments were made possible through the invention of an internet protocol that enabled computers to become communication devices that linked up each other, even across different computer brands and makes. Industrial Revolution 3.0 made it possible to create a collective knowledge base with information that can be shared with each other across the world. This universal collective knowledge base was known as the Internet. [The Internet of Things (IoT), a much later development, will be discussed in Part I Chapter 3.] Items from this global knowledge base can be drawn up using internet search engines that works on algorithms to index the search and make it more precise. Several generations of search engines emerged before one improved on and perfected the search through algorithms that proved to be more precise than its competitors and Google was born. The Internet was originally designed to survive a nuclear war and keep communications going among the US alliance network.

Finally, in the twenty-first century, the world arrived on the cusp of Industrial Revolution 4.0, a world that would include the emergence of A.I., robots, autonomous vehicles, algorithm-controlled machines, autonomous weapons systems, algorithm-based predictive behaviour software/apps, and the onset of a social media revolution. Facebook is a good example of this social media revolution. Facebook was created for users who were interested to put their personal data online in the form of comments, photos, emoticons and textual information and then share it with other members of their network or/and with the public in general. It was meant to be a free platform that allows people to share information easily and even do their own publicity stunts and self-marketing. Facebook was a democratic platform where people could post things easily without much technical knowledge needed. People could also fact-check their governments' materials and debunk propaganda. In fact, it facilitated revolutions like Arab Spring when incidents of abuse and inequity provoked the masses to topple an authoritarian government. Because Facebook could round up and connect friends, family and like-minded individuals together, ideas could be disseminated quickly to a target audience. But, at the same time, organizations and agencies other than Facebook could also hack into the database and/or data were sold by Facebook to paying parties legally. To many individuals who advocate privacy and cherish confidentiality, this was a negative aspect of Facebook's social media platform. Having said that, Facebook offers convenience for most users when tapping into their services and sharing.

Fake news, people getting jealous and emotional at each other's posts and racist/misogynistic posts now coexist with online friendships, greater inter-cultural/inter-religious understanding between societies and a smaller, more interdependent world. In other worlds, digital social media is a double-edged sword that can benefit societies as well as introduce more fissures into their social fabric. Fake news was in focus in the international media at the point of writing this volume. Fake news was cited for influencing governments and elections, something made possible by the fact that a large number of people now obtain their news feed from social media. These news are either recommended to them by the app (and its preference-detecting algorithm) or by family and friends through social media. The explosion of information, especially through the use of social media, facilitated the collection of massive amounts of data.

Human resource departments would also have to deal with the issue of transparency. Due to personal postings by individuals and, because of the ambiguous blurred lines between personal and work lives, materials related to company operations, workings, culture and workplace politics are sometimes posted online and made public. This applies to many companies in the world. Thus, suddenly, there is a rich tapestry of information about different work cultures, office political environments, personal celebrations and concerns available for all to see. It also empowers deep throat cultures, where gossips, rumours and scandals can break out easily. Such high levels of transparency is both an advantage and disadvantage for companies. On the positive side, it is a rich treasure trove of information for different stakeholders to extract precedents, case studies, empirical examples and cross-cultural comparative perspectives. On the negative side, issues of privacy, hacking, confidentiality, data protection, cybersecurity will come into play, especially if private, personal and/or confidential data is lost, stolen or hacked into.

How are some of these data gathered? All digital devices that humans use, especially if they are enabled online, will leave digital traces that can be tracked by companies and the state; so therefore they are all useful bits of metadata that can be reconstructed to reveal certain traits. On a daily basis, humans are already using a large number of digital devices and apps. When a human in the developed or fast-developing economy that is connected by the Internet wakes up, she/he will be messaging, Facebooking, WeChatting, Line-ing or social media communicating with other humans. When a human goes to work or school, either a smart card, a public transport payment app or Global Positioning System (GPS) in a car will be activated and more digital traces are left behind. In the course of the day, payments for consumer products, lunch and household shopping will leave more metadata through credit cards, phone payments and debit card systems.

During long rides of commuting home, another round of messages, social media checking in trains and buses is carried out. Some may even read e-books on electronic tablets or watch Netflix on smartphones. When the human individual goes for an evening jog or run in the park, the distance tracking and calorie-watching apps and smart watches clock up another round of metadata. At night before the human goes to sleep, she/he releases another round of metadata when the human checks the smartphone and social media apps again. All this data generation is made possible by the convergence of a large number of electronic devices, apps and software through online link-ups and smartphone use. When such individual routines are repeated over a sufficient period of time, it shows certain characteristics, inclinations, personality traits, consumption preferences and other patterns over time. Predictive analyses then becomes possible and eventually these machines, algorithms and apps will start prescribing choices for the individual users based on recorded or predicted preferences. And, when such data are collected from a large population, the analysis at the macro level becomes more accurate (that is why India and China are ideal labs for big data collection). That is why data mining is so profitable for the digital giants. Such data are then sold to third parties, including private sector firms and state-linked agencies. They are commercially useful and valuable for public security evaluations.

But Big Data can also be used in positive ways: tracking and predicting earthquakes, infections, logistical/transportation movements, etc. Therefore, regulators, state and society have to work together to decide how big data should be utilized in their own countries. Tech giants and titans can now collect and scan data from entire societies, countries, organizations and cities. These firms collect so much data that they are sometimes nicknamed or even self-identified as data firms. Data also allows their users to carry out mass marketing, garner feedback for products/services and even make predictive analyses on certain behavioural traits. For the first time, humankind could also connect physical machines and robots with autonomous decision making platforms so that the virtual and physical worlds are bridged together. This then brings humankind to debate and focus on a central focus for them: What is then the role of humankind in Industrial Revolution 4.0? The next chapter discusses this question in the context of the workplace of the future and the emergence of A.I. and Industry 4.0 smart technologies. In terms of chapterization, this volume is divided into three Parts:

Part I focuses on the theoretical and macro perspectives, contents, analyses/perspectives major arguments and theoretical frameworks.

Part II focuses on specific case studies (more focused micro examples) that are referenced and discussed in the Part I chapters.

Part III is the quizzes/exercises with their answer banks, organized in a way corresponding to each Chapter in Parts I and II.

BIBLIOGRAPHY

Leontiou, Andrea, "World's Shift from Analog to Digital Is Nearly Complete" dated 2 October 2011 in NBCNews.com [downloaded on 1 January 2017]. Available at http://www.nbcnews.com/id/41516959/ns/technology_and_science-innovation/t/worlds-shift-analog-digital-nearly-complete/#.WulhlqSFOUk.

CHAPTER 2

Digital Disruptions and the Workplace

Addressing the Digital Gap

There are lots of speculation, fallacies and pseudo-scientific statements about the potential impact of Artificial Intelligence (A.I.). Some are generated out of fear and anxieties about the unknown. Other versions claim that A.I. deep learning, convergence and singularity will happen so fast that humans will appear primitive in front of them and A.I. and their robots will study human societies like how humans observe animals (primitive lifeforms) at the zoo. Yet other versions claim that humans will be enslaved in a reversal of the originally intended scenario in which humans were supposed to be master to the machines. Many of these speculations are pseudo-scientific or speculation because nobody really knows how the digital, A.I. and robotics revolution will turn out and therefore the best bet and perhaps the only option is to be prepared for its social, economic and political impacts and address the digital gap within society.

In many economies of the world, there is a digital gap between individuals who have IT (Information Technology) skills and those who are not trained in such skills. The issue of digital gap is not new and had been debated and highlighted since the first IT boom in the 1990s. Robert Reich in US President Bill Clinton's administration has emphasized the need for training to bring everyone on board the digital revolution. In general terms, technological knowledge and knowhow have caused a differentiation between those who are highly skilled and others who have low levels of skillsets. Given the propensity for digital technologies and automation to replace humans in jobs that only requires basic skills, this has caused unemployment to increase significantly among those groups whose jobs were replaced by machines and software, resulting in the lesser skilled individuals probably belonging to low income households.

© The Author(s) 2019
T. W. Lim, *Industrial Revolution 4.0, Tech Giants, and Digitized Societies*,
https://doi.org/10.1007/978-981-13-7470-8_2

Some of the most vulnerable people when it comes to digital skills are youths. The gap in skills, availability of training and increased opportunities also motivate the mass migration of people from less to more developed economies. Host societies in the developed world as well as fast-developing large economies are keen to snap up human talents, skills labour and trained human resources in sectors where there is a global shortage of skills and digital skills is one of them. Coders, programmers, robotics engineers are among the most highly sought-after migrants. (Refer to Chapter 6 [Case Study 1] for more details on Japan's foreign talent policies to hire more Information and Communication Technology ICT personnel, especially from India.) Migration itself necessitates integration by host society and sometimes cultural differences have disrupted the harmony between host society and migrants. In the current context, this has led to political trends like Brexit and more insular policies by host governments in the US and European Union (EU). Therefore, there is also a sociopolitical element to the issue. In some societies like Japan, conservatives who adopt a cautious and meticulous approach towards immigration have looked towards technologies solutions like robotics to address the shortage of manpower brought about by an ageing population. Robots are believed to be incapable of committing crimes, able to work tirelessly and needs no social integration. (For more details on this, refer to Chapter 6 [Case Study 1].)

From the problem of unemployment caused by retrenchment to underemployment where people have not been able to access the workforce, the latest discussion has been on the topic of employability—are individuals good enough to be considered for a job? In the West alone, hundreds of millions of working-age individuals are left out of the workforce. Many more in the other parts of the world with even higher numbers of people without a job. The large economies (both developed and fast-developing) make up the bulk of these numbers and their youths needs to be equipped with digital skills or retrained for the digital economy. Besides youths, the other group that is disadvantaged are women and they are a buffer pool of labour that can be tapped upon by companies. Even elderly individuals can now be reskilled and/or re-equipped to handle physically demanding work. Elderly folks can now strap on robotic exoskeletons to enhance their physical strength to do work. (Some examples are provided in Chapter 6 [Case Study 1].) Handicapped and disabled people can potentially be fitted with bionic arms and prosthetics to lead normal productive lives. The silver generation can also be retrained in IT skills to continue with working lives beyond retirements. Technology in this sense offers beneficial solutions to humankind and their continued quest to create jobs.

But technology itself cannot offer a complete solution to job losses caused by Globalization 1.0 as the world becomes smaller and borderless. The large number of individuals who are unable to find work formed the bulwark of opposition against globalization, resulting in political phenomena like Brexit and "American First" policies. Populist calls to build a wall against immigration is based on genuine grievances and frustrations against globalization. The end of the Cold War has effectively integrated the former socialist world into its capitalist half, resulting in abundance of human labour for the world economy and large swathes of consumer markets at the same time. Globalization lifted millions of people out of poverty in world regions like East Asia (especially China), India and even Africa's economy are taking off and these rising middle-income countries have become ready consumers for the world's manufacturers and producers. But, in the advanced economies of the world, jobs have been subcontracted overseas with manufacturing jobs leaving for the "world factory" of China and the "backroom services workshop of the world" in India.

This has led to blue-collar and lower-skilled individuals in developed economies experiencing difficulties in getting jobs in the unskilled or less-skilled sectors. Developed economies have had to help ease the transition for these workers to be reskilled to get new jobs or provide welfare support for them till they are able to find jobs. Social welfare and safety nets will need to be tweaked to help individuals who are unable to find jobs or are retrenched due to outsourced jobs, jobs replaced by automation and other economic changes. Some media commentators believe that it may be possible to remigrate jobs that were previously subcontracted from developed economies to cheaper large developing economies like India and China back to the US and EU again. Automation holds the key to this great remigration of jobs back to the advanced economies. Robots that are efficient, armed with self-learning algorithms and A.I. and bereft of human attributes like fatigue, complaining and uneven levels of self-discipline can now perform manufacturing jobs better than cheaper human labour in the developing world. But, ironically and unfortunately in this sense, jobs that remigrate back to the developed world may not need human workers. The problem of employment may therefore still persist.

Governments and societies may also have to consider alternatives to conventional forms of incomes. They may need to come up with systematic ways to redeploy displaced workers, replaced by machines, cheaper foreign labour or economic migrants. Departments of Human Resource (HR), Chief Digital Officers and other stakeholders may have to reconfigure work to facilitate human workers in maximizing their productivity or multitasking in project management. Jobs can be redesigned to make better use of human skills. Versatility on the part of the workers in making such transitions (e.g. by retraining, picking up new skills or becoming an entrepreneur) will become a determinant factor in deciding their success in adapting to a digital economy. In this sense, it takes both hands to clap.

Companies may also want to adopt a gradual approach in integrating technologies into the manufacturing processes or retail services. The advantage of doing so is that it can buy some time for workers to get training or new skills for another position or a new job. Companies waiting to adopt new technologies can also have more time to evaluate their decision in adopting automation or digitalization/digitization and detect challenges and benefits. They can also determine if the move is profitable in the long run and whether it affects their traditional strengths in the face of technological changes. Moreover, other than the company's executives, customers and clients also need an adjustment period to get used to new digital platforms and technological solutions offered by the company. Customers do need time to adjust to interacting with a robot, app or software. Some scholars like Prof Gudela Grote of Switzerland's Eidgenössische Technische Hochschule (ETH) Zürich argued that a certain amount of "stability" in the company without ambiguous announcements and abrupt policy changes is needed to allow employees to exercise creativity and continuity at work without being afraid of abrasive changes.[1]

Morale is also affected when workers worry about the future of work for their children and there is widespread perception of a shrinking middle class. The disenfranchised start to blame their governments, politicians, wealthy elites, regional and global institutions for their economic situation. They also turn their sights on free trade regimes and organizations like World Trade Organization (WTO), countries supply cheap labour forces like India and China as well as global Multinational Corporations (MNCs) for their plight. In response to such sentiments, Alibaba has adopted a strategy in which the company tries to reassure its overseas market that it is not out to replace and snuff out the mom and pop shops but to work with small and medium sized enterprises (SMEs) to bring their products to the large Chinese consumer market instead. Alibaba is still in the process of this form of marketing persuasion. When Jack Ma met with US President Donald J Trump shortly after he was elected in 2017, Ma promised Trump that he would create new jobs in the US.

Meanwhile, as workers fret about the future of their jobs, employers simply do not have enough supply for skills that they need, including STEM (Science, Technology, Engineering and Mathematics) specialists and generalists who possess the skills and aptitude to work in a team, able to communicate and interact with others and are on time for their appointments and assignments. Other soft skills that are needed in today's workplace include the characteristics of empathy, persuasion skills, problem-solving solutions, decision-making processes, etc. Governments are gearing up their educational systems and syllabi to train individuals in such skills. One way to replenish the shortage of individuals in the economy with the appropriate skills is to absorb foreign talents but this option accentuate existing fears about globalization. (Refer to Chapter 6 [Case Study 1] for Japan's experience in this area.)

---

[1] Grote, Gudela, "The Digital Workplace: New Technologies, Same Old Story?" dated 2 February 2018 in the Eidgenössische Technische Hochschule (ETH) Zürich website [downloaded on 2 February 2018], available at https://www.ethz.ch/en/news-and-events/eth-news/news/2018/02/grote-digital-workplace.html.

People who fear jobs migrating overseas is just as fearful of economic migrants coming to their own country to take their jobs. They developed negative views about migration, thus adding on to the backlash against globalization and keeping them out of developed economies. However, global migration has become a reality regardless of resistance from the local populace. Economic migrants also play an important role in remitting their earnings back to their own home countries. Even if jobs are not subcontracted overseas or taken up by newly arrived migrants in the developed economies, they may be replaced by robots in the future. Thus, it is essential for governments and other stakeholders to provide training in job sectors where the skills are still needed.

Enlightened governments are tweaking skills and mass education to keep up with the digital economy. Some of the most enlightened governments in this aspect include Norway, Singapore, Taiwan and the US. The education system needs to be realigned with new jobs that will be created in place of those lost to automation. These new jobs will require new skillsets and therefore individuals will need to be retrained while the newer school-going generations will need new syllabuses taught by new pedagogies. McKinsey Global Institute projects 54 million Americans will be replaced by automation and are in acute need of acquiring new skills.[2]

Many smaller economies are also feeling anxious about their digital future. In 2017, the UAE (United Arab Emirates) came up with the post "Minister for Artificial Intelligence" (globally the first country to do so), coinciding this appointment with skills training to whip citizens into shape employability.[3] The difficult task for these government bureaucracies is identifying precisely trends in the digital economy. This is not easy given how fast things change. Governments also have to manage the pressures from other countries (especially their closest competitors) when the companies in those countries secure new technologies and pioneering status in implementing such technologies. There is pressure to keep ahead of the pack if not keep abreast them. The next wave and leap of innovation may have to be studied closely by the government alongside the private sector and other stakeholders like the unions and academia. In the next section, robotic development, a major trend in the tech world and complementary with digital technologies and industry 4.0, is cited as one example of such innovative trends.

[2] Robertson, Jennifer, "Digital Revolution Demands Changes to Education" dated 6 March 2018 in Forbes.com [downloaded on 6 March 2018], available at https://www.forbes.com/sites/gradsoflife/2018/03/06/digital-revolution-demands-changes-to-education/#1cfdf53e522a.

[3] GovInsider daily briefing news, "How AI Will Transform Taiwan's Economy" dated 10 April 2018 in the AI Taiwan website [downloaded on 10 April 2018] (Taiwan: Government of Taiwan), available at https://ai.taiwan.gov.tw/news/how-ai-will-transform-taiwans-economy/.

HUMAN SKILLS—SOFT SKILLS, JOBS AND EMPLOYMENT

Soft skills and people's skills are given new emphasis in the future of workplace. Communication skills, interactional capabilities, ability to show empathy, problem-solving on the spot, the art of persuasion, service to an organization, collaborative ease with fellow employees, strategizing and thinking long-term are all new skills sought after by contemporary employers. They are also regarded as the more humanistic parts of the job. Advocates of automation, A.I. and robotic sometimes argue that these tools facilitate emphasis on more humanistic assignments, enhancing their creativity, showing empathy for fellow human beings and working on higher order skills to promote strategic thinking and understanding among fellow human beings. Certain skills are classified as "soft skills" because they deal with human emotive elements and human interactions. For example, jobs in sectors such as early childhood, social work, human resource and leadership require soft skills such as empathy. It is not possible to work with children, urban poor humans, destitute persons, homeless/lonely persons and humans with special needs without the ability to show empathy for their challenges, celebrate their tribulations and provide advice for their trials. These are job sectors that are still short of humans and therefore the need to train human resources to fill up the capacities.

Besides the focus on soft skills, others believe that human–machine integration in the workplace is inevitable. Just as physical reality is now enhance-able with virtual reality and augmented reality, workers can now be complemented with science and technology to form an augmented workforce. Humans are better in some assignments (including those with soft skills requirements) while machines are better in others (repetitive, standardized, highly logical assignments). Analysts, policymakers and academics are now debating over optimal ways to deploy such augmented workforce and there are no conclusive ideas yet. Even a strategy that looks at separation of functions requires its own set of training. Meanwhile, companies and governments are struggling to prepare their general populace and workforce to match this emerging reality and outcome of the workplace of the future.

Besides soft skills training, digital education and hardware provision are also useful for empowering employees with digital access. Companies need to consider the investment returns of equipment used to provide this access, the security implications of using such devices and policies like whether workers are allowed to bring these devices to work. In high-security environments, some companies and organizations may choose to use only intranet for security of data and use only a few select stand-alone terminals for external connections to the Internet at the digital workplace. Some have defined the digital workplace as one that has all data stored in the cloud protected by cybersecurity. Given this definition, it implies the existence of a digital online security system within the company. Companies typically opt for a specialized department to take care of cybersecurity or set up a committee to oversee the security of data. For companies (and civil service departments) that rely on both intranet and internet external connection. Some ground rules setting may be useful for employees who use the intranet. Training is provided for the employees to remind them not to use intranet facilities for personal messages.

Some companies also provide external hardware devices to access the intranet and/or the Internet. Access to these devices elicit responses from the users. There is a psychological and emotive element to the use of digital devices at the workplace in that it could be a morale booster for some employees who feel prestigious and pride in owning such state-of-the-art devices. Others may feel excited about using the new tech in their workplace. In terms of mindset, a company, its employees, management and trade unions have to embrace and accept the reality of digital disruptions. Connectivity is no longer an option but a prerequisite to many work functions, including global collaborations, peer exchanges and teamwork facilitation. Even a device as simple as a smartphone can achieve this connectivity while other devices like the notepad (along with its connectivity to the Internet) can be used as a mobile catalogue of limitless featured items.

Changing mindset to adapt to digital technologies also requires patience and resilience as one is connected constantly and there are expectations by other parties of instantaneous or fast response time for replies. In some countries like France, they have acted against work-related emailing during the weekends for their citizens to achieve a better work–life balance. This may cause stress for certain individuals unused to such fast responses. To assist with smoother adaptation of new technologies, adequate training may be needed to transition workers to work with new technologies and processes. Due to the convenience that modern and contemporary communications devices bring to the ordinary workforce, it did away with some professions whose previous work functions were based on telecommunications in the previous industrial revolutions, e.g. Switchboard operators, telegram operators, etc. In the current Fourth Industrialization, there needs to be a detailed study to detect how many human jobs can be or have been eliminated with the convenience of digital telecommunications.

The way people worked would have also changed, with more mobility for teams that are spread out and keeping constant touch with the pulses, market supply-demand situations and partners in regional markets. People may have to get used to not being in the office for routinized work. Employees may even commute to the office only on demand and when there is need to so. Otherwise, they may just receive instructions through messages, emails, videos messaging and other communication formats. Employees who are posted overseas or provincially within the same country for assignments may also have to get used to the fact that they will stay in touch with their families electronically through digital communications. Work–life balance in this sense may have to be tampered with since employees may theoretically be on beck and call all the time. Some governments have turned to legislations to manage such high levels of work-related digital connectivity. France for example has frowned upon employers' emailing their employees in the weekend. Other countries like Japan are advocating greater work–life balance. Companies, workers, trade unions as well as individuals have to determine for themselves where to draw the line between on-call demand for work assignments and personal time.

Companies have their parts to play as well. When the lines between human and non-human are clearly ascertained, there is a need to reintegrate human communications (e.g. face-to-face dialogues/conversations) back into the company's operations and corporate culture. This is done so that the human component of communications is not missing from the company's operations. Just as parents are now trying to encourage their children to go outdoors and play in the park, companies may need to persuade its employees to have coffee dispenser machines conversations, chats across the partitions of an open office concept or even organize company activities like teambuilding and retreats to foster more interactions between individuals. Companies may also want to set up digital platforms for company discussions within a secure digital space so that employees do not take their disgruntled complaints to a public realm and hurt the company's standing or incur legal repercussions. Just like complaints procedures, such digital feedback spaces can curate employee information for a systematic presentation to senior management for further action or mitigation of the issue at hand.

Sometimes, it may be essential to utilize digital technologies simply because one's business partners have already switched to such systems and therefore it becomes necessary to catch up due to compatibility of systems. In the digital workplace, it becomes essential that employees are equipped with the appropriate technologies, including devices like tablets. Such equipment assist company employees in tapping into globalized networks and teams operating cross border. These equipment are time-sensitive in terms of the level of capabilities and need to be upgraded constantly, e.g. from push button to voice activation, in the near future from flat screen to 3-D projections. Mobility appears to be the keyword as workers can work from anywhere according to their assignment needs.

Technological use can sometimes translate into savings as videoconferencing for example can help to save money on travel costs like air tickets. Besides the hardware, companies need to better integrate their operations with the use of equipment. Staff members for example should adequately be exposed to and trained for using the system. Cloud computing has become a popular option for companies as it facilitates access to data from all locations but placing large volumes of data in the cloud exposes those data to security issues. Staff members should also be trained in cybersecurity so that their lines of communications and the contents of communications are safe and secure.

Lifelong Learning and Service Learning

Other than training humans in soft skills, far-sighted societies and governments are now encouraging lifelong learning. This is based on the belief that the moment individuals graduate from universities and high schools, their skills will be obsolete due to rapid changes in technologies and management knowhow. Therefore, the philosophy behind lifelong learning is that education does not end with a degree, individuals need to take responsibility to continually upgrade their knowledge, take refresher courses or retrain if existing skills are obsolete. It is a lifelong commitment to learning. Even after retirement, individuals are encouraged to keep their minds active, retrain for those who are still interested to work and/or pick up new skills in accordance with interest and post-retirement silver career opportunities.

Besides skills training, many believe that governments and societies need to extend more help to the disenfranchised and for those left out of the digital revolution. In this aspect, there is greater advocacy and attention paid to augmenting provision of social services and encouraging volunteerism within society to take care of those individuals who have fallen behind in preparing and tapping into the digital economy. Disciplines like service learning and social work are highlighted as career choices for caring about others, showing empathy to the needy and taking care of the less fortunate. This is a realization that, no matter how prepared a government or society is for economic restructuring to cope with the digital revolution, some individuals within that society will fall through the cracks. Therefore, there is a need for other humans to extend their help to this group of people through volunteerism, charitable work, social welfare, social work and service learning.

Service learning goes beyond just volunteerism, as service learning teams travel overseas to other societies to learn from those societies their needs as well as to self-reflect on one's own knowledge in order to contribute something positive and tangible to the host society. The experience is humbling. Service learning students learn from the society they serve as they volunteer their services to assist others. It is a two-way interactional platform. Service learning is discussed in greater details in Chapter 7 (Case Study 2). Some basic questions raised in reading this Chapter 7 (Case Study 2) include: Are displays of empathy, volunteerism engagement and helping others definitive elements of human behaviour? Will these traits separate us from machines?

Chapter 7 (Case Study 2) will be examining the following topics in the field of service learning in Japan: (A) surveying the increasing institutionalization and networking of Japanese universities involved in service learning as a possible model for outreach. (B) Comparing its curriculum with other youth leadership training programmes that the author has attended and highlight the idiosyncratic or unique features that stand out in each of these programmes. (C) Use service learning concepts to examine the author's previous cases studies of environmental and natural disaster relief volunteerism in Japan, along with some youth expedition training experiences. The idea of using service learning to shape social trends has been studied quite extensively in current literature on service learning in Japan but using service learning for creating awareness in other areas like environmental conservation and natural disasters is somewhat neglected or understudied in the existing literature.

Teaching service learning, encouraging community-based research and leading volunteer groups for missions related to environmental conservation and disaster relief efforts are important because the impacts of environmental damage and natural disasters tend to be long-term and so teaching the future generation to tackle these problems is crucial to managing the problems longitudinally. Continuing long-term community-based research also helps to understand the problems better to cope with their long-term impact. Chapter 7 (Case Study 2) pursues this line of enquiry to understand how Japan, which is well-known for its environmental management and sustainable development as well as natural disasters coping mechanism, has integrated environmental volunteerism and awareness as well as disaster relief work into its service learning curriculum for both schools and other non-governmental organizations, e.g. non-profit organizations (NPOs). (Refer to Chapter 7 [Case Study 2] for more details.)

FLEXIBLE EMPLOYMENT

In the service sector, some observers have advocated focusing more on service personnel and customer interface and the employee's enhancement of the customer experience as well as further improve the branding image of the company consequently. In other words, human centricity and the ability to think in a way that resonates with one's customers will become increasingly important, especially in the realm of persuasion, empathy and communication. Internally, within the companies, managers and senior executives are now required to be in tune with their organizational needs, able to mobilize fellow employees and harness unity to perform her/his tasks, something that has become just as important as effective interfacing with external customers. The mechanical aspects of service sector, for e.g. administrative procedures, payment processing, standard operating procedures found in manuals, clerical work no longer need human administrators. Instead, service sector employees previously carrying out such tasks will need to reskill to interact orally and emotionally with the customers, advising them on personalized matters like investment strategies, goal-setting, personal priorities and anxieties mitigation instead. The human dimensions of their jobs become the major value-add of their existence.

Employees and workers may also need to get used to flexibility and mobility at the workplace. Lifetime employment (LTE) or even stable employment may become increasingly tenuous as employees cope with the increasing need to manage projects that solve specific problems, the need to freelance when their skills are not in demand, constantly search for entrepreneurial opportunities, take up gigs that value-add to their career or financial needs, etc. These are non-traditional activities that cope with the unstable and fluctuating needs of the workplace. In fact, in some developed economies of the world, part-time jobs are becoming common and de facto major source of employment for young people.

An example is Japan whose scenario may be instructive. Japanese large companies used to practice LTE system where executives (called *sarariman* or salaryman in Japan) gave their loyalty and hardworking service to the companies in exchange for stable employment. These executives were not fired even when the economy was not doing well. They might be transferred to branches with a better title and a lower pay or posted to another company within the conglomerate network (known as *keiretsu* in Japanese). When the fast-growing economy of Japan came to a halt in 1989 after the economic bubble burst and as Japan entered decades of recessionary conditions, LTE broke down. Currently, some Japanese graduates and high school leavers have to take up non-stable employment. They could be doing subcontracting work similar to assignment-based work moving from project to project assignments. This mode of work is performed by what the Japanese call freeters. They jump from job to job (typically 1–3 years in duration per job) and are perpetually employed but in short-term contracts with the downside that it does not come with job security, insurance and welfare benefits. Nevertheless, it provides employment for these individuals. Others work in part-time jobs (*arubaito* in Japanese) taking certain hourly shifts or day shifts.

The upside of such arrangements is that it provides employment for various individuals but the downside is the emergence of some unanticipated social trends. In the case of Japan, some freeters and part-timers started to stay with their Showa-era parents who had stable jobs and now enjoying generous pension. Consequently, they began to be known as parasitic singles who live off their parents without paying rent and lead a carefree, sometimes high-consumption lifestyle. It also discourages these singles from getting married, accentuating Japan's birth rate problem, one of the fastest ageing society in the world. Some of these social trends may need to be taken into consideration eventually by the authorities, especially since almost all developed countries are facing ageing societal problems. Some developed economies that depended traditionally on migration to replenish their population stocks are facing antiglobalization/protectionist backlash from their native populations. See Chapter 9 (Case Study 4) for a detailed analysis of Japanese policies (comparing with Hong Kong) to cope with the impact of an ageing population.

Chapter 9 (Case Study 4)examines the policies in Japan and Hong Kong designed to alleviate the negative effects of an ageing population are of great interest to demographics, ageing and social welfare research. The two societies show a significant contrast in their approach towards coping with an ageing population. Hong Kong has spawned an NPO sector working with the bureaucracy, volunteers, social workers, community groups to look after the needs of the elderly. It is a laissez-faire approach dependent on community groups and volunteers with shared resources from the government. Japan's approach contrasts with Hong Kong in the sense that it too has a highly active NPO sector but the NPO sector works closely with the government in a civil society-state partnership with the state providing resources to local groups to manage certain programmes while steering it towards professionalization. Another area is the use of technologies to cope with an ageing population and to promote active ageing. Japan has some of the world's most advanced technologies in robotics designed to help with managing elderly care. They include assistive and therapeutic robots. (Some details are provided in Chapter 6 [Case Study 1].) Hong Kong is also keen to tap into technology to support its ageing population and active ageing narrative. In mid-2017, Hong Kong started looking into the idea of "gerontechnology". (See Chapter 9 [Case Study 4] for more details.)

Another group of advocates prefers a time-tested approach in coping with digital and robotic technologies. Go back to the drawing board and re-design jobs. In redesigning the workplace, entrepreneurs, governments, private sector and other stakeholders are now trying to differentiate human skills from standardized assignments or repetitive tasks based on logic that can be executed by robots. Human characteristics like empathy, creativity, leadership, listening, moralizing, soft communication skills, teamwork and collaboration, ethical thinking, socializing, EQ or emotional quotient and intelligence, and problem-solving for other humans are now emphasized in human resource (HR) hiring. Another human feature that excites HR departments is the quality of multiculturalism and diversity. In the new workplace environment, given that creativity and diversity of ideas are strengths that are not yet readily replaceable by algorithm-based A.I. or robots, human workers need to capitalize on diversity found at the workplace and consider it a strategic resource. Individuals with different genders, races, ethnicities, handicaps, sexual preferences and religions can come together as teams to brainstorm different ideas to come up with solutions to practice problems and challenges.

In order to continue to have a job, humans must now distinguish between jobs and assignments. Assignments are one-off projects that can be accomplished easily by robots when they are programmed for a certain task. But jobs require human skills that are part and parcel of daily activities at the workplace. This creates the demand for a new field known as design thinking which maps out how a job and its tasks are managed in a company. These maps are then analyzed by management to segregate assignments that require human skills named above and robot-capable tasks. This helps planners to identify the parts of the work process that still requires human inputs. It will also help companies plan ahead to project how many full-time workers and part-time/seasonal workers are needed. Augmentation of human inputs is a crucial process to create enough jobs for humans in workplaces of the future. It also helps the state plan ahead the kinds of resources needed to train such manpower and prepare the crucial skills training for them. In this way, learning will become a lifelong journey as skills need constant refreshment and upgrading. Jobs reserved for humans will also become increasingly knowledge-based and have less physical work in the long run.

Those who are slow in doing so will be eliminated and companies slow in identifying the humans and machine components of work assignments may also be eliminated. Companies that are slower in implementing technologies may also experience lower productivity and may be eliminated from competition. Some tech companies are leading the way in implementing technologies. Amazon.com for example is a successful example of integrated human-robot logistical delivery services for just-in-time logistical planning. The integration is so successful that some Amazon workers even gave their robots affectionate human names.

In the past, only manufacturing workers feel the danger from replacement by machines, especially from Industrial Revolution 2.0 onwards. However, even the service and retail sectors are not secure spaces from Industrial Revolution 4.0 today. E-commerce starting wiping out brick and mortar shops starting from the IT boom in the 1990s. Even earlier than e-commerce, automated bank tellers began to perform the same tasks as counter service staffs in financial institutions. Eventually, even automated tellers will disappear as all cash transactions become electronic and the world truly becomes a cashless society. Barcodes also make logistical delivery easier as deliverers, recipients and parcel senders are able to track the progress of the delivery online. China is probably the leading entity in this area as payments are now made through smartphones at the point of this writing (See Chapter 10 [Case Study 5] for a detailed treatment of this subject matter).

ROBOTICS

Aside from digital technologies, there are also advancements made in hardware-based technologies. Robotics is one such field and it has also become a complementary technology with A.I. and other digital applications. Robots developed for the military are usually controlled remotely (putting human operators out of harm's way) or are autonomous machines that can self-navigate for their mission (these may be operated through algorithms and self-learning capabilities). Many of these robot models are constantly upgraded so their level of adaptation to missions is enhanced constantly with each successive rollout of new models. The process is somewhat similar to constant improvement or kaizen in manufacturing ideologies. Robots have become well-adapted to performing tasks that are dangerous, dirty and demanding (the 3Ds). Formerly, these tasks were performed by humans who put their lives in danger and at risk of being injured or killed (bomb disposal work is a good example). Refer to Chapter 6 (Case Study 1) for a rundown on Japan's twin policies of importing foreign talents as well as implementing robotic replacements for humans in the context of manpower shortage and an ageing population.

In the "dangerous" jobs category, one rationale for developing robots is to reduce or even completely eliminate human casualties or injuries from the battlefield. Human operators will operate beyond visual range, from as far away from the battlefield as possible. Out of sight and out of range, the weapon systems human operators cannot be harmed by the enemy's weapon system. Other than weapons system, robots can manage dangerous and hazardous jobs like working in a nuclear reactor, spraying paint onto cars in the assembly line, etc. If robots are able to take over repetitive jobs, the logical questions may be what are skills that humans can possess that are not replicable by robots? Soft skills appear to be the response to this question. Certain skills are classified as "soft skills" because they deal with human emotive elements and human interactions. For example, jobs in sectors such as early childhood, social work, human resource and leadership require soft skills such as empathy. It is not possible to work with children, urban poor humans, destitute persons, homeless/lonely persons and humans with special needs without the ability to show empathy for their challenges, celebrate their tribulations and provide advice for their trials. These are job sectors that are still short of humans and therefore accounting for the corresponding need to train human resources to fill up those vacancies.

Meanwhile, robots are still some way away from being able to achieve these human skills in service learning or feel empathy for others. This can be explained using the uncanny valley theory. As robots still do not resemble human beings sufficiently, they are immediately differentiated from humankind cognitively and emotionally by humans. One can tell clearly they are machines and may lack the kind of human emotional bond needed by human nurses, caregivers, team colleagues, human leaders/managers, emotionally distressed patients, babies, children and the handicapped/disabled humans. This situation may change in the future if android development continues unabated. Japan is one of the countries that is technologically advanced in this area as its universities/companies have developed artificial skins, hydraulic parts, microelectronics and cloned robots after real humans as showcase technologies. Prof. Hiroshi Ishiguro from Osaka University is widely acknowledged as the father of Japanese android development and he cloned robot versions of his daughter, himself, a famous journalist and mixed race humans using android technologies.

However, the uncanny valley theory still applies. At the present moment, humans are still able to distinguish themselves from the androids and this accentuate fear and anxiety of the unknown among members of the human community. The author witnessed such emotions when he watched Ishiguro's Geminoid F android performing, conversing and singing to a Hong Kong audience in a shopping mall in 2012. At that point of time, this was one of the most advanced commercially developed androids in the world. Some audience members were intimidated by the human-like appearance of Geminoid F but were still able to tell her apart from real humans. Children in the audience, especially the younger ones, were confused and anxious. Other members of the audience were excited, elated and positive in experiencing android technologies for the first time in their lives.

The other possible area of development for robots in the field of caregiving are assistive and therapeutic robots. Again, Japan is one of the leading countries in the world in such robotic developments. One of its models, the RI-MAN series, is designed for providing caregiving to elderly patient in a fast-ageing Japanese society. The RI-MAN robot can smell, detect and execute human commands and has enhanced strength in lifting patients off beds horizontally. The other category, therapeutic robots, is represented by Paro the seal also developed by Japan. Paro is a cute-looking (*kawaii* in Japanese popular culture terminology) toy seal which has a baby pacifier masking electricity charging plug. Paro provides companionship to the elderly who may be suffering from dementia. Paro can substitute caregivers to the extent that it is able to provide 24 hours companionship to the patients tirelessly but cannot fully replace caregivers.

However, even if the technologies greatly improve in these cases, there are other challenges in implementing them. So far, much of the robotic case studies are applicable to Japan so they are not tested culturally in other countries such as the US and China. Japanese children are exposed to benign images of robots since young through animation series with robotic heroes portraying a positive coexistence between humans and robots but this may not be the same case in other countries, especially in the US where robots are often harbingers of apocalyptic dystopia to humankind. Thus, more studies have to be done on coexistence of robots and humans across cultures before wholesale job replacements are possible in some human-centred job sectors.

Dual-Use Technologies and Military Application

Robotics and A.I. has stoked the attention of many mass media observers and commentators. A major discussion revolving around A.I. is its potential to eliminate many jobs for human workers in the near future. The list reads long from accountants in danger of being replaced by accounting software to taxi drivers put out of work by autonomous vehicles. Relatively less discussion has been focused on the application of A.I. in weapons system. Just as industrial robots are replacing humans in factories, military robots will have the potential to replace humans in military jobs as well. A good example is the human pilot. With drones becoming more sophisticated, the era of humans flying planes may eventually pass. Humans are more susceptible to the high G-force (gravitational force) which takes a toll on their bodies and some may pass out at high G-forces scenarios. Human pilots also get fatigued when they are on long lonely missions. Drones can correct such issues through technologies. Drones are even being developed to eventually replace human-operated aircrafts on the deck of aircraft carriers. The X-47 is a good example carrier-based drone in this aspect. Again, this can save lives as carrier landings and take-offs over a short runway are extremely complicated and dangerous. Robots enjoy greater precision in navigational and guidance systems.

What are the issues involved when it comes to military use of such technologies? There is also an ethical dimension to the issue at hand. In April 2018, a group of researchers decided to boycott a major Korean technological university due to its alleged involvement with A.I. weapons. This brings to mind several questions. When should civilian researchers withdraw from projects that can lead to weaponization that they oppose on ethical grounds. Sometimes, this is difficult given the dual-use nature of many weapons system. Past and current technologies used by a majority of civilians in society like the Internet, tin cans and microwave ovens were initially military technologies. Human dignity is sometimes at stake when military robots and drones kill and/or injure civilians by mistake. At the same time, there are battlefield robots whose mission is not to fight but to rescue. Medic robots can get into the danger zone to extract wounded human soldiers. But of course, there are limits to such deployments as well because of the human factor. Some soldiers may still prefer to see human faces when they are down or recuperating. Nevertheless, while the preference is still pro-human in the military profession, most militaries remain accountable to their civilian governments to ensure casualties are kept to a minimum. Many soldiers serving in the battlefield and as combat medics are young men and women who otherwise have a productive life and career ahead of them.

Some jobs are simply too dangerous for humans. US drones had to be deployed in the aftermath of Japan's "3.11" Great East Japan Earthquake triple disaster. The drones carried out missions in the form of flying over an exploded nuclear reactor (Fukushima reactor). In this sense, there is good potential for robot deployment in non-traditional security (NTS) missions, like disaster relief. This helps to prevent humans from being exposed to radiation. Due to Japan's constitutional limits imposed after WWII (Peace Constitution No. 9) on developing weapon systems and waging war on others, they could not develop and did not have an equivalent robot to the US Predator Drone. Tapping on American help, the US launched such drones from their aircraft carriers to help Japanese efforts in earthquake/nuclear leakage recovery work. The drones took vital photos of the damaged nuclear plant for radiation leakage diagnosis. It would have been dangerous to fly humans over the damaged plant. They would have been exposed to leaked radiation that can have serious long-term effects.

With drones flying the skies and unmanned vehicles diving in the depths of seas and oceans, the next frontier for robot deployment is outer space. After all, the Cornell University-developed Mars Rover had traversed the difficult terrain of the planet Mars, collected soil samples and analyzed them as well as beamed information back to NASA (National Aeronautics and Space Administration). The entry of robots into space raises ethical questions. Will militaries wage high tech warfare fought through robots in outer space? What are the consequences of weaponizing space? The initial space race was carried out by the US and Soviet Union during the Cold War. The Soviets placed the first cosmonaut into space while the Americans landed the first man on the moon. This was in the 1950s and 1960s. In the 1980s, near the final stages of the Cold War, the Ronald Reagan administration unveiled the Star Wars programme, again stirring up debates about weaponizing space.

In the weaponization of robotic technologies, the idea of A.I.-enabled killer robots scare and intimidate many people. Some EU-based advocates and some groups of scientists and activists have long lobbied for legislating a "killer switch" in some technologies including some sensitive and important A.I.-enabled technologies that can have an impact on sustained human existence. A killer switch would enable humans to switch off a certain technology, including A.I.-enabled ones, if they prove to be dangerous to humankind in the future. It is unclear if this is a universal view shared by all stakeholders. Other humans are concerned about ethical questions like: should A.I.-enabled robotics technology have the power to make decisions over which groups or should individual humans that prove to be harmful to the collective/society be eliminated? Some fear this may be the outcome of the development of a class of technologies now known as "autonomous systems". Pro-human advocates argue that humans should ultimately remain as the operators of weapons systems and not A.I. or other forms of technologies. According to this belief, humans should be the ultimate arbitrator of decisions over other human lives. Some of these advocates are busy lobbying the United Nations to ban such weapon systems that can make decisions and behave autonomously of their human owners.

Among their numbers (anti-autonomous system advocates) include well-known philosophers like Noam Chomsky, technologists and entrepreneurs like Steve Wozniak and Elon Musk as well as prominent scientist Stephen Hawking who passed away recently. Added to their numbers are human rights groups who argue that any bans should be complemented/preceded by national legislations to govern these technologies first. Others worry that a complete ban on autonomous weapons system may affect the development of human-operated and/or semi-autonomous systems since loopholes for skirting the law can often be found in human-drafted legislations. It will take an international panel of esteemed lawyers to carefully draft such agreements, although this measure by itself does not completely eliminate the difficulties in enforcement and detection technologies to identify cheaters.

The EU, including Germany, appears to be the major world power most resistant to development of autonomous systems. Outside the EU, other countries that oppose the development of autonomous weapons include countries like Mexico, Egypt, Cuba, Chile, etc. Russia argues that it will continue to develop robotic systems that are still human-operated. But others, including some Europeans, argue that it is difficult to enforce the non-use of autonomous systems. There will always be suspicions that some countries will skirt or disobey any laws or rules on non-development and/or non-use of autonomous systems. Difficulties in monitoring and enforcement may prevent more countries from agreeing to a universal ban on autonomous systems. Moreover, there are economic incentives in developing autonomous systems and other technologies. Many robot technologies, including the cutting-edge ones, are dual-use technologies. These technologies are potentially usable in both civilian and military applications. Therefore, besides the military industrial complex developing high tech robotic weapons as defence contractors, the same technology can be adapted for civilian use. If successful, they can be commercialized for the mass markets (made cheaper and aesthetically more attractive). Besides serving domestic markets, these dual-use technologies can be exported to overseas customers. Even the humble robotic carpet cleaner is related to technologies developed for military robots. The combination of military and civilian applications makes a strong justification for the development of such technologies. So far, this chapter has been discussing the emergence of smart devices and Industry 4.0 technologies like robotics used by various individuals, groups and organization. The next chapter discusses the unified platform through which smart devices and Industry 4.0 technologies can communicate with each and with humans. Finally, machines and robots have a unified platform through which all devices are connected, hitherto known as the "Internet of Things (IoT)".

BIBLIOGRAPHY

GovInsider daily briefing news, "How AI Will Transform Taiwan's Economy" dated 10 April 2018 in the AI Taiwan website [downloaded on 10 April 2018] (Taiwan: Government of Taiwan). Available at https://ai.taiwan.gov.tw/news/how-ai-will-transform-taiwans-economy/.

Grote, Gudela, "The Digital Workplace: New Technologies, Same Old Story?" dated 2 February 2018 in the Eidgenössische Technische Hochschule (ETH) Zürich website [downloaded on 2 February 2018]. Available at https://www.ethz.ch/en/news-and-events/eth-news/news/2018/02/grote-digital-workplace.html.

Robertson, Jennifer, "Digital Revolution Demands Changes to Education" dated 6 March 2018 in Forbes.com [downloaded on 6 March 2018]. Available at https://www.forbes.com/sites/gradsoflife/2018/03/06/digital-revolution-demands-changes-to-education/#1cfdf53e522a.

CHAPTER 3

The Internet of Things (IoT)

INTRODUCTION: WHAT EXACTLY IS THE INTERNET OF THINGS (IoT)?

For the Internet of Things (IoT) to flourish, one of the pre-requisite is the proliferation of broadband technologies. Portable pieces of hardware to tap into wireless broadband technologies are also proliferating. Besides connectivity, the IoT also proliferated on the back of the availability of affordable, energy conserving and low power chips with the capability of wireless communications. All these developments lead to an expansion of connectivity. Connectivity is the pre-condition for IoT to take off in any settings. IoT allows any sort of hardware to be connected to the Internet. Because of the proliferation of internet use, electronics manufacturers are also tailoring their devices for compatibility with Wifi wireless internet access systems. The two greatest technologies that enable users to detach themselves from desktops and go mobile are smartphones and cloud. The invention of smartphones, pioneered by Apple, means that humans can now carry a small portable phone with microprocessors and computer chips as powerful as their personal computers (PCs) with them 24 hours a day. Users are no longer constrained by the presence of network machines, private sector commercial network systems and geographical locations. They can now access their accounts and apps from most locations.

There are now billions of devices connected to the IoT and they are connecting with each other. The only criteria that these devices need is an on (O) and off (I) switch to become potentially smart since the most basic capabilities of IoT-connected devices is to be able to turn them on or off. Application Programming Interfaces (APIs) facilitates the linkage of smart devices to the Internet. Their embedded chips allow these devices to have computing

T. W. Lim, *Industrial Revolution 4.0, Tech Giants, and Digitized Societies*,
https://doi.org/10.1007/978-981-13-7470-8_3

power. In the future even objects as small as particles can be tagged with chips to communicate with other devices. The IoT is an aggregator of data and information coming from all sides and is the conduit to pass on the signals to their end destination devices. The IoT is also analogized as physical objects expressed as digital information and, using the latter, the IoT can manipulate physical objects, turn them on or off, activate them or operate them using remote control.

IoT and Mobile Devices

This provides the avenue for physical devices to be connected with the Internet. Although the process started in the 1980s, the proliferation of internet-capable devices is a much more recent phenomenon due to leaps in technological capabilities. There is an economic factor involved as well, as improvements in productivity, manufacturing technologies and economy of scale with increased demand brought down the prices of these internet-accessible devices, such as the smartphones. Because smartphones are now an extension of the individual self, humans can stay in touch with their schedules and other humans via machines, the human-operated smartphone machine can now communicate with other machines. Siri and other electronic personal assistants are able to communicate the needs of human users and connect them with other humans. Google has already developed a version in which electronic personal assistants are able to autonomously connect with humans to perform daily human tasks and needs. This will be the beginning of machines' direct autonomous communications with humans.

Machine to machine communication is not entirely new, it has occurred in the manufacturing sector. They are mostly performing the function of breakdown alerts and maintenance indicators. They warn humans or other machines about the near end of life phases of smart devices and such pre-emptive measures can help to nip defective devices in the bud before they can do real damage to human users/consumers. Diagnostic functions will continue to intensify greatly in the IoT age. But IoT allows more two-way formats of communications, involving both machines and humans. This gives rise to the three sets of relationships: human–human direct or machine-intermediated interactions, human–machine interactions (through devices carried on their body) and through machine–machine communications (sending and receiving signals between machines). Conventional thinking on device connections appears to have a deterministic nature, the momentum appears to head towards connecting anything and everything. Someday, these devices may anticipate your daily habits and start planning your routine everyday tasks even without your requests or instructions. Smart machines will also have the capabilities to track the human individual and anticipate her/his arrival and be able to activate everyday tasks even before the human sets foot in the next destination.

Stand-alone, these equipment are considered mechanical machines but when they are connected to the Internet and are operable online, these devices became "smart" instantly. Conversely, devices that are not connected to the IoT, cannot be operated remotely and are unable to transmit collected data to other machines. Thus, machines that cannot operate autonomously of human actions/inputs and/or receive data are considered "dumb". Because of wireless access via smartphones, devices related to daily use can be activated and deactivated using mobile control platforms. It also implies that everyday devices can now receive and transmit data when they are connected to the Internet. IoT brings all these devices together and connects machines that are otherwise standalone equipment. Therefore, some scholarly and trade professional publications only regard internet-connected everyday devices that were not usually associated with internet connection as part of the definition of IoT.

Manufacturing gurus and commentators believe that the function of IoT-enabled smart devices will eventually move beyond maintenance work and into the realm of productivity-monitoring. Sensors embedded in each phase of the conveyor belt system feeds real-time data into a collective pool of data. The data are precise and accurate and, because they are fed into a common pool of data, the big picture is visible and so cohesive and integrated coordination of different sections of the conveyor belt system becomes possible. Human technicians or managers will only be needed to look at the big picture to ensure the entire system is moving along fine and/or make some minor adjustment to address productivity issues. The information presented to human technicians will be parsimonious, summarized and easy to read/analyse. These information may be presented in a digital dashboard, monitor, palmtop, tablet, tabphone or even ipad for easy reading and data accessibility. Having accurate real-time data means the entire production cycle can be speeded up.

IoT and Smart Cities

Everyday individual mobile devices are not the only platforms controllable via the Internet. Individual devices can be embedded all over a larger area, including those as large as a city, and they can then be activated for feeding information back to a centralized platform for effective urban management or be turned out for specific application purposes. This effectively means humans are now able to control the environment (at the very least take readings from the environment) through a large number of sensors embedded in the urban environment. These sensors can also increasingly allow machines to take the readings and make autonomous decisions affecting the physical environments on their own accord without the need for human inputs. There are some visible advantages in managing the environment through sensors. Their readings are trackable through the Internet in a real-time fashion. Sensors are able to collect readings from the environment that can rationalize the use of energy (e.g. monitoring energy use, tracking carbon emissions, etc.) and mitigate negative impacts of energy use in cities and urban spaces (e.g. taking pollution index readings from the air, monitoring water quality, etc.). A city in which these sensors and readings are constantly taking readings while human decision-makers are processing the information and taking steps to run the city functions more efficiently is sometimes known as a "smart city".

A major incentive for embedding IoT-enabled smart technologies into a smart city is to manage overcrowded urban cities. Some cities are overcrowded to the extent that they are becoming supercities. Resources in these crowded cities need to be re-distributed more evenly and environmental problems arising from intense use of resources needs to be managed carefully. Most first-tier cities already feature technologies like Closed Circuit Television (CCTVs), sensors and smartphone app-activated devices. Some more advanced cities have integrated facial recognition capabilities into their CCTVs. Others incorporate devices with autonomous capabilities in monitoring, tracking and identifying. Usual functions for these smart equipment are controlling and monitoring traffic, coordinating essential urban services like trash collection/public street lamp controls/etc., and evaluating environmental conditions (e.g. air, water, etc.). Energy conservation is a big plus in IoT-enabled smart devices. Such functions are made all the more crucial due to the explosion in urban population. (See Chapter 8 [Case Study 3] for the case study of China smart cities projects.)

Pro-transparency groups are advocating the public sharing of these data sets for the benefit of all stakeholders in the city. They believe that data sharing can help to demystify the workings of IoT for the public. Data sharing and even conducting workshops and mobile displays can help to create greater public awareness of the IoT-enabled smart devices out there and inform the ordinary consumers on the product offerings, their specifications and the advantages and pitfalls of using such technologies (as well as the protection needed against viruses and hacking activities). Progressive no-detriment agendas and/or campaigns can be carried out in such public awareness sessions, including explaining the mechanisms behind energy conservation smart devices and how sensors work to reduce household wastage/usage of energy/electricity, making individual households more environmentally friendly while reducing the costs of using electricity for them.

Big data appears to be more accurate in representation if they are agglomerated with data from different sources through sharing. In advanced countries, their governments have been collecting and accumulating data longitudinally for many years. But they are locked up in some archives, records vault or stand-alone terminals/servers. Advocates of data-sharing suggest that they should be freed up to assist in the provision of public services. Based on such longitudinal data collection, the authorities can understand how social issues arose over time, where resources are distributed unevenly, conversely the locations and sites with excessive provision of resources/public services. Moreover, making public such data can translate to profit-making opportunities. According to McKinsey & Co., data silos could generate up to US$5 trillion in revenue, because transparency advocates argue that "[information] becomes more valuable as it is shared, less valuable as it is hoarded".[1]

IoT and Data Collection/Transmission

The collection of large amounts of data also opens up another avenue which is big data analytics. One example of collected information will be medical information and data. Personal smart watch devices can now constantly monitor heart rate and health readings. Real-time data empower a healthy lifestyle, allowing individuals to spot health risks earlier and track their exercise regimes to optimize longevity. In addition to heart rate measurements, other health readings include the surface temperature of skin, analysis of sweat and perspiration, air intake, etc. The constant collection of health-related readings are sometimes referred to as "the quantified self". These medical tracking devices belong to a class of technologies known as "biometric sensors". Their functions are specialized in the field of measuring and quantifying.

Sharing data between companies and their customers locks both of them into more intense relationships as data allow companies to serve their customers better by customizing services/products for the latter. Similarly, customers are given an important avenue to supply feedback through data in terms of deficiencies and gaps arising from the service provided. To fully benefit from the availability of data, companies need to groom a strong analytics department to analyse the data sets and translate them into practical use. At the same time, they would also need to train a strong cybersecurity team to prevent the data from being hacked and/or stolen. Data collected from customers over a period of time can also contribute to calibrating the maintenance, servicing and parts replacement intervals and durations, so that these functions can be systematized.

Pro-data sharing advocates argue that releasing data to the public or even to competitors can sometimes help to promote the efficiency of the entire industry. They can better learn from each other's silo-ed data. They believe that companies can learn from each other's best practices and high performances, spurring competition within the industry. Even individual plants and factories within the same conglomerate can learn from each other's data and try to outcompete each other's performances, as a form of internal competition. Ultimately, pro-data sharing advocates believe that even with data-sharing and mutual emulation, a production system that is efficient, productive and effective cannot be easily copied in its entirety because of its unique strengths that are not completely replicable in other conditions and settings.

[1] Horwitz, Lauren, "Can Smart City Infrastructure Alleviate the Strain of City Growth?" undated in Cisco.com website [downloaded on 1 September 2018], available at https://www.cisco.com/c/en/us/solutions/internet-of-things/smart-city-infrastructure.html.

Data-sharing advocacy is also based on the assumption that no one single company can collect data so comprehensively that it has absolute dominance over others. There are likely to be gaps and loopholes in the data that can be filled or corroborated from data originating from other sources. But data-sharing across an industry is not easy to achieve due to traditional distrust of one's rivals and the tendency to hoard data in the belief that it represents an advantage over others. Ultimately, companies within an industry may turn to the government for the same purpose of hoping that the authorities would share macro data with them so that they have a bigger picture of how to use those data to their advantage. Sometimes, the government shares big data in the interest of public safety, for e.g. sharing public transportation data with car manufacturing firms in the interest of developing technologies that can reduce car accidents.

IoT and Its Impact on Jobs/Workplace/Economy

Real-time information makes just-in-time logistics and delivery possible. Micro-positioning systems emit beacons and signals that are integrated with a smartphone and can tell where nearby retailers and service providers are located. Inventory management is facilitated by these capabilities as warehouse human personnel and robots can stock up on goods that are running short on supply. The goods are therefore delivered upon anticipated demand. At the individual level, Amazon has come up with a dash button concept where, with the single push of a button, the smartphone app will immediately place an order for a favourite product. Just one button settles the specific retail and consumption need of that individual. Even consumption is tracked. When purchases are made through online retailers, the time, date and frequency of purchases are kept as part of its rolling data collection. Consumption patterns, inclinations, range of preferences, and other data associated with the purchases are then analysed and mapped out for more effective marketing, promotional and predictive purposes. If consumption preferences and inclinations are tracked more accurately, then the conscious human action of decision-making processes are greatly minimized in favour of accurately tracked and pre-selected products purchases based on informed instincts and impulse.

Smart machines and infrastructure, in this sense, leads to smart decision-making. Machine learning helps smart devices carry out actions without human inputs/actions. The ultimate individually tailored smart device is a virtual assistant that is synchronized between the scheduler and Siri-like function in the smartphone with the personal housekeeper at home. This personal assistant can remind the user of when to stock up supplies, make suggestions on lighting intensity, activate devices like television/radio/washing machines and other appliances, adjust climate controls and air conditioning and, in some Japanese systems that the author has observed, even suggest the colour of dresses and clothes to wear. These suggestions are made based on information gathered from sensors and monitoring devices embedded all over the residence.

In the service sector or traditional human-centred communication functions in the workplace, face-to-face communication may gradually give way to communication via electronic means. The latter method saves costs and is generally more convenient for busy executives. It provides SMEs with a wider reach without blowing a hole in its budget. Because IoT-enabled smart machines can diagnose faults and can directly handle such problems speedily, IoT can host the platform of the customer relations management (CRM) system itself. Oral face-to-face communications between humans are no longer crucial. Sometimes, self-diagnosing capabilities are inbuilt into mechanical machines so that machines can check other machines to ensure overall safety for humans. Jet plane engines have such inbuilt self-diagnosis systems to ensure the working order of the engines with constant real-time feedback.

Governments around the world need to train their citizens in IT skills so that they are able to harness the full benefits of IoT. For the vast majority of people in the world, they are not coders, engineers, programmers or IT specialists. They have to be exposed to such technologies and knowledge in order to understand how to use them or even build their careers on such specialized knowledge. For the small group of elite programmers, IT specialists and coders in the high tech capitals of the world, such knowledge is normative and the foundations of their innovative research and development efforts. These tech elites lead the way in developing new products which they consider intuitive and instinctual to use but are often considered cutting-edge and stuff of sci-fi by others. The commercialized fruits of the tech elites' research slowly percolate throughout the rest of the world and the masses than normalize the use of these devices and became a daily fixture. While tech elites need little introduction to different technological offerings and developments out there, the mass consumers and users need training and familiarization to get used to the new technologies. In this aspect, the state can step in to provide such familiarization training and exercises so that their citizens can keep up with the latest technologies for enhancing productivity in their workplaces and daily lives.

IoT has connected even the remotest areas in the world from deepest African Sahara to the coldest winter lands of Siberia. For the first time, IoT affords the opportunities for individuals in these areas as well as the most poverty-stricken parts of the world to connect with the rest of the world. It gives them the opportunity to leapfrog over conventional economic development stages and reach for the more advanced consumer electronics technologies and information and communications technological (Infocomm or ICT) infrastructures. While developed economies built their infrastructure using copper wires and telephone/telegraph technologies, developing and emerging economies are able to rely on wireless/wifi technologies for their communication needs. If more citizens can have access to IoT technologies and use them effectively, IoT can help distribute resources more effectively, i.e. to the most rural parts of the country, or to minority tribes living in secluded locations, or disenfranchised women and children living in peripheral impoverished areas and/or people living in war zones/crime-infested areas or disaster stricken locations.

IoT Meets Social Media Networks

The IoT makes it possible for machines to interact with human-based social media networking. Devices that emit signals and readings can send their output to human social media networks. When humans interpret those readings and use the data for interactions with other humans, devices have effectively been integrated into human networking. Some call this process the socialization of objects and their data. Devices can also communicate with each other via the IoT. One of the foreseeable application for social media working in conjunction with the IoT is in the medical and healthcare field. Increasingly, patients/recovered former patients/individuals concerned about their health can communicate and interact with their doctors/medical practitioners/healthcare professionals through social media which makes it easier for doctors to access their patients' records, take constant readings from health monitoring devices and dispense advice via the same platform. In the same way, portable fitness devices including watches can send health data via social media to the user's family members and friends or even jogging/physical fitness circles.

Patients and individuals in general wearing portable watch-like health monitoring devices are able to collect data on their heath readings constantly and feed these data back to health professionals. Low power chips embedded on pharmaceutical medicinal bottles can communicate with smartphones with regard to dosage information, frequency of administering and inventory/re-stocking needs. The chips can also act as early warning systems to remind patients when their stock of medicines deplete and require replacement. For some individuals with medical conditions, having enough medicine supplies, taking the right dosage and the need for constant reminders to take the medicines in the accurate frequency can be a matter of life or death for some of them. Some vulnerable groups can really benefit from such constant monitoring of health conditions and needs.

For example, babies who are doli incapax and still unable to articulate their physical conditions in human words can benefit from such technologies. Smart devices can monitor their heart rates, breathing and other vital signs to feedback to concerned parents that their young children are doing alright. This is especially useful when both parents have to be away and the baby is left in the hands of a third party (nanny, helper, maid, healthcare professional or amah). Another group is the elderly. The function of using IoT-enabled technology to monitor the whereabouts of the elderly is especially important in ageing societies. Most of the developed world, as well as the fast-emerging economies of East Asia are ageing rapidly. (See Chapter 9 [Case Study 4] for two examples of ageing populations in East Asia and their coping mechanisms.) Thus, the potential marketability and sales of such devices are likely to be sunrise growth markets. Some of these devices are highly innovative.

For example, Japanese companies have come up with hot water dispensing flasks that emit signals every time an elderly individual dispenses hot water to make green tea. The signal is then transmitted via a computer server to the recipient's (concerned family member related to the elderly users) email as well as mobile phone. The signal puts the concerned family member at ease because it implies that the elderly person is making green tea at home and therefore the whereabouts of the aged family members are trackable and in the know. The reason for such elaborate use of smart devices instead of simply monitoring the elderly through CCTV is due to privacy concerns. Culturally, Japanese may feel uncomfortable if they are constantly tracked in the privacy of their own home through a camera. The hot water flask on the other hand is inconspicuous and blends in with the kitchen setting. Moreover, making green tea is a widespread traditional habit in Japan, so the elderly is not performing something unusual or unnatural.

Besides healthcare, smart devices have also been used in the sports arena, with chips tagged to marathoner shoes and chips for monitoring how human individuals used their sports equipment. Such equipment will be useful in managing large sports events like marathons. They are also used for more accurate tracking and monitoring in case of disputes arising in competitive events. Besides sports events, the same smart technologies are useful for improving the game and ball skills. In golf, embedded chips can track the golfer's swings and the coach can better diagnose technique issues and recommend better strokes for the golfer, especially crucial for competitive individuals and fulltime professionals. Both healthcare and sports/fitness devices can be modified to monitor public hygiene or obtain health readings from public spaces, especially in the context of a smart city, when embedded in large numbers.

It is not only human health which requires monitoring. Machines also require regular checkups. The IoT can also help connect members of an interest-based community or a community of users who bought the same product together through the use of social media. Thus, individuals who bought the same car for example can now connect with other users through social media. Newer buyers can learn from the experiences of older car owners and receive tips on how to manage certain idiosyncrasies of a particular make or model. As with all other smart devices connected to the IoT, cars can also be embedded with chips that can send signals to their owners' social media account the state of their vehicle's health and maintenance alert, much like how humans are reminded of their medication and vital health-related signs. The car companies also gain from the data in learning about the problems faced by car owners, the regularities of breakdowns of certain components and improve those designs or eliminate these problems in future models. In such cases, all stakeholders benefit from the data generated and shared through IoT and social media.

The Security and Political Implications of IoT

Smart devices are also potentially surveillance devices. Smartphones ensure that all individuals are constantly tracked as the phone leaves behind meta data. Use of apps also allows the smartphones to track the daily activities of an individual smartphone user. Data are sent from home to private sector data collectors, marketing firms, and in some cases, they end up in third parties. Data can also be hacked and stolen. Usual hacking tools when it comes to smart devices are viruses like malicious software or malware that can infiltrate cloud, smart devices, monitoring sensors, etc. Some hackers are driven ideologically, believing in the need to break the tech industry's hold on source code and technological blueprints by hacking into their systems and stealing the blueprints/sources codes and then publishing them openly in the Internet for all to see. If attacks are widespread and uncontrollable, it may end up hurting IoT development, deterring users and consumers from using IoT-enabled smart devices and their platforms. Therefore, some cybersecurity advocates argue that the IoT should not be allowed to grow faster than the ability of security products to protect smart devices from being hacked.

Privacy issues are also another challenge in an IoT-enabled world. A residence that has become "smart" may end up becoming a constant data lab for private sector companies that manufactured the home appliances and hackers keen on selling the data for their own sinister causes. There are also some personal items that may become smart in the near future, e.g. personal intimate products like bras, underwear, etc. Embedding low-power chips in them may mean that these personal-use products can be tracked or/and monitored by unwelcomed parties such as hackers. Sometimes legal loopholes or legal complexities allow companies to collect data when their appliances are used. Some companies may include a clause in the contract of use for privacy. The fine print in these clauses may have the legal effect of signing away the right to bar manufacturers from using the data collected from smart appliances for commercial purposes. Besides the private sector's possible misuse or abuse of data, other security, criminal and military groups may be tempted to weapon-ize smart devices for intelligence purposes or they may use the data for character assassination and other sinister purposes to bring down targeted governments or companies.

The Europeans are taking a lead in the fight for privacy and confidentiality having successfully sued some American tech giants for invading personal spaces in people's lives. Their governments have also taken actions against dolls that record information and transmit them to servers. In trying to understand the impact of privacy loss, European institutions and foundations have commissioned studies like the Helsinki Privacy Experiment whereby researchers try to observe and study the psychological impact of constant surveillance on human test subjects. The study showed that it led to behavioural modifications where humans utilized IoT-enabled technologies for their own purpose and simply got used to higher levels of constant surveillance. At the end of the experimentation, respondents did not feel anxious about technologies constantly monitoring them, although in some cases and specific scenario, they felt some anger and discomfort. Apparently, humans are more resilient than previously thought when it comes to adapting to privacy. Some critics of IoT are already visualizing the emergence of the technology as a colonizer of personal information and data. Many of the apps and devices have proprietary rights to the data generated. Some may require brick and mortar retailers to buy or rent the platform for connecting to these electronic systems. The fear therefore is that suggested consumption options and advice provided by electronic personal assistants may not be entirely neutral or free of biasness towards certain digital tech companies that run these apps and systems. Conscientious objectors who are against inbuilt biasness to these systems therefore bypass the convenience of online options and directly communicate with the brick and mortar retailers for their consumption needs.

There has been a rethink of the Internet itself in the arena of personal freedom and individual rights. The 1990s was an era of irrational exuberance on how the Internet represented freedom and democracy. But it soon dawned on users that the same tools to advocate convenience and openness can also be used to monitor individuals. They were further disappointed with the willingness of telecommunications and IT companies to share or sell their data to third parties. But aligned against them are pro-tech groups or technologists who argue that standardization of technologies and adopting global technological standards for regulating them can lead to geopolitical stability. This is because technologies rely on networks and collaboration work to function well. Therefore, the functionalists, constructivists, idealists among them believe that the world will become more peaceful with more big data-sharing, research collaboration, states and big companies sharing financial/data resources, etc. Some characterize the debates between the two factions as one of productivity-centric machine-based efficient governances versus democratic human-centric effective governance. Eventually, humans will have to find a balance between the two priorities.

Critics also argue that, with such a vast array of smartphones, smart devices and IoT-enabled equipment, energy use is set to go up. This may lead to energy shortage and subsequently, greater global competition for energy. The world is already short of energy based on existing use of tech devices, piling many more devices onto them may exacerbate the situation further. On the other hand, the idea of smart machines enables them to regulate energy use according to functionalities and scenarios. They are self-adjusting and can adapt to external environmental conditions. Energy conservation and the conflicting scenarios of greater energy use due to larger numbers of smart devices versus energy self-regulating functionality in smart machines point out the complexities of urban management.

Another fear of reliance on smart devices is escalating costs and need for manpower. In order to install smart devices throughout a smart city, manpower is not only needed for the installation but also the maintenance and repairs of these smart devices. Given that the number of smart devices now run into billions numerically, the scale of installation of such devices in a smart city is mammoth. Any upgrades to these devices will also face the same problems and challenges. Such public infrastructure installation drives up costs which may eventually translate to higher taxation contributions from the public. Therefore, this highlights the complicated nature urban management and critics of IoT remain unconvinced that such complex tasks can be left to machines, algorithms and smart mechanical systems. Moreover, humans are complex animals and they show great diversity of individual differences. Culturally, they are heterogeneous rather than homogenous in their political, economic, social thoughts and differ even in lifestyles too. Embedded sensors in individually used smart devices or sensors embedded throughout a smart city are unable to capture fully human instincts, emotions and random changing of minds.

The military industrial complex and defence industries conceptualize the IoT as a potential weapon. Devices that share information can be modified for extracting information from others. This translates to advantages on the battlefield. Electromagnetic pulses have long been used on the battlefield to disable enemy telecommunications systems. Electromagnetic emissions can be re-diverted for use in extraction of digital information from others. The weapon-ization of IoT may cause security concerns among governments and intelligence agencies, fearing their information and communication infrastructures may be compromised. It also brings to question the ethics of IoT research since devices invented through design and research may be dual use in nature (usable by both civilian and military end users). Even toy dolls that are IoT-enabled with the capabilities of recording conversations and sending recorded messages as meta data to servers has been classified as an illegal spying tool by certain EU (European Union) government. Given that a lot of personal and confidential information are stored in cloud and in IoT informational systems, it can make many people vulnerable to identity thefts and cyber hacking. A conversation between stakeholders including intelligence agencies, law enforcement departments, manufacturers of smart devices, internet regulators, software developers and product designers is urgently needed to address the issue of privacy.

IoT and Trends

IoT in the US has become a normative vocabulary among the Silicon Valley elites, tech geeks, technology-savvy members of the public. Some smart devices have become ubiquitous. For example, in the arena of personal smart devices, 12 million pieces of smart watches were sold in the US by November 2017.[2] Therefore, a substantial number of Americans

---

[2] Press, Gil, "10 Predictions for the Internet of Things (IoT) in 2018" dated 9 November 2017 in Forbes website [downloaded on 9 November 2017], available at https://www.forbes.com/sites/gilpress/2017/11/09/10-predictions-for-the-internet-of-things-iot-in-2018/#5289dda735e7.

are already wearing health-monitoring personal smart devices, generating health data while they are working, sleeping and living their daily lives. Even as the use of personal smart devices proliferate, the US authorities continue to warn about cybersecurity. In 2016, the then Assistant Secretary for Cyber Policy at the Department of Homeland Security Robert Silvers warned at a symposium hosted by the Coalition for Cybersecurity Policy and Law:

> We have a rapidly closing window to ensure that security properly accounted for, (because) once an ecosystem is already built and deployed it's infinitely harder to try to bolt on security at the back end.[3]

This is a highly persuasive argument that it is eminently easier to build strong cybersecurity foundations to protect smart devices than to plug the loopholes in the future when the system is already up and running. A pre-emptive measure instead of a patch-up.

While privacy and confidentiality advocates are going uphill to fight for privacy for the individuals in the US, others are franker in admitting that there is no longer a concept of "absolute privacy" in the US. Former Federal Bureau of Investigations (FBI) Director James Comey (tenure of directorship: 4 September 2013–9 May 2017) pointed out:

> …[Americans should not have expectations of] absolute privacy…There is no such thing as absolute privacy in America; there is no place outside of judicial reach. Even our communications with our spouses, with our clergy members, with our attorneys are not absolutely private in America. In appropriate circumstances, a judge can compel any one of us to testify in court about those very private communications…[Americans] have a reasonable expectation of privacy in our homes, in our cars, in our devices…It is a vital part of being an American. The government cannot invade our privacy without good reason, reviewable in court.[4]

Without including smart devices into the conversation, Comey is basically arguing that all communications in America are subject to legal obligations of public hearing and testimonies provided legal procedures are met and the courts judge these contents' disclosure to be in the public interest. All legal

[3]Weise, Elizabeth, "Feds Offer Ways to Make Internet of Things More Secure" dated 15 November 2016 in *USA Today* website [downloaded on 15 November 2016], available at https://www.usatoday.com/story/tech/news/2016/11/15/feds-offer-ways-make-internet-things-more-secure/93925944/.

[4]Mallonee, Mary Kay and Eugene Scott, "Comey: 'There Is No Such Thing as Absolute Privacy in America'" dated 9 March 2017 in CNN website [downloaded on 9 March 2017], available at https://edition.cnn.com/2017/03/08/politics/james-comey-privacy-cybersecurity/index.html.

procedures for disclosure are also subject to courts' review. Human adaptability to dissipation of privacy (as the Helsinki Privacy Project shows) as well as lawfully enforced legal procedures appear to be the most reliable safeguards on protecting privacy in the US.

Meanwhile, the IoT revolution continues unabated. Even the most un-industrialized sector of America's economy are undergoing IoT-enabling revolution. There are now groups within the US specialized in providing IoT solutions to agricultural and rural communities. Sensors and tech solutions are needed for monitoring crops, feeding livestock, etc. Rationalization in terms of increasing the productivity of agricultural output and scientific ways of improving yields are some of the priorities for the application of IoT-enabled smart devices in the agricultural sector. These are industry-based niche communities that share information, best practices and technology know-how with each other. As with all advocated reasons for data-sharing, it promotes intra-industry competition while benefitting from each other's information and data to streamline and improve existing products.

The US appears to be self-reflecting and debating about ethical issues surrounding the use of IoT while maintaining its lead as the world's most advanced developer and user of IoT. Another country is trying to play catch-up. As for China, an economy often caricatured as the world's manufacturing workshop, IoT is a possible platform for increasing productivity, especially in the context of a maturing economy. Unlike the US which has a laissez-faire economy that has an inbuilt creative destruction process for innovation, China's state-led system has a masterplan for guiding its net lap of economic development. The authorities have put in place a "Made in China 2025" blueprint and one of the features of this scheme is to integrate IoT with China's manufacturing sector. Specially, China hopes to integrate big data, IoT, cloud and mobile smartphone internet access into the same platform. In some aspects, China wants to work with the firms and manufacturers in Germany and learn from their successful features. Germany's Siemens and Chinese tech giants like Alibaba.com are active in providing IoT solutions. Both countries have ambitious plans for Industry 4.0, therefore they can learn from each other's experiences.

In one area of China's infrastructure, this integration is already in its advanced stages, as trains, buses and even individual shared bicycles have all turned smart, with every single piece of equipment embedded with chips. Ofo, mobile and other bike-sharing, smartphone-paying companies are the pioneers in tracking bicycles and making them available to users. Some of these smart transportation technologies are exported overseas, including Singapore. Another successful digitally plugged transportation company is Didi which runs like Uber and able to call for cabs for app users. It is also one of the world's most environmentally friendly company with a large fleet of electric vehicles (EVs). Because of this association with EVs, it made sense for Didi to enter the business of EVs. In manufacturing cutting-edge world-class products by 2025, China hopes to integrate these smart technologies into its smart cities project. China is ambitiously building 500 smart cities all across its country and looks poised to become the world's largest market for smart technologies that are useful for smart cities.

With the government pushing the agenda, China provides tax breaks for IoT manufacturing companies. China is also scouring the US to headhunt for big data analytics, Artificial Intelligence (A.I.) and IoT solution providers. Both the academic community and the IoT-skilled personnel are working hard to implement the government's top-down policies. The way forward is fraught with challenges, especially since conservations in the US have labelled "Made in 2025" an existential threat to US lead in science and technology (an issue festering in the trade tensions between the two countries). It may also yield benefits if success is achievable. The rest of the economies in the world are not standing still as China forges ahead with its smart cities project while the Association of Southeast Asian Nations (ASEAN) intends to create a network of smart cities. (See Chapter 8 [Case Study 3] for the case study of China smart cities projects.) In fact, the region that China is located in, the Asia-Pacific, is also steaming ahead with smart cities construction.

TRENDS IN THE SINGAPORE CASE STUDY

Besides China and the US, Singapore is also rapidly developing its IoT platform. Like its smart city initiative and big data sharing in the SingStat website and its overall regional and global trade worldview, Singapore opts for an open and transparent platform with global normative standards in building its own access to the IoT. Singapore is against the idea of silo-ed approach erected by tech giants and dominant players. It advocates open standards for all entrepreneurs, IT developers/providers and other companies to tap into those standards for their own product and services development. Fostering an open standard is not possible without the strong hand of the state to pry open access to IoT platforms. A state-appointed IoT government committee was established in 2013 to form IoT basic standards in sectors like architecture, interoperability, security and data protection. Industry advocates/lobbies like Open Connectivity Foundation (OCF) are contributing to the framing of IoT specifications for better coordination between IoT suppliers, working with the Singapore Semiconductor Industry Association in March 2017 to have its IoT specifications taken up by small and medium-sized enterprises (SMEs) in Singapore.

Open standards can also promote the idea of having IoT-compatible systems in buildable blocks so that additional complex units can be added on or taken off according to current and near-future needs. The important point behind this thinking is to have a pluralism of choice so that consumers can pick from an offering of suitable technologies. Choices also promote price competition and drive companies to outcompete each other. Having various kinds, brands, levels of capabilities of technologies to choose from is especially important since technologies have very short upgrade cycles and short shelf life that quickly enter obsolescence quite rapidly. Moreover, not all smart cities, companies, organizations and individuals need every single function that a smart device can offer at the same time. Less complicated devices or high performing devices with less complicated functions can make it simpler to use and reduce exposure to hacking and other cybersecurity risks. Therefore, a buyer beware caution as well as adopting a longer term utilization vision may be helpful when acquiring such equipment, for the government, private sector as well as individuals. Technologies become obsolete quickly, they need to be upgraded fast and cutting-edge technologies have a short shelf life and quickly become a discounted item in the tech world.

The other cautionary attitude taken by the Singapore government is in the sector of cybersecurity. Adopting any IoT-enabled required corresponding acquisition and installation of relevant security measures to protect the integrity of those devices. This is also to protect the data contained within them. Security patches are needed for the operating systems found in the companies and businesses. Encryption is also needed to protect the online communications and industrial secrets found in the servers of these companies. Other measures include the use of biometric markers. Many manufacturers and retailers not located in security-sensitive industries are not sufficiently sensitized to the importance of security. Therefore, industry experts, as well as senior Singapore government officials urged all Singaporean businesses to integrate security measures from the onset so that the foundations are strong. Even individuals need to be vigilant since they have to take responsibility in leaving behind digital footprints, meta-data and other personal data. In the very near future, remote devices embedded in the confines of the home can constantly monitor the health indicators of the individual. This connotes a high level of intrusion into the daily lives of humans. Individuals, like companies, have to be sensitized to protecting the privacy of their confidential data. The technology allows humans to monitor their health closely and spot anomalies that can be resolved quickly before it becomes a health risk. IoT and smart devices are expected to bring a lot of convenience to Singapore, especially in managing complex problems like the effects of an ageing population but, with enhanced convenience, comes the individual responsibility to protect those data, especially since more human tasks will now be relegated to machines to perform.

Responsibility for cybersecurity is now a collective one since hackers can now infiltrate large computer system from personal devices (PDs) as basic as a notebook computer. Some stakeholders (private sector executives, bureaucrats/technocrats, thought leaders, in Singapore are urging for a set of best practices and regulatory framework to prevent ordinary electrical appliances from communicating personal data to marketing companies and e-commerce retailers. They want some form of industry norms and practices to guide the use of data in everyday life. In addition to installation of security technologies and measures, appropriately qualified personnel are needed to ensure those systems are operated in the proper manner and maintained consistently without lapses. In this sense, once again, the Singapore government can be a model for the private sector to follow. Systems should also be appropriately secure enough to withstand hostile attacks from state and non-state sources. The Singapore government had hoped to be a model for the private sector to emulate. In addition, its agencies are taking additional security measures. The private sector is also calling upon the government to provide funding and incentives for research work on developing new technologies.

In 2017, Singapore's Government Technology Agency (GovTech) had begun work on a sensor network spanning the country (the Smart Nation Sensor Platform) that features standardized security infrastructure like the data-sharing gateway, video and data analytics machines. Public transportation infrastructure is a common feature targeted for smart device conversion many first-tier smart cities around the world. The urgency in instituting smart technologies in the smart city infrastructure is to deal with or pre-empt paralyzing traffic jams in first-tier cities. Singapore is not an exception as it intends to install sensors in its public lamp posts that have evaluative monitoring capabilities to determine humidity, temperature and other climatic conditions. The next chapter will bring the discussion to a macro level, implementing Industry 4.0 technologies and smart devices on the scale of an entire city.

BIBLIOGRAPHY

Horwitz, Lauren, "Can Smart City Infrastructure Alleviate the Strain of City Growth?" undated in Cisco.com website [downloaded on 1 September 2018]. Available at https://www.cisco.com/c/en/us/solutions/internet-of-things/smart-city-infrastructure.html.

Mallonee, Mary Kay and Eugene Scott, "Comey: 'There Is No Such Thing as Absolute Privacy in America'" dated 9 March 2017 in CNN website [downloaded on 9 March 2017]. Available at https://edition.cnn.com/2017/03/08/politics/james-comey-privacy-cybersecurity/index.html.

Press, Gil, "10 Predictions for the Internet of Things (IoT) in 2018" dated 9 November 2017 in Forbes website [downloaded on 9 November 2017]. Available at https://www.forbes.com/sites/gilpress/2017/11/09/10-predictions-for-the-internet-of-things-iot-in-2018/#5289dda735e7.

Weise, Elizabeth, "Feds Offer Ways to Make Internet of Things More Secure" dated 15 November 2016 in *USA Today* website [downloaded on 15 November 2016]. Available at https://www.usatoday.com/story/tech/news/2016/11/15/feds-offer-ways-make-internet-things-more-secure/93925944/.

CHAPTER 4

The Rise of Smart Cities

On a more macro-scale, robotic applications, algorithm-based applications, Artificial Intelligence (A.I.) and other digital technologies will be implemented on a city-wide scale, turning entire cities into "smart cities". The utilization of cloud computing, energy management and enhancing the standards of living, practice sustainable development and bringing about liveable cities are also criteria for defining smart cities. The urgency and significance of building smart cities lies in the reality that more than half the globe's denizens now live in urban cities and this number is projected to increase to 70% by 2050 (Asia will be the lead here) with exponential growth in megacities.[1] Therefore, today's first-tier cities are now keen to come up with innovative solutions to allocate resources, manage sustainable growth and practise good governance. Another reason for studying smart cities is that they are normally engines of economic growth for most countries. Their abilities to handle logistics, contribute to law enforcement, and manage economic competitiveness by keeping ahead of the pack will be crucial nationally.

In Taiwan, for example, there are interested stakeholders who want to embed Internet of Things (IoT) technologies into the public transportation system, especially a system that can manage scooter traffic and drivers in the near future.[2] The most significant progress regarding smart city development in Taiwan has been made in the areas of smart transportation, smart energy, and smart healthcare. This includes the development of smart energy grids by

[1] Carmodyon, Patrick, "Taiwan Leads in Smart Cities" dated 13 November 2016 in *Taiwan Business Topics* [downloaded on 13 November 2016], available at https://topics.amcham.com.tw/2016/11/taiwan-leads-smart-cities/.

[2] Salmonsen, Renée, "Connecting Cars and IoT at Taipei Smart City Summit—A.I. on the Road: Applying IoT Solutions to Traffic in Taiwan" dated 28 March 2018 in *Taiwan News* website [downloaded on 28 March 2018], available at https://www.taiwannews.com.tw/en/news/3392486.

© The Author(s) 2019
T. W. Lim, *Industrial Revolution 4.0, Tech Giants, and Digitized Societies*,
https://doi.org/10.1007/978-981-13-7470-8_4

the local electric scooter company, Gogoro, and the EasyCard, a card with an embedded chip that can be used for borrowing books from the public library and drive popular consumption.[3] YouBike, a bike-sharing scheme, is integrated with an app that is both a fitness tracker and lifestyle guide (e.g. to restaurants). YouBike can monitor, keep tabs on and know the whereabouts of thousands of bikes under its scheme at any one time. Car parking spaces are also under electronic surveillance. In these ways, Taiwan, especially its capital city Taipei, is already a smart city.

In addition, Chunghwa Telecom has scanners, monitors and sensors placed on public lighting to manage the intensity of energy use for lighting and also to monitor temperatures, pollution indexes, and precipitation/rainfall.[4] Changhwa's Smart City for All system ensures no one is left behind and is inclusive of all Taiwanese including those who are physically handicapped. Changhwa is coming up with innovations for the impaired and senior citizens who may be incapacitated to differing extents. For example, its app i4Blind provides 4G location tracking signals, direction guidance functions, location info provider, warnings of dangers/obstacles and local community/business info; all of which can help community volunteers to guide their charges through schools, subway platforms, high speed rail (HSR) terminals and museums.[5]

Even within Taiwan, there is already a network of smart cities, including Taichung which has a strong telecommunications industry that provides advanced broadband reach into the distant districts of the city, creating cloud libraries for the rural children to read books and facilitating rural teachers' video conferencing needs.[6] Taichung has also worked with the French Dassault Systems to acquire rapid calculation equipment to enable Taiwanese researchers to develop entire lines of smart factories and production systems that can be sold directly to Southeast Asian (SE Asian) customers.[7] In a way, this was a precursor of the current Tsai Ing-wen administration's "Go South"

[3] Salmonsen, Renée, "Connecting Cars and IoT at Taipei Smart City Summit—A.I. on the Road: Applying IoT Solutions to Traffic in Taiwan" dated 28 March 2018 in *Taiwan News* website [downloaded on 28 March 2018], available at https://www.taiwannews.com.tw/en/news/3392486.

[4] Carmodyon, Patrick, "Taiwan Leads in Smart Cities" dated 13 November 2016 in *Taiwan Business Topics* [downloaded on 13 November 2016], available at https://topics.amcham.com.tw/2016/11/taiwan-leads-smart-cities/.

[5] Carmodyon, Patrick, "Taiwan Leads in Smart Cities" dated 13 November 2016 in *Taiwan Business Topics* [downloaded on 13 November 2016], available at https://topics.amcham.com.tw/2016/11/taiwan-leads-smart-cities/.

[6] Fulcoon, Matthew, "Taiwan's Cities Smarten Up" dated 15 August 2017 in *Taiwan Business Topics* (Taipei: American Chamber of Commerce Taipei AmCham Taipei), available at https://topics.amcham.com.tw/2017/08/taiwans-cities-smarten/.

[7] Fulcoon, Matthew, "Taiwan's Cities Smarten Up" dated 15 August 2017 in *Taiwan Business Topics* (Taipei: American Chamber of Commerce Taipei AmCham Taipei), available at https://topics.amcham.com.tw/2017/08/taiwans-cities-smarten/.

policy. The Taiwanese leadership was eager to avoid economic overdependence on China by reaching out to Southeast Asia and India for trade and commerce.

Taiwan has started its external collaborations with Indian companies like Bengaluru in India in the field of information and communications technologies (ICT). In developing smart cities, the complementarity between the two lies in Taiwan's expertise in hardware development and manufacturing while Taiwanese companies seek Indian strengths in ICT, virtual reality, and A.I.[8] Bengaluru is already seeking Taiwanese companies' expertise in electronic bike sharing systems, subway management and electronic toll system while Taiwan plans to invest US$10 billion in India.[9] Taiwan's domestically eTag system has installed sensors, computerized monitors and computer servers in highway toll gantries run by Far Eastern Electronic Toll Co. that can scan cars for electronic toll payment without slowing them down to a stop, thereby saving fuels on cars (millions of litres annually) in the process.[10]

Taiwan is well placed to capitalize on its strengths in ICT as well as experiences in managing an urbanized smart city (like Taipei). Taiwan can export such expertise to the global smart cities marketplace which is estimated to reach US$1.57 trillion in 2020 (Asia accounts for US$1 trillion yearly in smart city market by 2025), built on the foundation of current figures of more than one thousand cities currently in various stages of smart city programmes.[11] At the same time, the Taiwanese government is aware that neighbouring governments are also going full blast into smart city projects. For example, Tokyo is already testing A.I. systems that can track the large numbers of medical claims in nursing care, Moscow is researching on A.I. cancer detection/diagnosis systems and locate new properties for residents, Hong Kong is utilizing A.I. softwares that can foresee landslides/erosions.[12]

---

[8] *Economic Times (ET)*, "Taiwan to Empower Bengaluru's Quest to Become a Smart City" dated 13 March 2018 in *Economic Times (ET)* website [downloaded on 13 March 2018], available at https://economictimes.indiatimes.com/magazines/panache/taiwan-to-empower-bengalurus-quest-to-become-a-smart-city/articleshow/63279696.cms.

[9] *Economic Times (ET)*, "Taiwan to Empower Bengaluru's Quest to Become a Smart City" dated 13 March 2018 in *Economic Times (ET)* website [downloaded on 13 March 2018], available at https://economictimes.indiatimes.com/magazines/panache/taiwan-to-empower-bengalurus-quest-to-become-a-smart-city/articleshow/63279696.cms.

[10] Carmodyon, Patrick, "Taiwan Leads in Smart Cities" dated 13 November 2016 in *Taiwan Business Topics* [downloaded on 13 November 2016], available at https://topics.amcham.com.tw/2016/11/taiwan-leads-smart-cities/.

[11] Carmodyon, Patrick, "Taiwan Leads in Smart Cities" dated 13 November 2016 in *Taiwan Business Topics* [downloaded on 13 November 2016], available at https://topics.amcham.com.tw/2016/11/taiwan-leads-smart-cities/.

[12] GovInsider daily briefing news, "How AI Will Transform Taiwan's Economy" dated 10 April 2018 in the AI Taiwan website [downloaded on 10 April 2018] (Taiwan: Government of Taiwan), available at https://ai.taiwan.gov.tw/news/how-ai-will-transform-taiwans-economy/.

In terms of infrastructure, a smart city is likely to have embedded sensors and other data-collecting gauges or devices located throughout the city. The collected data are then used to make improvements in allocation of resources, regulation of traffic/human flows, and adjust intensities of light sources to save energy. In constructing smart cities, it may be useful for the technocratic planners to bear in mind that each city is unique and different. Therefore, any solution designed for urban problems must take into consideration the unique characteristics of every city. In the case of Taiwan, for example, specific features include the high density of scooters in the country. Taiwan is generally more prepared than many other cities in constructing a smart city since it is technologically advanced economy itself with a formidable electronics manufacturing industry. In fact, some private sector leaders who bemoaned Taiwan's missed opportunities to go into smartphone technologies (hardware) argue that the economy can leapfrog and enter the digital application realm by becoming a digital solution provider instead of being stuck at subcontracting OEM manufacturers.[13]

The other world-class smart city in East Asia is Singapore. Singapore is not only interested in building a smart city but a smart nation as well where people have "meaningful and fulfilled lives".[14] Singapore's approach is inclusive and involves all stakeholders from the government to the private sector and the individuals, otherwise known as the "whole of nation" approach. There are several objectives set out for forging a smart nation and city. First, there are incentives to make as many citizen-based transactions online as possible. Second, there is motivation to ensure e-payments are safe and secure. Third, build sensors that can make the city as secure and responsive to its inhabitants as possible. Fourth, use the latest technologies like A.I. to make urban transportation as seamless as possible and pave the way for autonomous vehicles (AVs) to arrive. Fifth, institute the "moments of life" and make public services as relevant and complementary as possible to every Singaporean at different stages of their lives.

Through the smart nation approach, the authorities appear to focus on the software of building a smart nation/smart city. Singapore is not keen to follow the data centric approach but rather prefer to make their data as usable and accessible to local communities and residents as far as possible. In other words, it is a human-centric approach to make data work for humans rather than mechanistically compiling and churning out data. Human communities (or even an entire society) then get together to determine how they wish to use the collected data and provide feedback for suitable solutions and policies to sociopolitical and socioeconomic issues. Even data accumulated by

[13] Fulcoon, Matthew, "Taiwan's Cities Smarten Up" dated 15 August 2017 in *Taiwan Business Topics* (Taipei: American Chamber of Commerce Taipei AmCham Taipei), available at https://topics.amcham.com.tw/2017/08/taiwans-cities-smarten/.

[14] Smart Nation and Digital Government Office, "Smart Nation" dated 2018 in the Smart Nation website [downloaded on 1 May 2018], available at https://www.smartnation.sg/.

public agencies are made available to Singaporeans and the general public so that they can work with the authorities to come up with people-centric solutions.[15] Singapore is keen to attract R&D firms and multinationals to the city to trial their technologies and use Singapore as a test bed. Singapore fully understands how creativity generally sprouts from entrepreneurs with good ideas but lack practical experience. Therefore, the authorities have paired up technopreneurs with experienced industry practitioners and leaders.

Singapore is already leading in smart cities rankings in many areas. For example, its ability to handle and manage traffic is acknowledged globally as a golden benchmark showcase model. The use of smart technologies by Land Transport Authority (LTA) to manage traffic flows have saved the average Singaporean driver as much as 60 hours annually.[16] At the heart of traffic management capabilities, Singapore's philosophy has always been to control the population of cars on the road. Faced with an ageing population, Singapore is also installing monitoring devices to ensure the safety of elderly individuals and to reduce crime, Singapore has also implemented smart surveillance devices to monitor illegal activities. Besides the innovative nature of these measures and the extensiveness of implementation, the rapidity of changes in becoming a smart city has caught the attention of leading smart cities ranking and experts/specialists.

There are a number of ways through Taipei and Singapore can cooperate and learn from each other. In terms of quality public transportation system, Singapore ranked No. 1 and Taipei second in the 2017 Smart Cities Index from EasyPark Group.[17] Taipei has more experience in managing a large number of scooters in its public transportation system, therefore Singapore may wish to learn from such experiences for application to its motorbike, scooters, 2-wheeled vehicles and bicycles population. Similarly, both Taipei and Singapore use the electronic gantry systems, they can exchange notes on common challenges facing the two systems in the advent of the AVs. Singapore's measures to control car populations may be useful as a form of reference for city-sized entities like Taipei.

Singapore may be ahead in terms of human centricity when it comes to building a smart nation but it can also learn from Taipei's attempts to make the city friendlier to handicapped individuals. Similarly, Taipei may wish to learn from Singapore how to test bed new technologies and attracting foreign

[15] Smart Nation and Digital Government Office, "Smart Nation" dated 2018 in the Smart Nation website [downloaded on 1 May 2018], available at https://www.smartnation.sg/.

[16] Sregantan, Navin, "Singapore Tops Global Smart City Performance Ranking in 2017: Study" dated 13 March 2018 [downloaded on 13 March 2018], available at http://www.businesstimes.com.sg/government-economy/singapore-tops-global-smart-city-performance-ranking-in-2017-study.

[17] Hynes, Casey, "Singapore Ranks as World's No. 2 Smart City, Report Says" dated 10 November 2017 in Forbes.com [downloaded on 10 November 2017], available at https://www.forbes.com/sites/chynes/2017/11/10/singapore-ranks-as-one-of-the-top-smart-cities-in-the-world/#c234bb5717d6.

direct investments and/or foreign multinational companies to test new technologies in the city. Taipei's economic outreach is focused on high tech cities in South and Southeast Asia, e.g. Bengaluru while Singapore, as the ASEAN (Association of Southeast Asian Nation) Chair in 2018, is proposing linking up smart cities within ASEAN. This was proposed in the 32nd ASEAN Summit meeting. One advantage in creating a smart city network is the larger pool of potential solution providers drawn from the entire ASEAN region. Any challenge faced by one single smart city in ASEAN can search for innovative solutions offered by tech companies located throughout the region. Such solutions may even come from intra-regional home-grown companies, giving small and medium sized enterprises (SMEs) economic opportunities to work with state bureaucracies in solving regional problems.

While Singapore is one of the first-tier cities in the region, it can benefit more by being embedded within a larger network of smart cities. Singapore led the charge within ASEAN to propose linking up smart cities so that the first-tier cities within ASEAN can form a network to compete with other larger countries that also have integrated smart cities regionalism. China has publicly released the news that it wants 500 of its cities to become smart and have started this process for these 500 cities in 2017.[18] (Refer to the Chapter 8 [Case Study 3] for a detailed treatment of Chinese smart cities projects.) Therefore, Taipei may learn more about regional connectivity among smart cities from the Singapore initiative in the different stages of implementation. A couple of points can be observed from the Singaporean regional initiative. First, smart cities can only succeed if technologies are adapted to local conditions. ASEAN smart cities offer the diversity for Taipei to learn from in terms of localization and indigenization of technologies for implementation. Second, Taipei and its sister cities in Taiwan are more homogenous in racial/ethnic makeup and level of economic development. Therefore, it may be useful to learn from Singapore's experience in navigating through a diverse region, especially since Taipei is keen to have closer economic cooperation with Southeast Asian economies.

JOBS AND EMPLOYMENT

Soft skills and people's skills are given new emphasis in the future of workplace. Communication skills, interactional capabilities, ability to show empathy, problem solving on the spot, the art of persuasion, service to an organization, collaborative ease with fellow employees, strategizing and thinking long term are all new skills sought after by contemporary employers. They are also regarded as the more humanistic parts of the job. Advocates

---

[18] Hynes, Casey, "Singapore Ranks as World's No. 2 Smart City, Report Says" dated 10 November 2017 in Forbes.com [downloaded on 10 November 2017], available at https://www.forbes.com/sites/chynes/2017/11/10/singapore-ranks-as-one-of-the-top-smart-cities-in-the-world/#c234bb5717d6.

of automation, A.I. and robotic sometimes argue that these tools facilitate emphasis on more humanistic assignments, enhancing their creativity, show empathy for fellow human beings and work on higher order skills to promote strategic thinking and understanding among fellow human beings.

Besides the focus on soft skills, others believe that human–machine integration in the workplace is inevitable. Just as physical reality is now enhance-able with virtual reality and augmented reality, workers can now be complemented with science and technology to form an augmented work-force. Humans are better in some assignments (including those with soft skills requirements) while machines are better in others (repetitive, standard-ized, highly logical assignments). Analysts, policymakers and academics are now debating over optimal ways to deploy such augmented workforce and there are no conclusive ideas yet. Even a strategy that looks at separation of functions requires its own set of training. Meanwhile, companies and gov-ernments are struggling to prepare their general populace and workforce to match this emerging reality and outcome of the workplace of the future.

Besides soft skills training, there are many considerations involved in empowering employees with digital access. Companies need to consider the investment returns of equipment used to provide this access, the secu-rity implications of using such devices and policies like whether workers are allowed to bring these devices to work. In high security environments, some companies and organizations may choose to use only intranet for security of data and use only a few select stand-alone terminals for external connections to the Internet at the digital workplace. Some have defined the digital work-place as one that has all data stored in the cloud protected by cybersecurity. Given this definition, it implies the existence of a digital online security sys-tem within the company. Companies typically opt for a specialized department to take care of cybersecurity or set up a committee to oversee the security of data. For companies (and civil service departments) that rely on both intranet and internet external connection. Some ground rules setting may be useful for employees who use the intranet. Training is provided for the employees to remind them not to use intranet facilities for personal messages.

Some companies also provide external hardware devices to access the intranet and/or the Internet. Access to these devices elicit responses from the users. There is a psychological and emotive element to the use of digi-tal devices at the workplace, which is that it could be a morale booster for employees who feel prestige and pride in owning such state-of-the-art devices. Others may feel excited about using the new tech in their workplace. In terms of mindset, a company, its employees, management and trade unions have to embrace and accept the reality of digital disruptions. Connectivity is no longer an option but a prerequisite to many work functions, includ-ing global collaborations, peer exchanges and teamwork facilitation. Even a device as simple as a smartphone can achieve this connectivity while other devices like the notepad and its connectivity to the Internet can be used as a mobile catalogue of limitless featured items.

Changing mindset to adapt to digital technologies also requires patience and resilience as one is connected constantly and there are expectations by other parties of instantaneous or fast response time for replies. This may cause stress for certain individuals unused to such fast responses. To assist with smoother adaptation, adequate training may be needed to transition workers to such working modes. Due to the convenience that modern and contemporary communications devices bring to the ordinary workforce, it did away with some professions whose previous work functions were based on telecommunications in the previous industrial revolutions, e.g. Switchboard operators, telegram operators, etc. In the current Fourth Industrialization (Industry 4.0), there needs to be a detailed study to detect how many human jobs can be or have been eliminated with the convenience of digital telecommunications.

The way people worked would have also changed, with more mobility for teams that are spread out and keeping constant touch with the pulses, market supply–demand situations and partners in regional markets. People may have to get used to not being in the office for routinized work. Employees may even commute to the office only on demand and when there is need to so. Otherwise, they may just receive instructions through messages, emails, videos messaging and other communication formats. Employees who are posted overseas or provincially within the same country for assignments may also have to get used to the fact that they will stay in touch with their families electronically through digital communications. Work–life balance in this sense may have to be tampered with since employees may theoretically be on beck and call all the time. Some governments have turned to legislation to manage such high levels of work-related digital connectivity. France for example has frowned upon employers' emailing their employees in the weekend. Other countries like Japan is advocating greater work–life balance. Companies, workers, trade unions as well as individuals have to determine for themselves where to draw the line between on-call demand for work assignments and personal time.

Companies have their parts to play as well. When the lines between human and non-human are clearly ascertained, there is a need to re-integrate human communications (e.g. face-to-face dialogues/conversations) back into the company's operations and corporate culture. This is done so that the human component of communications is not missing from the company's operations. Just as parents are now trying to encourage their children to go outdoors and play in the park, companies may need to persuade its employees to have coffee dispenser machines conversations, chats across the partitions of an open office concept or even organize company activities like teambuilding and retreats to foster more interactions between individuals. Companies may also want to set up digital platforms for company discussions within a secure digital space so that employees do not take their disgruntled complaints to a public realm and hurt the company's standing or incur legal repercussions. Just like complaints procedures, such digital feedback spaces can curate employee information for a systematic presentation to senior management for further action or mitigation of the issue at hand.

Sometimes, it may be essential to utilize digital technologies simply because one's business partners have already switched to such systems and therefore it becomes necessary to catch up due to compatibility of systems. In the digital workplace, it becomes essential that employees are equipped with the appropriate technologies, including devices like tablets. Such equipment assist company employees in tapping into globalized networks and teams operating cross border. These equipment are time-sensitive in terms of level of capabilities and need to be upgraded constantly, e.g. from push button to voice activation, in the near future from flat screen to 3-D projections. Mobility appears to be the keyword as workers can work from anywhere according to their assignment needs. Some of these uses of technologies can translate into savings as videoconferencing for example can help to save money on travel costs like air tickets. Besides the hardware, companies need to better integrate their operations with the use of equipment. Staff members for example should be adequately exposed to and trained for using the system. Cloud computing has become a popular option for companies as it facilitates access to data from all locations but placing large volumes of data in the cloud exposes those data to security issues. Staff members should also be trained in cybersecurity so that their lines of communications and the contents of communications are safe and secure.

In the service sector, some observers have advocated focusing more on service personnel and customer interface and the employee's enhancement of the customer experience as well as further improve the branding image of the company consequently. In other words, human centricity and the ability to think in a way that resonate with one's customers will become increasingly important, especially in the realm of persuasion, empathy and communication. Internally, within the companies, managers and senior executives are now required to be in tune with their organizational needs, able to mobilize fellow employees and harness unity to perform her/his tasks, something that has become just as important as effective interfacing with external customers.

The mechanical aspects of service sector, for e.g. administrative procedures, payment processing, standard operating procedures found in manuals, clerical work no longer need human administrators. Instead, service sector employees previously carrying out such tasks will need to reskill to interact orally and emotionally with the customers, advising them on personalized matters like investment strategies, goal-setting, personal priorities and anxieties mitigation instead. The human dimensions of their jobs become the major value-add of their existence.

Employees and workers may also need to get used to flexibility and mobility at the workplace. Lifetime employment (LTE) or even stable employment may become increasingly tenuous as employees cope with increasing need to manage projects that solve specific problems, the need to freelance when their skills are not in demand, constantly search for entrepreneurial opportunities, take up gigs that value-add to their career or financial needs, etc. These are non-traditional activities that cope with the unstable and fluctuating needs of the workplace.

In fact, in some developed economies of the world, part-time jobs are becoming common and de facto major source of employment for young people. An example is Japan whose scenario may be instructive. Japanese large companies used to practise LTE system where executives (called *sarariman* or salaryman in Japan) gave their loyalty and hardworking service to the companies in exchange for stable employment. These executives were not fired even when the economy was not doing well. They might be transferred to branches with a better title and a lower pay or posted to another company within the conglomerate network (known as *keiretsu* in Japanese). When the fast-growing economy of Japan came to a halt in 1989 after the economic bubble burst and as Japan entered decades of recessionary conditions, LTE broke down.

Currently, some Japanese graduates and high school leavers have to take up non-stable employment. They could be doing subcontracting work similar to assignment-based work moving from project to project assignments. This mode of work is performed by what the Japanese call freeters. They jump from job to job (typically 1–3 years in duration per job) and are perpetually employed but in short-term contracts with the downside that it does not come with job security, insurance and welfare benefits. Nevertheless, it provides employment for these individuals. Others work in part-time jobs (*arubaito* in Japanese) taking certain hourly shifts or day shifts.

The upside of such arrangements is that it provides employment for various individuals but the downside is the emergence of some unanticipated social trends. In the case of Japan, some freeters and part-timers started to stay with their Showa-era parents who had stable jobs and now enjoying generous pension. Consequently, they began to be known as parasitic singles who live off their parents without paying rent and lead a carefree, sometimes high-consumption lifestyle. It also discourages these singles from getting married, accentuating Japan's birth rate problem, one of the fastest ageing society in the world. Some of these social trends may need to be taken into consideration eventually by the authorities, especially since almost all developed countries are facing ageing societal problems. Some developed economies that depended traditionally on migration to replenish their population stocks are facing anti-globalization/protectionist backlash from their native populations. See Chapter 9 (Case Study 4) for a detailed analysis of Japanese policies (comparing with Hong Kong) to cope with the impact of an ageing population.

Chapter 9 (Case Study 4) examines the policies in Japan and Hong Kong designed to alleviate the negative effects of an ageing population are of great interest to demographics, ageing and social welfare research. The two societies show a significant contrast in their approach towards coping with an ageing population. Hong Kong has spawned an Non-Profit Organization (NPO) sector working with the bureaucracy, volunteers, social workers, community groups to look after the needs of the elderly. It is a laissez-faire approach dependent on community groups and volunteers with shared resources from the government. Japan's approach contrasts with Hong Kong in the sense that it too has a highly active NPO sector but the NPO sector works closely with the government in a civil society–state partnership with the state providing resources to local groups to manage certain programmes while steering it towards professionalization. (Refer to Chapter 7 [Case Study 2] for some details on service learning in Japan that involves NPOs as well.) Another area is the use of technologies to cope with an ageing population and to promote active ageing. Japan has some of the world's most advanced technologies in robotics designed to help with managing elderly care. They include assistive and therapeutic robots. (More details available in Chapter 6 [Case Study 1].) Hong Kong is also keen to tap into technology to support its ageing population and active ageing narrative. In mid-2017, Hong Kong started looking into the idea of "gerontechnology".

Another group of advocates prefers a time-tested approach in coping with digital and robotic technologies. Go back to the drawing board and re-design jobs. In re-designing the workplace, entrepreneurs, governments, private sector and other stakeholders are now trying to differentiate human skills from standardized assignments or repetitive tasks based on logic that can be executed by robots. Human characteristics like empathy, creativity, leadership, listening, moralizing, soft communication skills, teamwork and collaboration, ethical thinking, socializing, EQ or emotional quotient and intelligence, and problem-solving for other humans are now emphasized in human resource (HR) hiring. Another human feature that excites HR departments is the quality of multiculturalism and diversity. In the new workplace environment, given that creativity and diversity of ideas are strengths that are not yet readily replaceable by algorithm-based A.I. or robots, human workers need to capitalize on diversity found at the workplace and consider it a strategic resource. Individuals with different genders, races, ethnicities, handicaps, sexual preferences and religions can come together as teams to brainstorm different ideas to come up with solutions to practise problems and challenges.

In order to continue to have a job, humans must now distinguish between jobs and assignments. Assignments are one-off projects that can be accomplished easily by robots when they are programmed for certain tasks. But jobs require human skills that are part and parcel of daily activities at the workplace. This creates the demand for a new field known as design thinking which maps out how a job and its tasks are managed in a company. These maps are then analysed by management to segregate assignments that require human skills named above and robot-capable tasks. This helps planners to identify the parts of the work process that still requires human inputs. It will also help companies plan ahead to project how many full-time workers and part-time/seasonal workers are needed. Augmentation of human inputs is a crucial process to create enough jobs for humans in workplaces of the future. It also helps the state plan ahead the kinds of resources needed to train such manpower and prepare the crucial skills training for them. In this way, learning will become a lifelong journey as skills need constant refreshment and upgrading. Jobs reserved for humans will also become increasingly knowledge-based and have less physical work in the long run.

Those who are slow in doing so will be eliminated and companies slow in identifying the humans and machine components of work assignments will also be eliminated. Companies that are faster in implementing technologies will also experience lower productivity and may be eliminated from competition. Some tech companies are leading the way in implementing technologies. Amazon.com for example is a successful example of integrated human-robot logistical delivery services for just-in-time logistical planning. The integration is so successful that some Amazon workers even gave their robots affectionate human names.

In the past, only manufacturing workers feel the danger from replacement by machines, especially from Industrial Revolution 2.0 onwards. However, even the service and retail sectors are not secure spaces from Industrial Revolution 4.0 today. E-commerce starting wiping out brick and mortar shops starting from the IT boom in the 1990s. Even earlier than e-commerce, automated bank tellers began to perform the same tasks as counter service staffs in financial institutions. Eventually, even automated tellers will disappear as all cash transactions become electronic and the world truly becomes a cashless society. Barcodes also makes logistical delivery easier as deliverers, recipients and parcel senders are able to track the progress of the delivery online. China is probably the leading entity in this area as payments are now made through smartphones at the point of this writing. Refer to Chapter 10 (Case Study 5) for a detailed treatment of China as possibly the world's first cashless society.

THE INDUSTRIAL REVOLUTION 4.0

Besides human individuals, even companies need help to cope with changes. The advent of digital technologies has also created a dual-track economy whereby large multinational companies (MNCs) have greater capabilities in implementing digital technologies while the small and medium sized sectors face greater difficulties. Even among large multinational corporations, the implementation of technologies is uneven. Companies that have a faster rate of technological adoption tend to enjoy higher rates of growth, productivity and cost savings. Companies alone (especially SMEs) may not have these kinds of resources to retool themselves for the future. For smaller economies like Hong Kong and Singapore, the need for state resources is acute in coping with the current Industrial Revolution 4.0 changes. In the area of digital technologies implementation, it is no surprise that tech companies are the fastest to integrate digital tech into their company operations. The trend also indicates that American and Chinese companies tend to have faster integrations than their European counterparts. Part of the reason for tech companies' adaptability to digital technologies arises from having horizontal hierarchies, flexible and fluid work schedules, rapid decision-making procedures, nimble work processes, etc.

From Budget 2018, Singapore has tried to tackle challenges at the future workplace head-on. One of the major points spotted from 2018 onwards is the need to adapt to changing patterns of production and consumption behaviour. Singapore can no longer compete on costs but on deep skills, capabilities and value-add. It takes all stakeholders to work this out. The government for example is supporting all firms in Singapore to purchase new solutions for their industrial/economic/commercial needs, construct their own solutions or work with external parties to do so and this applies to all categories of firms across the value chain. The Singapore government is astute in striking a balance between encouragement of automation to increase productivity and reduce overdependence on foreign workers. The world-class visionary bureaucracy understands the needs of local SMEs in loosening the quota on influx of foreign workers as they tend to be more manpower intensive. But, at the same time, the government is keen to provide suitable grants for these business owners to acquire technologies or/and training. In order not to impede human talents from entering Singapore, the government has put in place skills transfer schemes that facilitate SME needs for hiring non-local human talents so that they can transfer their knowledge and skills to a local employee.

Other stakeholders mustered to manage and navigate Singapore through the changing economy are Singapore's universities which have been called upon to build strong research capabilities and shore up its knowledge base and creation and the government is providing opportunities to commercialize its own public sector research output. There is also a particular accent on digital platforms, robotics and automation, and their applications in practical sector-specific settings like the seaports and airports. These facilities will literally become test-beds and living labs for companies to test out their new tech and gear through specific programmes.

Certain skills classified under the need to build "deep capabilities" are emphasized and accentuated. They include the need to internationalize. Globalization and a neoliberal flow of talents, capital and labour have fostered economic development in many parts of the world. As a small economy, Singapore needs external markets to function so therefore, its government has always been pro-globalization and pro-free trade. This is the only way for small and medium sized economies to survive as there is little option for self-reliance or isolation. In the same way, the peoples of an economy need tools for globalization to tap into large markets, more diversified consumers and also reach out to the marketplace of ideas, capital and consumers. In this sense, language training, usage of electronic tools of communication, cross-cultural exchanges are all helpful in this process.

The second element of digitalization is the ability to use digital technologies to harness information needed for economic purposes. Skills Future programmes in Singapore may offer some form of training in this area and all individuals can spot courses on the menu that enhances their ability to tap into globalization. Moreover, the need for programmers, data analytics-trained personnel, the recruitment of A.I. and cybersecurity operators and coders as well as architecture designers will increase as the economy goes through digitalization. The attention given to these technologies will also create an ecosystem for all stakeholder engaged in designing, operating and implementing these technologies. It is a growth area that is likely to witness increased demand for manpower. Eventually, demand may grow to such an extent that there is a need to bring in foreign talents to meet the anticipated demand for such skills.

Besides individuals, the Singapore government is concerned with raising the competitiveness and technological capabilities of Singapore SMEs. The government has begun a slew of programmes to encourage Singapore's SMEs to go digital and train their existing tech personnel to either be equipped with digital skills or up-skill to higher capabilities. The Productivity Solutions Grants are meant to support Singapore SMEs in adopting available technologies solutions to increase productivity. The grant provides up to 70% of the costs of SMEs taking up these ready-made solutions. In addition, there is a nationwide encouragement of robotic use, starting with the construction industry from 2018. Refer to Chapter 11 (Case Study 6) in this volume for an example of an SME in a traditional business and retail sector in Singapore utilizing digital technologies.

GLOBALIZATION 2.0 AND ITS TECHNOLOGIES

There is a lot more work to be done. Many in the world are still left without access to digital technologies and the Internet. The most pressing need in the developing economies is to provide digital infrastructure facilities for the population so that they are empowered to have access to the Internet. Minorities, women, physically disabled, rural folks, the poor are the most vulnerable groups in this aspect. There is also a need to promote more digital lessons for them, encourage them to carry on lifelong learning, pick up skills related to science and technology, promote soft skills among them and train students/workers in soft skills like communication and teamwork. Eventually, learning and work will converge as skills are constantly refreshed according to workplace requirements and changes in technological skills. This is sometimes carried out by upskilling through dedicated training workshops for workers in specific skills.

If skills are not available domestically or if training is not fast enough to satiate market demand for certain skills, companies and bureaucracies will have no choice but to open up floodgates for highly skilled highly trained migrants to come in. This has caused a backlash against globalization in some societies. In the UK, Brexit is often cited as an example of British middle-class frustration with the European Union (EU) and migrants from former Eastern European states from taking their jobs. Such frustrations may be based on perceptions rather than objective assessments of reality. In the case of North America, the election of President Donald J. Trump, who is extremely popular with some elements of the US middle class (with the following typical profile: divorced, non-college educated white voters), was voted into power with an "America First" policy. His administration plans to stem the flow of Mexican migrants to the US (even building a wall to carry this out) and encourage offshore American companies to return back to the homeland again. Frustrations with globalization has encouraged the emergence of political populism in the US and this trend is visible in the EU as well.

Outside the workplace, geopolitically, while Globalizations 1.0 and 2.0 have made the world smaller, technologies also afford the option for states, especially those with strong governments and strongman regimes, to regulate and control the flow of information. China is a good example in this aspect. The Chinese government has set up a Great Firewall to censor incoming information from the outside world and also to track and monitor messages sent and received within China itself. Virtual Private Networks (VPNs) that can bypass the Firewall are banned in China, so are Google, Gmail, Facebook while Whatsapp was facing some intermittent blocking by the authorities. Posts or information that crossed the red line, making fun of Chinese elite leadership or critical of the Communist Party's governance, as well as popular cultural characterizations like Winnie the Pooh, George Orwell's *Animal Farm*, are scrubbed from the Internet. This enables China to restrict information that are critical of the government and augment news that are complementary to state thinking. Continuing with the theme of smart cities, the next section examines how smart devices and the smart city concept makes urban spaces friendly to the disabled.

SMART CITIES BREAKING BARRIERS: MAINSTREAMING DISABILITY IN EAST ASIA COMMUNITY

Smart Cities and the Community Stakeholders

Continuing with the theme on smart cities, this section looks at the ambitions of making smart cities friendly to the disabled in the context of East Asia. Part of becoming a smart city entails an inclusive approach that reaches out to all segments of society, including people with disabilities, and integrates their needs into urban planning. Smart cities often deploy technologies and design to ease mobility and connectivity in an all-inclusive manner, including assisting those with disabilities or challenged in some ways. Very often, smart technologies to help the handicapped and disabled navigate around the city may also be usable by other vulnerable groups. These groups may include the elderly and, in some cases, even children. Inclusive thinking may have other benefits as well, including bonding previously marginalized members of the community back into mainstream society, lessening discrimination against disadvantaged members of the community and integrate the very human element of empathy into urban planning, infrastructure design and use of public funding for public works. The injection of empathy means that even deliberation and brainstorming sessions must involve disabled or handicapped individual so that their needs are taken into consideration before the implementation of any smart cities scheme, plans or blueprints.

Under the United Nations Development Programme (UNDP) auspices, community meetings for the Smart Cities and Social Governance Research index research collaboration outdoor meetings were held in September and October 2016 in Guiyang with combined Appreciative Inquiry and Study Circles coming together to formulate innovative ideas through mutual learning for bringing about policy changes.[19] All members of the community (including the disabled) participated in this UNDP collaborative meeting to contribute their ideas for smart cities governance with the dissemination of attractive brochures that featured cartoon figures, digital tools/applications and accessible language that resonates with youngsters (these brochures are also distributed to members of the general public).[20] Yi Broadcasting, Weibo and WeChat were involved in the deliberations that were taped and broadcasted and the community meetings served as brainstorming sessions for opportunities, solutions and problems by studying the daily needs of various members of the different communities (including the disabled and handicapped community).[21]

The very fact that the city is an urban environment inevitably means that it will be cluttered and difficult to manoeuvre even for normal healthy individuals. Urban environments are concrete jungles, often with grid systems or standardized modular unit structures that can be identical or similar to each other. In taking care of a large population of handicapped/disabled in any urban environment, disabled needs are often closely intertwined with public health, health policies and health care in general. Medical facilities in smart

[19] United Nations Development Programme (Zhou, Steven, Samantha Anderson, Boshu Cui, and Shenglin Zhang), *Smart Cities and Social Governance: Guide for Participatory Indicator Development* (New York: UNDP), 2017, pp. 50–52.

[20] United Nations Development Programme (Zhou, Steven, Samantha Anderson, Boshu Cui, and Shenglin Zhang), *Smart Cities and Social Governance: Guide for Participatory Indicator Development* (New York: UNDP), 2017, pp. 50–52.

[21] United Nations Development Programme (Zhou, Steven, Samantha Anderson, Boshu Cui, and Shenglin Zhang), *Smart Cities and Social Governance: Guide for Participatory Indicator Development* (New York: UNDP), 2017, pp. 50–52.

cities tend to practice smart healthcare with multiple avenues of interactions between patients, medical practitioners, medical organizations and equipment for the informatization of health records, platforms for accessing those records and cutting-edge technologies.[22]

CONCEPTUALIZATIONS OF SMART CITIES RELATED TO CARING FOR THE DISABLED/HANDICAPPED

Some definitions of smart healthcare include the construction of smart hospitals, health systems and family health platforms, all of which are equipped with digital systems that can collect, archive, keep, process, access, take out, interact with data for the purposes of diagnosis, health screening, medicine dispensing, administrative work, medical treatment, unit transfer, surgical procedures, etc.[23] More advanced applications and technologies enable remote imaging, data transfers, data computational functions, disease prevention, recovery assistance, vital symptoms monitoring, flash alerts with regards to conditions, movements of patients in larger countries/regions, chronic diseases care, alarms/scheduling for prescription medication and cost-cutting measures.[24]

Assistive technologies designed for smart cities have been implemented to a significant extent in countries like Japan where assistive robot technologies are now applied to cater to disabled and handicapped needs. For example, Paro robotic seals are therapeutic robots that can help provide companionship and therapeutic care for the elderly and people stricken with dementia. The Hybrid Assistive Limb (HAL) is a robotic exoskeleton suit that enhances the strengths of elderly workers and those stricken with

[22]EU SME Centre and China-Britain Business Council, "Sector Report Smart Cities in China" dated 2015 [downloaded on 1 January 2018], available at http://ccilc.pt/wp-content/uploads/2017/07/eu_sme_centre_report_-_smart_cities_in_china_i_edit_-_jan_2016_1_1.pdf. It was compiled by Ms Kelly Yang (Consultant, China Britain Business Council CBBC), Ms Aideen Clery (China Britain Business Council CBBC) and Mr Domenico Di Liello (Knowledge Centre Coordinator, EU SME Centre).

[23]EU SME Centre and China-Britain Business Council, "Sector Report Smart Cities in China" dated 2015 [downloaded on 1 January 2018], available at http://ccilc.pt/wp-content/uploads/2017/07/eu_sme_centre_report_-_smart_cities_in_china_i_edit_-_jan_2016_1_1.pdf. It was compiled by Ms Kelly Yang (Consultant, China Britain Business Council CBBC), Ms Aideen Clery (China Britain Business Council CBBC) and Mr Domenico Di Liello (Knowledge Centre Coordinator, EU SME Centre).

[24]EU SME Centre and China-Britain Business Council, "Sector Report Smart Cities in China" dated 2015 [downloaded on 1 January 2018], available at http://ccilc.pt/wp-content/uploads/2017/07/eu_sme_centre_report_-_smart_cities_in_china_i_edit_-_jan_2016_1_1.pdf. It was compiled by Ms Kelly Yang (Consultant, China Britain Business Council CBBC), Ms Aideen Clery (China Britain Business Council CBBC) and Mr Domenico Di Liello (Knowledge Centre Coordinator, EU SME Centre).

weaker muscle strength. HAL helps these people and patients lead normal lives, e.g. elderly farmers and/or people with weaker muscle strength can carry heavy farm produce with their suits. Assistive robots are also used in Japan to look after patients and the elderly in the hospitals and hospices. The RI-MAN robot can lift patients, carry out facial recognition identification, smell/taste medicines and other features that make it an ideal assistive robots.

ASSISTIVE TECHNOLOGIES IN SINGAPORE

Likewise, Singapore's official GovTech website approaches smart nation digital and IoT projects with all-inclusiveness, including the disabled and physically challenged, using basic technologies like touchscreen smartphones for the visually handicapped to cutting edge technologies. Singapore's NPOs are also active in such ventures. The Specialised Assistive Technology Centre (Specialised ATC) established and managed by SPD (voluntary welfare organisation or VWO) uses Assistive Technologies to empower handicapped and disabled individuals. Different technologies can help various disabled groups cope with their challenges. For example, patients with speech challenges, cerebral palsy, motor neurone diseases, stroke survivors and other ailments cannot express themselves well, feel marginalized, isolated and frustrated with not being understood by others.

Therefore, writing and text-to-speech converters can potentially assist with communications (known technically as augmentative and alternative communication [AAC] methods) and they are convenient as the technology can be integrated with smartphones and tablets.[25] Another example is the advanced eye-tracking technology camera monitors that follow eye movements' minute motions to manipulate a computer cursor, facilitating users to express ideas in their eyes. The eyes focus on a virtual keyboard with letters, words or phrases that can be typed into the text through blinking or staring at their intended target for milliseconds longer before the complete text is read out by an integrated voice assistant.[26] These technologies can be made available in public spaces for those who lack the budget to acquire them.

[25] GovTech Singapore, "An Inclusive Smart Nation: 5 Ways Tech Can Empower Persons with Special Needs" dated 9 February 2018 in GovTech Singapore [downloaded on 9 February 2018], available at https://www.tech.gov.sg/TechNews/Innovation/2018/02/An-inclusive-Smart-Nation-5-ways-tech-can-empower-persons-with-special-needs.

[26] GovTech Singapore, "An Inclusive Smart Nation: 5 Ways Tech Can Empower Persons with Special Needs" dated 9 February 2018 in GovTech Singapore [downloaded on 9 February 2018], available at https://www.tech.gov.sg/TechNews/Innovation/2018/02/An-inclusive-Smart-Nation-5-ways-tech-can-empower-persons-with-special-needs.

Singapore's medical institutions have integrated technologies that can be helpful for the disabled and handicapped. For example, the Tan Tock Seng Hospital's Help Me Speak initiative uses advanced eye-tracking technology to facilitate its patients in indicating discomfort, initiating emergency distress calls, conduct dialogue and access the Internet with a loaning service for such eye tracking devices.[27] Besides individuals with vocalization challenges, smart technologies are also available for people with visual challenges. Individuals with cataracts, macular degeneration, low vision, text recognition can now use apps, devices and software to increase the font size, distinguish between texts by sharpening the contrast, listening to audio voiceover, using braille-able platforms, electronic magnifiers, lifestyle talking devices, etc.[28] Similarly, these devices, software and apps can be made available in public spaces for all socioeconomic disabled/handicapped groups to use.

INTIMIDATING SPACES

Statistically, hundreds of millions of people with disabilities who live in cities around the world. By 2050, 15% of 6.25 billion urban dwellers in the world (940 million) will consist of disabled individuals who live in cities, prompting the UN's acute announcement that poor accessibility "presents a major challenge".[29] Even a task that is considered non-challenging for a healthy individual like moving around a subway station or/and using a public toilet can be intimidating for the handicapped or disabled individual. These urban environments also reach upwards to skyscraper heights and underground through tunnelling for the subway system. Thus, the city is a three-dimensional space that extends into the air and tunnels deep into the ground. Environments are often cluttered, complex and at its best, a form of organized chaos. Megacities are a superlative and extreme form of these physical landscapes, bigger in scale and even more intimidating.

While cities are intimidating to ordinary individuals, they may also generate fear among the disabled. In this sense, besides the physical impairment, there is also a psychological barrier to the disabled and handicapped individual living in the urban environment of a large city. The idea of smart cities is

[27] GovTech Singapore, "An Inclusive Smart Nation: 5 Ways Tech Can Empower Persons with Special Needs" dated 9 February 2018 in GovTech Singapore [downloaded on 9 February 2018], available at https://www.tech.gov.sg/TechNews/Innovation/2018/02/An-inclusive-Smart-Nation-5-ways-tech-can-empower-persons-with-special-needs.

[28] GovTech Singapore, "An Inclusive Smart Nation: 5 Ways Tech Can Empower Persons with Special Needs" dated 9 February 2018 in GovTech Singapore [downloaded on 9 February 2018], available at https://www.tech.gov.sg/TechNews/Innovation/2018/02/An-inclusive-Smart-Nation-5-ways-tech-can-empower-persons-with-special-needs.

[29] Salman, Saba, "What Would a Truly Disabled-Accessible City Look Like?" dated 14 February 2018 in *The Guardian* [downloaded on 14 February 2018], available at https://www.theguardian.com/cities/2018/feb/14/what-disability-accessible-city-look-like.

to use technologies to bring about normal life for the disabled by normalizing their daily routine activities that the rest of society have taken for granted. Some of these technologies need not be cutting-edge, they can be as simple as touchscreens and audio voice functions that can read out textual materials for those with hearing challenges. The other smart technologies now applicable to smart cities are Personal Mobility Devices (PMDs) including bikes, smart powered motorized wheelchairs (some sophisticated enough to manoeuvre with finger pressure), electronic scooters that are usable in public facilities like airports, etc.

Intimidating spaces are applicable not only to public urban spaces and can include indoor living/residential spaces as well. Handicapped and disabled individuals may find it difficult to navigate their own residences and properties as well. For example, turning off switches, operating electronic appliances, turning on heaters, all of which can now be handled by using smart sensors, remote controls, motion sensors, security/alarm warning systems, etc. Thus, this opens up another space for smart city development, not just in terms of public infrastructure but also individual atomized living spaces as well.

The Next Generation of Technologies

Of course, curiosity, inquisitiveness, human ingenuity and necessity have not stopped technicians, engineers and scientists from pursuing further cutting-edge technological research. Based on a national action plan on A.I. from 2018 to 2020, China is looking at mass producing neural network processing chips, assistive robots for disabled people and machine learning aiding radiologists interpreting X-ray scans.[30] In the field of digital identity, the Chancheng district in southern China is utilizing Blockchain to confirm Chinese nationals' identity prior to using digital public services known as the "intelligent multifunctional identity" that works by pairing encryption keys to verify identities on their smartphones.[31] *China Daily* mentioned that this technology can also be used to download or read insurance certificates, tax records, pensions and disability allowances through a mobile app.[32] It can also be used to access services at local hospitals and libraries. All these cutting-edge technologies are contributive towards a smart city's handicap or disabled-friendly features.

[30] He, Wei, "Chipmakers Seek New Edge" dated 24 April 2018 in *China Daily* [downloaded on 24 April 2018], available at http://www.chinadaily.com.cn/a/201804/24/WS5ade7ffaa3105cdcf651a11e.html.

[31] Basu, Medha, "Three Innovative Data Projects from China" dated 20 March 2018 in GovInsider [downloaded on 20 March 2018], available at https://govinsider.asia/security/three-innovative-data-projects-china/.

[32] Basu, Medha, "Three Innovative Data Projects from China" dated 20 March 2018 in GovInsider [downloaded on 20 March 2018], available at https://govinsider.asia/security/three-innovative-data-projects-china/.

THE SINGAPORE CASE STUDY

In Singapore, the CapitaGreen Building is seen as an exemplary example of a smart infrastructure that is disabled-friendly. The building is 82,000 square metres in spatial size, designed by Japanese architectural firm Toyo Ito and Associates Architects and completed in 2015.[33] The facility has a lowered front desk and concierge that makes it convenient for the disabled and handicapped individual to access and internal spaces are designed free of columns for the handicapped to move around easily.[34] It is ergonomically designed for disabled and handicapped individuals that is equally accessible to other members of the public. Such developments are encouraged by Singapore's Building Construction Authority (BCA, established in 2007) which have put in place Universal Design principles that guide building designs to be more handicapped-friendly. These initiatives have won accolades from the United Nations (UN). Besides being handicapped and disabled friendly, the Capitagreen Building is also constructed efficiently using new piling methods and has a lush green environment. Wind funnelling technologies also make it energy-efficient by bringing in cool air drafts.

Within the Asia Pacific region, some of the leading smart cities have begun to instal technologies to aid the impaired individuals to lead normal lives. For example, in Melbourne, the Southern Cross Train Station has a beacon navigation system that emits audio instructions via smartphones to guide visually impaired people walking around the city, warning them about escalators and other areas that can pose a hazard to them.[35] Smart cities catering to the disabled makes economic sense for the private sector because such initiatives can attract substantial funding and may be a potential gold mine for private sector companies and entrepreneurs that can come up with the appropriate and innovative technologies. In other words, it can spur economic growth as well. Since countries like China are targeting the construction of 500 smart cities (see Chapter 8 [Case Study 3] for more on this topic), the large number of smart features for the disabled can also translate to significant economic windfall for innovative companies that can come up with the problem-solving ideas for enhancing accessibility and/or mobility.

[33] RSP, "CapitaGreen One of the Greenest, Crowned with Cool Void" in RSP website [downloaded on 1 January 2018], available at http://www.rsp.com.sg/project/show?id=170.

[34] Salman, Saba, "What Would a Truly Disabled-Accessible City Look Like?" dated 14 February 2018 in *The Guardian* [downloaded on 14 February 2018], available at https://www.theguardian.com/cities/2018/feb/14/what-disability-accessible-city-look-like.

[35] Salman, Saba, "What Would a Truly Disabled-Accessible City Look Like?" dated 14 February 2018 in *The Guardian* [downloaded on 14 February 2018], available at https://www.theguardian.com/cities/2018/feb/14/what-disability-accessible-city-look-like.

THE INDIAN CASE STUDY IN THE INDO PACIFIC ARENA

East Asia is not the only region that is striving to create smart cities that are friendly to the handicapped and disabled. It is significant to look towards the Indo Pacific region to look for other inspirations as well, including the IT powerhouse of India. India is targeting about 100 buildings each in 50 cities (50 out of the planned 100 smart cities in total) through the Accessible India Campaign, to convert at least 25–50 of the most significant buildings into disabled/handicapped friendly buildings.[36] By end of 2018, about 50% of all state building structures of the national and state capital cities in India will be included and in the same year, all international and domestic airports will become more accessible (25 out of 32 airports are made more accessible for visually handicapped with disabled-friendly washrooms).[37] There are other initiatives as well. Giving a Unique Disability ID (UDIDs) to the disabled, developing skills training programme to enhance productivity of disabled people, protecting them through legislations (e.g. Rights of Persons with Disabilities Act 2016, implemented in 2018), and instituting Mobile Courts to handle complaints by the disabled/handicapped communities are just some of the initiatives to make Indian smart cities friendlier to all.[38]

MUCH TO LEARN FROM EACH OTHER

With the 100-city smart city initiative in India, the 500-city smart city Chinese vision, Japan assistive robot development, and Singapore's advocacy for networking smart cities in Southeast Asia within the rubric of ASEAN integration and economic community, there are abundant opportunities for East Asian countries to learn from each other. East Asian smart cities can also interact and learn from the Indian case study. The net result may be a hybridization or cross-fertilization of technologies and know-how that can result in new innovations through collaborations and joint ventures. Best practices and successful technologies may also stand a chance of being exported to other countries within the region that need them. Similarly, negative implementation and failures may also serve as reference for other countries in the process of mutual interactions over smart technologies for the handicapped and disabled.

---

[36] *The Hindu*, "Disabled People Not to Be Left Behind in Smart Cities" dated 30 July 2017 in *The Hindu Business Line* [downloaded on 30 July 2017], available at https://www.thehindubusinessline.com/economy/disabled-people-not-to-be-left-behind-in-smart-cities/article9794091.ece.

[37] *The Hindu*, "Disabled People Not to Be Left Behind in Smart Cities" dated 30 July 2017 in *The Hindu Business Line* [downloaded on 30 July 2017], available at https://www.thehindubusinessline.com/economy/disabled-people-not-to-be-left-behind-in-smart-cities/article9794091.ece.

[38] *The Hindu*, "Disabled People Not to Be Left Behind in Smart Cities" dated 30 July 2017 in *The Hindu Business Line* [downloaded on 30 July 2017], available at https://www.thehindubusinessline.com/economy/disabled-people-not-to-be-left-behind-in-smart-cities/article9794091.ece.

Given that adaptations to local conditions are important for smart city technologies to be successful, working with local partners can also enhance mutual understanding, confidence-building measures and bonding over a no-detriments cause like helping the disabled. Universal empathy and care for another fellow human being will become increasingly important in an age where A.I., robots and machines will take over many human functions. Smart cities initiatives for the handicapped and disabled may be another convenient platform for social integration and regional cooperation.

BIBLIOGRAPHY

Basu, Medha, "Three Innovative Data Projects from China" dated 20 March 2018 in GovInsider [downloaded on 20 March 2018]. Available at https://govinsider. asia/security/three-innovative-data-projects-china/.

Carmodyon, Patrick, "Taiwan Leads in Smart Cities" dated 13 November 2016 in Taiwan Business Topics [downloaded on 13 November 2016]. Available at https://topics.amcham.com.tw/2016/11/taiwan-leads-smart-cities/.

Economic Times (ET), "Taiwan to Empower Bengaluru's Quest to Become a Smart City" dated 13 March 2018 in *Economic Times (ET)* website [downloaded on 13 March 2018]. Available at https://economictimes.indiatimes.com/magazines/ panache/taiwan-to-empower-bengalurus-quest-to-become-a-smart-city/article-show/63279696.cms.

EU SME Centre and China-Britain Business Council, "Sector Report Smart Cities in China" dated 2015 [downloaded on 1 January 2018]. Available at http://ccilc. pt/wp-content/uploads/2017/07/eu_sme_centre_report_-_smart_cities_in_chi-na_i_edit_-_jan_2016_1_1.pdf. It was compiled by Ms Kelly Yang (Consultant, China Britain Business Council CBBC), Ms Aideen Clery (China Britain Business Council CBBC), and Mr Domenico Di Liello (Knowledge Centre Coordinator, EU SME Centre).

Fulcoon, Matthew, "Taiwan's Cities Smarten Up" dated 15 August 2017 in *Taiwan Business Topics* (Taipei: American Chamber of Commerce Taipei AmCham Taipei). Available at https://topics.amcham.com.tw/2017/08/taiwans-cities-smarten/.

GovInsider daily briefing news, "How AI Will Transform Taiwan's Economy" dated 10 April 2018 in the AI Taiwan website [downloaded on 10 April 2018] (Taiwan: Government of Taiwan). Available at https://ai.taiwan.gov.tw/news/ how-ai-will-transform-taiwans-economy/.

GovTech Singapore, "An Inclusive Smart Nation: 5 Ways Tech Can Empower Persons with Special Needs" dated 9 February 2018 in GovTech Singapore [down-loaded on 9 February 2018]. Available at https://www.tech.gov.sg/TechNews/ Innovation/2018/02/An-inclusive-Smart-Nation-5-ways-tech-can-empower-persons-with-special-needs.

He, Wei, "Chipmakers Seek New Edge" dated 24 April 2018 in *China Daily* [downloaded on 24 April 2018]. Available at http://www.chinadaily.com. cn/a/201804/24/WS5ade7ffaa3105cdcf651a11e.html.

Hynes, Casey, "Singapore Ranks as World's No. 2 Smart City, Report Says" dated 10 November 2017 in Forbes.com [downloaded on 10 November 2017]. Available at https://www.forbes.com/sites/chynes/2017/11/10/singapore-ranks-as-one-of-the-top-smart-cities-in-the-world/#c234bb5717d6.

RSP, "CapitaGreen One of the Greenest, Crowned with Cool Void" in RSP website [downloaded on 1 January 2018]. Available at http://www.rsp.com.sg/project/show?id=170.

Salman, Saba, "What Would a Truly Disabled-Accessible City Look Like?" dated 14 February 2018 in *The Guardian* [downloaded on 14 February 2018]. Available at https://www.theguardian.com/cities/2018/feb/14/what-disability-accessible-city-look-like.

Salmonsen, Renée, "Connecting Cars and IoT at Taipei Smart City Summit—A.I. on the Road: Applying IoT Solutions to Traffic in Taiwan" dated 28 March 2018 in *Taiwan News* website [downloaded on 28 March 2018]. Available at https://www.taiwannews.com.tw/en/news/3392486.

Smart Nation and Digital Government Office, "Smart Nation" dated 2018 in the Smart Nation website [downloaded on 1 May 2018]. Available at https://www.smartnation.sg/.

Sregantan, Navin, "Singapore Tops Global Smart City Performance Ranking in 2017: Study" dated 13 March 2018 [downloaded on 13 March 2018]. Available at http://www.businesstimes.com.sg/government-economy/singapore-tops-global-smart-city-performance-ranking-in-2017-study.

The Hindu, "Disabled People Not to Be Left Behind in Smart Cities" dated 30 July 2017 in *The Hindu Business Line* [downloaded on 30 July 2017]. Available at https://www.thehindubusinessline.com/economy/disabled-people-not-to-be-left-behind-in-smart-cities/article9794091.ece.

United Nations Development Programme (Zhou, Steven, Samantha Anderson, Boshu Cui, and Shenglin Zhang), *Smart Cities and Social Governance: Guide for Participatory Indicator Development* (New York: UNDP), 2017, pp. 50–52.

CHAPTER 5

Conclusion

In this concluding chapter, some of the major points in the previous chapters are recapped here. Technology in the form of much vaunted categories like robotics and Artificial Intelligence (A.I.) has provided pathways to achieve higher productivity and economic growth for companies that tap into such technologies. Technology brings about many benefits, including the possibilities of increased productivity leading to better salaries, skills trainings, careers and even convenience to the workplace and its functions as well. Such conveniences can include Human Resource (HR) matters where software like LinkedIn have made it possible for easier job search online as apps connect personal CVs with an appropriate position. Companies are also turning to such apps to hire people. Many jobs will be disrupted by technology and automation. Historically, one of the manufacturing jobs/functions in the US auto-making industry that was first replaced by robots was the vehicle body-painting assembly line. Automation in this area facilitated the automakers' ability to customize body paint colours for customers. Digitization and robotic automation will eventually affect both manufacturing and service sector jobs. Self-driving autonomous vehicles may makes deliveries and carry out other logistics assignments for industries and factories. Digital platforms and online payment systems may replace tellers and human service providers.

No job is considered sacred and many monotonous, standardized, repetitive or/and mechanical tasks can be replaced by machines. Automation will also exert pressure on workers' salaries, particularly the lower-skilled jobs. Experts focus on the accelerated pace of disruption which will pose a challenge never experienced before in the evolutionary history of the workplace. The scope is also extensive with all industries and occupations affected, from blue to white-collar jobs. Many find it inevitable that they will have to adapt to technology or even integrate technologies fully into their jobs to increase their productivity. Machines and software will eventually acquire self-learning capabilities and be able to achieve more tasks than humans, if not equalize

© The Author(s) 2019
T. W. Lim, *Industrial Revolution 4.0, Tech Giants, and Digitized Societies*,
https://doi.org/10.1007/978-981-13-7470-8_5

with them. Programmed in the right way, they are likely to make less mistakes and errors than humans. They are also less likely to complain and begrudge working conditions and hours. Robots are also highly deployable in jobs that are dirty, demanding and dangerous. Manufacturers, employers and firms will make a strategic decision in deploying these robots, taking into consideration their long-term costs and investments. In the short run, if there is still availability of cheap affordable human labour, the use of robotics, A.I. and apps may be delayed. The challenge is how to help humans coexist and work together with A.I. and robots.

Pro-automation, pro-robotics and pro-A.I. experts argue that all is not lost. Technologies can actually empower humans in their search for the ideal matching careers. Digital software and algorithms make it possible for individuals to be connected to their matching jobs or at least best-fitting ones. This will alleviate HR challenges to a certain extent. Digital technologies also make CVs, bio-data and HR records of job-hunting individuals more transparent to employers. Another advantage of technologies is that it allows humans to work in more flexible hours and even from home. Access to technologies makes it easier for groups who are not enjoying full mobility, working mothers who need to look after their children, individuals who need to be at home to look after the elderly, people who choose to work from home for various reasons, etc. It also facilitates the lifestyles of individuals who cannot work according to regular working hours to work at their own pace, schedule and preferred locations. Some of these individuals may be previously working in the informal sectors of the economy, they are brought back into the fold of formal employment.

The power apps with search engines and sieving functions of algorithms can also help to spot human talents in certain fields and with certain skills easily for firms. This will ease efforts by HR managers to look for such talents and companies can save costs putting out advertisements and calls for such talents as well. By sieving through large amounts of data and information, these software increases the efficiency of HR departments and also promote the right person for the right job. This process is made possible by digital trends pointing to the expansion of online data storage capabilities and superfast data processing speeds in contemporary computer systems. When individuals are matched with the optimal job selection, they tend to show more job satisfaction, motivated by self-interest and exhibit higher morale in the workforce.

Finally, technologies also empowers the entrepreneurs, self-employed individuals and independent contractors. These individuals may want a higher degree of freedom in picking the assignments that interest them. Another group of individuals in this category may have difficulties getting a regular job and therefore decided to strike it out on their own. Yet others may have a creative idea and wants to drive it to fruition. In other words, technologies can empower the entrepreneurs and the creative individuals driven to realize a creative idea. It can drive innovation when applied on creative entrepreneurial individuals.

In this sense, technologies can actually help to create new jobs and accentuate demands for certain skills (e.g. data analytics) that were not present before. This has spurred the non-profit organizations, non-governmental sector, the state and the private sector to work together to empower more people to tap into the use of technologies. They help to train coders in African villages, coach women in technological skills in Indian villages, reaching out to rural areas to bring more people into the fold of employability. Some of these organizations donate or subsidize infrastructure, equipment and facilities in addition to training individuals. Many became inspiring stories for others. The author met an African lady who was sold as a sex slave and landed on the shores of France where she was rescued and eventually made her home in the UK. She was then trained as a coder in Britain and has gone on to great success commercially and therefore decided to set up non-governmental organizations and foundations to help train African women in coding so they can have a better future.

PREPARING FOR THE FUTURE WORKFORCE

Some argue that, before the advent of A.I. or algorithm-enabled machines, previous industrial revolutions had already eliminated some human jobs but aligned against them are narratives that Industrial Revolution 4.0 will be faster in speed, more global in coverage and covering a broad extent of existing jobs. Yet others point to the benefits that the new technologies will bring about, allowing humans to move to higher-value added jobs. Service counter staff personnel for example can be retrained to become designers that requires the faculty of creativity. The technologies will also gather better feedback to create better products, and make them more complementary with individual customer's tastes at cheaper prices and at faster speeds. Whichever side of the debate one stands on, it is clear the workforce will be affected by technological changes. Therefore, a number of private sector and state stakeholders may need to do something about this.

The mind-sets of the workforce will need to change with the times. Senior management especially chief digital officers in companies may have to take the lead in spearheading digitization of their companies and lay out the vision and roadmap ahead for the companies. Senior management must also encourage their executives to try out digital platforms personally (especially those technologies that are utilized by consumers) and be willing to experiment with new technologies. Besides the manufacturing sector, even those in the retail and services sector needs to be acquainted with digital platforms and ultimately engage in e-commerce.

Many of today's tech giants are multitaskers: data collectors, marketing/retail companies; and some like Alibaba are even functioning like banks offering micro loans. Some believe there is even an archiving function for information technology. As older generations of human executives (those who were born before the internet age) pass away, they bring their knowledge to the grave. Some of these knowledge are valuable and can be mined for company operational details that can benefit future operations. They are also useful information to distinguish assignments and tasks that are performable by robots who are better at repetitive, standardized and/or highly logical work than humans.

The future workplace is also likely to see the convergence of workplace and personal lives. In China, this has been taken to the farthest extent with the emergence of the Social Credit System. The social credit system works to the same tune as the bank credit system in the US. In the US, banks keep records of an individual's credit-worthiness based on her/his ability to pay back bills, the spending patterns, income earned and assets that a person owns. The bank credit system is crucial for an individual in the sense that bank can access such information to determine if they should forward a loan to an individual applicant and also determine the quantum of the loans. Tencent founded China's first WeBank on 18 January 2015 while, in the same year, Alibaba launched MYbank which offers financial services for customers in the rural areas. These companies are keen to finance the small and medium sized enterprises (SMEs). Many are wondering if the social credit system will eventually be utilized to determine eligibility for bank loans. Right now, these banks using big data to determine this. Baidu's Baixin Bank utilizes behaviour analysis and risk management algorithms for customized solutions. In this sense, loan dispensing has become instantaneous, conveniently online and the transactions are cashless. (Refer to Chapter 10 [Case Study 5] for details on Chinese efforts to go cashless.)

The Chinese social credit system keeps records on more aspects of an individual lives. It keeps track of an individual's environmental record, criminal activities (if any), credit worthiness, track record of volunteerism, traffic offences, online interactions with other individuals, etc. Eventually, many believe that this social credit system will be used to determine a person's eligibility for jobs, loans, school entries, and other crucial social functions. All these are made possible because of the high level of surveillance in China, country that has large numbers of state-owned Closed Circuit Televisions (CCTVs), A.I.-enabled security monitoring equipment and even traffic violations tracking systems. Many consider Xinjiang, a restive autonomous region in China with the presence of some independence/autonomy-seeking groups and militant extremists, to be a living laboratory of how A.I., algorithms, robots and behaviour analytics will be used in the future to monitor, control and secure a human population.

Differing from China in the social credit system aspect, it shares a commonality with Chinese tech giants in the sense that there is a social consensus within the US to help grow small and medium sized businesses in the US. In the US, SMEs are often considered the fertile soil that spawns innovative companies and ideas. The platforms offered by US-based social media companies and other digital tech giants have extended the reach of SMEs globally. Social media platforms allows these businesses to market their products and services to a much wider global audience and consumer base. This wider reach has inspired some observers to nickname SMEs "micronationals". Ebay's PayPal system also facilities online payment by customers who buy products and services online in addition to the global shipping service provided by the same company. This enables more SMEs to have a global presence in terms of marketing and deliver logistically worldwide. Having discussed the general points in Section A, the next section, Section B, of this volume moves on to examine specific case studies. The final section of this concluding chapter will take a macro perspective and discuss the issues of integration, cooperation, collaboration among countries in managing Industry 4.0.

TRACK II DIPLOMATIC INSTITUTIONS' INITIATIVES, NARRATIVES AND IDEAS ABOUT INDUSTRY 4.0

The author has participated in a series of Track II diplomacy meetings that discussed the implications of Industry 4.0 and its impacts/influences on global media and audiences. Government officials remain quite consistent in their calls for engagements in frank and open discussions about the future of Industry 4.0, smart cities and Internet of Things (IoT). Some questions are consistent in all these meetings, how can organizations and countries pull together online resources and tackle challenges and opportunities brought about by Industry 4.0. Regionally, Track II diplomatic institutions and other stakeholders are concerned about how they can use Information and Communications Technology (ICT) for the benefit of the (East Asian) region. Regional resource-sharing and information-sharing are suggested by regionalism stakeholders under the umbrellas of Asia Pacific Economic Cooperation (APEC), Regional Comprehensive Economic Partnership (RCEP), Comprehensive Progressive Trans Pacific Partnership (CPTPP), ASEAN Plus Three (APT) ministers, etc.

While ASEAN (Association of Southeast Asian Nations) continues unabated to try to set up a network of smart cities, there is regional interest on how to manage the mass media communications, contents and coverage. Regional organizations like ASEAN are trying to include such cooperation and collaborations in their work plans based on mutual consensus. Technologically, there are calls to enhance, augment and improve technical capacity in information and media management. Some countries that are not liberal democracies even suggested working on managing access to the international printed press, radio and TV programmes, accusing them of spreading falsehoods on occasions. They claimed to be smeared and attacked by groups using social media. Authoritarian government fear the use of social media to incite public opinion against their tight control and human rights issues.

They also fear the snowballing of critical opinions against them. On the other hand, liberal democracies are keen to widen the platforms for discussions while keeping out hackers, criminal organizations and terrorist elements from infiltrating these platforms and spreading messages of misogynistic narratives, extremist messages and radicalism.

Regional organizations therefore promote more exchange programmes, mutual consultation, personnel training, content generation collaboration and cooperation among regional (e.g. East Asian) public broadcasting stations. Regional organizations also place an emphasis on less developing countries (LDCs) like Myanmar in areas of communications and economic development. Only a segment of Myanmarese have phone access. Even for basic technologies that are taken for granted by the people of developed economies like SIM cards, they still cost of thousands of kyat dollars (Myanmarese currency), which is out of reach for many Myanmarese citizens. Thus, due to market pressures in 2013, Myanmar opened the telecommunications market to foreign telecoms operator with the entry of international operators like KDDI.

Some stakeholders in the ASEAN ICT sector urged all members to look at ICT for the development of health and welfare sectors. They argue that ASEAN countries should have better procedures and measures to prevent cybercrimes, particularly in face of alleged Russian interference of US election. Apparently, digital technologies transcend distances and, despite the fact that Russia is geographically far away from the US, they are said to have the capability of creating millions of electronic accounts to elicit responses to the machine generated communications that can shape public opinions. These accounts can remotely interact with each other and collecting information and data related to socioeconomic, military and national security issues of importance. If such allegations are true, it is weaponized form of data warfare at little cost to the perpetrator, who may only spend a modest amount of money compared to costs involved (and the real damage done).

But, Industry 4.0 can also be a force for good. Alibaba.com apparently has a corporate social responsibility (CSR) agenda to help China with poverty alleviation. Alibaba is teaching villagers on how to open up a small businesses and retailing their products and would arrange for urbanite business operators to go down to the villages to assist these small businesses with their day to day operations. Villagers can then keep in tandem with market pricing. Apps and software can also help out with online resolution/mediation of disputes on e-commerce platform and increase consumer confidence in online shopping and retailing. As these systems mature, they can even become pre-court procedures or help courts become more efficient in their handling of court cases. Stronger enforcement can help to decrease fraud, encourage regulation, protect the rights of the consumers, prevent abuse and misuse of the

Internet, etc. Evidence presentation and identification may be facilitated by the fact that the internet technologies can now recognize individual users. This can help with enforcement of legal actions against individuals who abuse the Internet.

The Internet infrastructure is set up in most parts of the world. It is almost a universal system globally. Internet use and procedures are standardized in many parts of the world, which is becoming a collective of ideas, people and communities. Many retailers are trying to meet the consumption demand created by the availability of such infrastructures. Such infrastructures can also encourage cross-boundary trade and can reduce inequities between regions in each country in the region and between countries themselves. All these cross-boundary trade require coordination, leadership and compromises. The architecture should be open with strong collaboration in technology sharing, friendly innovation competition, and treaties for cooperation can be signed. The fact that countries should cooperate in fostering Industry 4.0 technologies is also a sign that technologies have progressed by leaps and bounds.

The pre-Industry 4.0 and 3.0 means of communication was mainly through copper wire-based telephones lines. Phone calls used to be limited in geographical reach and costly to operate. Even textual word processing was primitive in the recent past. Typewriters are much slower than word processors, and it took much more efforts to type out the contents. Mistakes could not be erased with the click of a mouse. The leap from this situation to having a powerful computer in the palm of one's hand is a great leap forward. Many are keen to use Industry 4.0 technologies and social media as a force for good. This can include countering Non Traditional Security (NTS) threats, crimes, drug trafficking, regional integration for trade, increasing mutual trust and world peace through cross-cultural communications, increased levels of communications between all stakeholders in the world, counter cyberthreats collectively, exchange of critical information, telemedicine, agricultural development, combating radicalism/extremism/terrorism by spreading messages of peace and moderation.

Some argue that technological advancement should not be viewed with fear. In the past, even with the advent of primitive technologies, the publication of books and their ideas broke certain particularistic views and their monopoly over personal opinions. In Germany, reformist Christian ideas spread through printed bibles. Radios then spread the public messages over a wider area. Television brought visual images further ashore. Whether it was books, radio or television, some contents were fluffier than others and this is no different from the rise of social media which also contains non-value-added contents. But every wave of technological change also brought about progress and change. Even in terms of epistemology and knowledge creation, social media and industry 4.0 communication technologies can bring about successes in the field of education. The Internet is after all an aggregator of worldwide knowledge and can be piped into classrooms easily and, through different apps, software and programming, made more enjoyable and user-friendly.

Internet can access all topics, and some universities in the developed world, particularly the US, is already offering free knowledge. This can spread development to impoverished areas. A.I. is also being adopted for navigating children to complete assignments, homework, language learning, etc. Knowledge will no longer be restricted to a degree programme and can be lifelong in nature. There are endless possibilities that are only restricted by the speed of internet access in developing economies. When Internet is made accessible, social media platforms like Facebook can connect communities of educators together, share their materials, involve parents in online chats as well. ICT experts, electrical engineers, coders and programmers may have a social responsibility in bringing about technological accessibility to a wide spectrum of stakeholders in Industry 4.0 developments.

PART II

Section on Specific Case Studies

Case Study 1: Japan's Foreign Talent Policy and the Future of Robot Replacements

The projected impending labour shortage in Japan arising from its rapidly aging population is the greatest impetus for Japan to initiate policies for foreign talent attraction. After Japanese Prime Minister Shinzo Abe came into power in late 2012, reconstruction of Japan's northeast devastated by the Great East Japan Earthquake (also known as "311") and preparations for the 2020 Tokyo Olympics infrastructure needs added pressure on manpower supply. Such manpower needs increased the inflow of non-Japanese workers 40% compared to 2013 figures, and Chinese workers made up more than 33.3% of the total (Vietnamese, Filipinos and Brazilians followed suit).[1] Fields that are reeling from labour shortage like agriculture (labour pool reduced by 40% from 2008 to 2018), construction industry and nursing jobs (projected shortfall of 380,000 personnel by 2025) are given priority in this scheme.[2]

---

[1] Sieg, Linda and Ami Miyazaki, "Japan Eyes More Foreign Workers, Stealthily Challenging Immigration Taboo" dated 26 April 2016 in Reuters [downloaded on 26 April 2018], available at https://www.reuters.com/article/us-japan-immigration/japan-eyes-more-foreign-workers-stealthily-challenging-immigration-taboo-idUSKCN0XN07X.

[2] Nikkei Staff Writers, "Japan to Allow Foreign Interns to Work Five Additional Years" dated 11 April 2018 in *Nikkei Asia* website [downloaded on 11 April 2018], available at https://asia.nikkei.com/Politics/Japan-to-allow-foreign-interns-to-work-five-additional-years.

This case study is derived from a limited circulation background brief working paper for National University of Singapore (NUS EAI): Lim, Tai Wei, "Japan's Foreign Talent Policy" dated 2018 in EAI Background Brief, (Singapore: National University of Singapore East Asian Institute NUS EAI), 2018 [Unpublished at the time of submission of this manuscript].

© The Author(s) 2019

T. W. Lim, *Industrial Revolution 4.0, Tech Giants, and Digitized Societies*, https://doi.org/10.1007/978-981-13-7470-8_6

Japan also has an internship scheme that had traditionally allowed non-Japanese to work in Japan without becoming a formal employee. Some of these interns have made valuable contributions to their jobs and/or communities, incentivizing the Japanese government to create policies to allow them to stay. Most of these manpower needs were blue collar workers working in manpower intensive industries. But Prime Minister Abe's government is also interested in white collar highly skilled workers, and individuals with skills that the countries needs badly, in other words, a foreign talent attraction policy. In end October 2016, Japan's Ministry of Justice figures indicated that there were 1,083,769 foreign workers in Japan, mostly high skilled non-Japanese professionals (coaches, engineers, etc.) and trainees.[3] As of June 2017, the Ministry of Justice approved 8515 individual as highly skilled professionals attaining 70 or more points and the Ministry is also working with other agencies to increase the number of intake to 20,000 by the year 2022.[4] By October 2017, the number of foreigners working in Japan's 66 million-strong workforce reached 1.27 million people.[5]

Japanese Prime Minister Abe's government is keen to have more professionals and high skilled individuals, including research personnel, professional lawyers, doctors, engineers, and even creative entrepreneurs. The Japanese government's embrace of overseas professionals in sectors like nursing and construction resulted in an all-time high of 2.38 million foreign residents in 2016.[6] According to the METI, the information technology (IT) industry in Japan is aggressively trying to hire more foreigners (including those from South Asia/India) as the industry is constrained by a deficit of 200,000 IT engineers, likely to expand four times to 800,000 by 2030.[7] To achieve an increase in

[3]Mehta, Dhriti, "A New Deal for Japan's Foreign Workers" dated 28 November 2017 in the Journal of International Affairs Columbia University website [downloaded on 28 November 2017], available at https://jia.sipa.columbia.edu/online-articles/new-deal-japans-foreign-workers.

[4]Nagata, Kazuaki, "With Fast-Track Permanent Residency Rule, Japan Looks to Shed Its Closed Image" dated 4 January 2018 in *Japan Times* [downloaded on 4 Jan 2018], available at https://www.japantimes.co.jp/news/2018/01/04/national/fast-track-permanent-residency-rule-japan-looks-shed-closed-image/#.WvtswaSFOpo.

[5]Nikkei Staff Writers, "Japan to Allow Foreign Interns to Work Five Additional Years" dated 11 April 2018 in *Nikkei Asia* website [downloaded on 11 April 2018], available at https://asia.nikkei.com/Politics/Japan-to-allow-foreign-interns-to-work-five-additional-years.

[6]Chandran, Nyshka, "Foreigners Could Ease Japan's Labor Shortage, but Tokyo Prefers Robots" dated 9 March 2018 in CNBC Asia [downloaded on 9 March 2018], available at https://www.cnbc.com/2018/03/09/foreigners-could-ease-japans-labor-shortage-but-tokyo-prefers-robots.html.

[7]Aiyar, Pallavi, "Rhetoric and Reality of Japan's Skilled Labor Dilemma" dated 27 November 2017 in *Nikkei Asian Review* [downloaded on 27 November 2017], available at https://asia.nikkei.com/Economy/Rhetoric-and-reality-of-Japan-s-skilled-labor-dilemma2.

number of incoming high skilled workers, Japan's authorities have emulated Western countries to institute a points system for evaluating immigration eligibility, based on criteria such as qualifications, language abilities, professional experience with points allocated to them added up to a total. The final marks can then determine whether the foreign talent is able to attain permanent residence (PR) and, with this point system, Japan appears to have shortened waiting time to be the fastest PR approval system globally.[8] It then takes additional half a decade and relevant forms to fill to become a Japanese citizen.

The government offers fast track options for skilled foreigners, including PR rights. From 2012 onwards, Japanese point system for skilled foreign workers adopted the criteria of case-by-case biodata (e.g. age, salary, ability to speak Japanese, qualifications) to fast-lane proficient employees to become PR. Applicants with 70 points or more based on such criteria are eligible for permanent residency after five years, down from a decade waiting time in the past. In 2017, the five-year requirement is further reduced to three for employees with 70–79 points and down to just 365 days for employees scoring 80 points and above. Starting from April 2017, there is a fast track option for skilled non-Japanese workers. They can be eligible for a one-year stay in Japan before applying for PR in a bid to attract and keep those who studied in Japan and/or who have been working in Japan. According to the Ministry of Justice, among the 40,000 non-local students in Japan who went into the job market in 2017, 19,400 found jobs which is 24% higher than the equivalent number of jobs taken up in 2016 and about 90% of those who applied for jobs were successful in 2017.[9]

Non-Japanese students studying in Japan accumulate points for graduating from Japanese tertiary institutions. There are also changes in the internship schemes. Foreigners who complete a half decade-long technical internship can continue to work in Japan for five more years and get their family to join them from their originating countries. Japanese PM Shinzo Abe's administration, which is a conservative government in most aspects, takes a liberal approach when it comes to welcoming foreign workers to Japan. PM Abe intends to expand the scope of residency eligibility for non-Japanese workers to professional and technical fields, something previously set aside mainly for highly skilled individuals like researchers, professional managers and academics.[10]

[8] Smith, Noah, "Japan Struggles to Attract Immigrants as Shrinking Population Time Bomb Keeps on Ticking" dated 30 November 2017 in *The Independent* [downloaded on 30 November 2017], available at https://www.independent.co.uk/news/world/asia/japan-immigrants-migrants-worker-shortfall-shrinking-population-demography-a8084436.html.

[9] Aiyar, Pallavi, "Rhetoric and Reality of Japan's Skilled Labor Dilemma" dated 27 November 2017 in *Nikkei Asian Review* [downloaded on 27 November 2017], available at https://asia.nikkei.com/Economy/Rhetoric-and-reality-of-Japan-s-skilled-labor-dilemma2.

[10] *The Asahi Shimbun*, "Editorial: If Japan Wants More Foreign Workers, More Flexibility Needed" dated 26 February 2018 in *The Asahi Shimbun* website [downloaded on 26 February 2018], available at http://www.asahi.com/ajw/articles/AJ201802260027.html.

In 2016 and without much fanfare, a senior Liberal Democratic Party (LDP, political party of PM Abe's government) panel increased the categories of occupations and positions non-Japanese can apply.[11]

SOURCING FOR IT TALENTS FROM INDIA

Besides retaining talents in Japan, Japanese companies are also sourcing from overseas locations like India. Chief Executive Officer (CEO) Yohei Shibasaki of Fourth Valley Concierge Corp (a leading talent recruitment firm in Japan attracting high skilled talents from 130 countries) and a Ministry of Labor task force member on immigration policy, worked with approximately 30 Indian universities (like the Indian Institutes of Technology or IIT) from 2010 to 2017 to hire fresh graduates for Japanese multinationals.[12] Overall, only approximately 20 of Japan's leading headhunting firms hire from India while others look to China for this purpose due to language aspects, despite the fact that some of the world's top IT talent are found in India.[13] However, these Indian talents tend to use English as their main language of communication and Japanese firms that uses non-Japanese language in interviews is below 1%.[14]

Some Japanese companies adopt a strategy of focusing on exclusively recruiting the second tier of Indian Institute of Technology graduates as they realize that cream of the crop either end up in the US or are hired for lucrative projects at home in India where they can also enjoy creature comforts of home ground, native culture and home-grown social networks.[15] The number of Indians employed in Japan is going up with approximately 7–8000 of

[11] Sieg, Linda and Ami Miyazaki, "Japan Eyes More Foreign Workers, Stealthily Challenging Immigration Taboo" dated 26 April 2016 in Reuters [downloaded on 26 April 2018], available at https://www.reuters.com/article/us-japan-immigration/japan-eyes-more-foreign-workers-stealthily-challenging-immigration-taboo-idUSKCN0XN07X.

[12] Aiyar, Pallavi, "Rhetoric and Reality of Japan's Skilled Labor Dilemma" dated 27 November 2017 in *Nikkei Asian Review* [downloaded on 27 November 2017], available at https://asia.nikkei.com/Economy/Rhetoric-and-reality-of-Japan-s-skilled-labor-dilemma2.

[13] Aiyar, Pallavi, "Rhetoric and Reality of Japan's Skilled Labor Dilemma" dated 27 November 2017 in *Nikkei Asian Review* [downloaded on 27 November 2017], available at https://asia.nikkei.com/Economy/Rhetoric-and-reality-of-Japan-s-skilled-labor-dilemma2.

[14] Aiyar, Pallavi, "Rhetoric and Reality of Japan's Skilled Labor Dilemma" dated 27 November 2017 in *Nikkei Asian Review* [downloaded on 27 November 2017], available at https://asia.nikkei.com/Economy/Rhetoric-and-reality-of-Japan-s-skilled-labor-dilemma2.

[15] Aiyar, Pallavi, "Rhetoric and Reality of Japan's Skilled Labor Dilemma" dated 27 November 2017 in *Nikkei Asian Review* [downloaded on 27 November 2017], available at https://asia.nikkei.com/Economy/Rhetoric-and-reality-of-Japan-s-skilled-labor-dilemma2.

the 23,000-strong Indian community in Japan working in the IT sector, but growth is held back by factors cited by critics (e.g. compulsory tax returns in Japanese language, inheritance tax for global assets regardless of length of stay in Japan, and rentals requiring a guarantor who will have to pay the rent if a tenant defaults).[16]

Critiques of Japan's Foreign Talent Policies and Systems

Every system has its own critics. Foreign professionals in Japan pointed out that they had to pay compulsorily into the Japan's National Pension system (applies to all individuals between 20 and 59 years old residing in Japan). The payee would receive benefits when they are older, handicapped or passed away (in this case left to the estate) after being employed for a decade but individuals with less than 10 years of employment would not qualify for the benefits.[17] Other critics of Japan's foreign talent attraction measures argue that the world outside Japan has changed tremendously. Even the large emerging economies are developing so fast that their first-tier cities have become expensive and costly areas to live in. For e.g. property prices in Sao Paulo Brazil's downtown is higher than Tokyo's suburban property prices like the district of Hachioji and Brazilian minimum wage multiplied three times while Japan's equivalent stayed unchanged and so Brazilians working in Japan drawing on Japanese salaries are no longer able to purchase a property in Brazilian first-tier cities back home.[18] Therefore, to attract highly talented people from first-tier cities in the world to Japan now requires a complete mind-set change. The Japanese companies and their government may have to stop thinking of talented migrant workers as economic migrants. Instead, they can re-conceptualize them as mobile talents who have access to many jobs in the globalized economy, much like how Richard Florida's concept of the "Creative Class" is able to travel freely around the world in search of ideal lifestyle choices, attractive jobs and cultural offerings.

Another critique of Japan's foreign talent policy revolves around the idea of permanence. When Japan has attracted talents to its shores, the offspring of these talent people may choose to reside in Japan and became Japanese,

[16] Aiyar, Pallavi, "Rhetoric and Reality of Japan's Skilled Labor Dilemma" dated 27 November 2017 in *Nikkei Asian Review* [downloaded on 27 November 2017], available at https://asia.nikkei.com/Economy/Rhetoric-and-reality-of-Japan-s-skilled-labor-dilemma2.

[17] Mehta, Dhriti, "A New Deal for Japan's Foreign Workers" dated 28 November 2017 in the *Journal of International Affairs* Columbia University website [downloaded on 28 November 2017], available at https://jia.sipa.columbia.edu/online-articles/new-deal-japans-foreign-workers.

[18] *Mainichi Shimbun*, "Learning to Coexist with Foreign Workers, on Whom Japan Relies Heavily" dated 28 February 2018 in *Mainichi Japan* [downloaded on 28 February 2018], available at https://mainichi.jp/english/articles/20180228/p2a/00m/0na/016000c.

having been educated there. For example, both highly skilled as well as blue collar workers Japanese Brazilians' children who followed their parents to live in Japan are native Japanese speakers and have acclimatized to Japanese culture and therefore some can be prime candidates for citizenship.[19] But, some international media sources reveal that, in February 2018, PM Abe made public his plan to let in more professional and skilled foreign workers but wants a limit on their duration of stay without family members from joining them.[20] Many children who've accompanied their Japanese-Brazilian parents to Japan can speak Japanese. Regardless of whether the Japanese government decides to change its policies to accept more immigrants, many may become immigrants in the future. Therefore to attract highly skilled talents and their children, the government may have to create a "Japanese dream" so that they can succeed multi-generationally and contribute their skills permanently to the destination country. If the "Japanese dream" is not attractive in terms of material gains, lifestyle choices and perceptions of Japan's reception of global talents around the world, some argue Japan may continue to feature low on the radar screen of international global talent migration.

Without the "Japanese dream" imagery, Japan's attempt at talent immigration faces challenges, according to its critics. In 2017, it scored low on the IMD World Competitiveness Center ranking, even lower than other Asian countries that are authoritarian, have polluting cities, and unsafe—the very antithesis of Japan.[21] Japan on the other hand has good public order, high environmental standards, high tech infrastructure, Tokyo is the city with the largest number of Michelin starred restaurants in Asia, Japanese in general are polite people and their service industry has highly trained professional staff. All these factors should attract economic migrants and highly mobile global talents.

However, according to domestic critics and the international media, a major obstacle in attracting skilled migrants is language as the working language and language medium of its education system is still Japanese. Some private sector human resource professionals appear to agree with this view.

[19] *Mainichi Shimbun*, "Learning to Coexist with Foreign Workers, on Whom Japan Relies Heavily" dated 28 February 2018 in *Mainichi Japan* [downloaded on 28 February 2018], available at https://mainichi.jp/english/articles/20180228/p2a/00m/0na/016000c.

[20] Chandran, Nyshka, "Foreigners Could Ease Japan's Labor Shortage, but Tokyo Prefers Robots" dated 9 March 2018 in CNBC Asia [downloaded on 9 March 2018], available at https://www.cnbc.com/2018/03/09/foreigners-could-ease-japans-labor-shortage-but-tokyo-prefers-robots.html.

[21] Smith, Noah, "Japan Struggles to Attract Immigrants as Shrinking Population Time Bomb Keeps on Ticking" dated 30 November 2017 in *The Independent* [downloaded on 30 November 2017], available at https://www.independent.co.uk/news/world/asia/japan-immigrants-migrants-worker-shortfall-shrinking-population-demography-a8084436.html.

Foreign talents, according to Tim Eustace who runs Next Step headhunting consultancy in Tokyo Japan, prefers to send their children to English medium international school and still hope to be able to use English as a working language at least partially at work.[22] Besides the medium of communication, working long hours is another often cited challenge for non-Japanese who are less keen on overtime work and prefer to gauge performances based on productivity.

Another issue is the seniority based salary payment is less attractive to global talents. Highly mobile foreign talents have less patience for seniority-based promotion despite the stability and certainty that it brings. In terms of corporate culture, Japanese companies and society in general frown upon job-hopping. Therefore, career changes at an advanced age or competitive bidding for manpower are frowned upon in Japan, making job mobility and mid-career changes challenging. Mobility appears to be an important quality that draws global talents through meritocratic and competitive systems of performance. Due to global demand for their skills, global talents tend to have shorter stays in any one particular job. Certain communities have their own specific cultural issues.

Other cultural factors cited by V. Sriram (establisher of Infosys Japan) is work culture contrasts where in Japan, each and every assignment is treated with careful attention to possible unconventional outcomes and little work ethical space for improvising but Indians for example pay more attention to some outcomes more than others.[23] Besides cultural factors, there were also procedural legal ones for certain groups of foreign talents like Indian professionals. V. Sriram, a Japanese resident who founded the pioneering Japanese branch office of Infosys in 1997, remembered he had to put up at a hotel for more than 365 days because he could not meet the guarantor condition for renting but such rules have effectively been improved by the Japanese authorities over the years.[24]

Governmental Assistance

Besides the fact that Japan needs skilled manpower due to an aging population and the need to catch up with other advanced developed countries that are also attracting global talents, Japan has other incentives to lure foreign talents

[22] Smith, Noah, "Japan Struggles to Attract Immigrants as Shrinking Population Time Bomb Keeps on Ticking" dated 30 November 2017 in *The Independent* [downloaded on 30 November 2017], available at https://www.independent.co.uk/news/world/asia/japan-immigrants-migrants-worker-shortfall-shrinking-population-demography-a8084436.html.

[23] Aiyar, Pallavi, "Rhetoric and Reality of Japan's Skilled Labor Dilemma" dated 27 November 2017 in *Nikkei Asian Review* [downloaded on 27 November 2017], available at https://asia.nikkei.com/Economy/Rhetoric-and-reality-of-Japan-s-skilled-labor-dilemma2.

[24] Aiyar, Pallavi, "Rhetoric and Reality of Japan's Skilled Labor Dilemma" dated 27 November 2017 in *Nikkei Asian Review* [downloaded on 27 November 2017], available at https://asia.nikkei.com/Economy/Rhetoric-and-reality-of-Japan-s-skilled-labor-dilemma2.

to its shore. Director Satoshi Kurimoto, Technical Cooperation Division at the Ministry of Economy, Trade and Industry (METI) argue that non-Japanese workers can introduce "fresh perspectives to management and production development and help expand to global markets" and at the same time, the Ministry is "hoping that this will erase the closed image of Japan".[25] There is therefore a strong element of wanting to introduce diversity into the workplace and project a cosmopolitan image of Japan when it comes to attraction of global talents.

Agencies are chipping in to resolve the problem of language barriers, Japan External Trade Organization (JETRO) operates online facilities for foreigners providing advice for residing in Japan, procedures for establishing bank accounts and smartphone registration while the Ministry of Education (Monbukagakusho) comes to the assistance of kids who are not Japanese-proficient. Critics also argue that, while immigration law is eased up, all those who apply must go through a Japanese language test. They also argue that because English proficiency among Japanese people is not strong, Japanese may not constantly feel at ease in conversing with foreigners. The METI has supported Fourth Valley Concierge (a leading Japanese human resource firm) to propose the concept of building Japan Centres in some IITs (Indian Institutes of Technology) to instruct students on how to pick up Japanese language and expose them to cultural norms in presentation and culinary cultures.[26] Moreover, community-based help is also coming. Some Tokyo-based Indian institutions of learning have taking in students and assisting with settling down and integrating into family lifestyles while apartments with basic conditions for renting are built and Indian communities have popped up in areas like Nishikasai (an eastern Tokyo district).[27]

ALTERNATIVES—TECHNOLOGICAL MEANS

Besides foreign talent policies, there are other alternatives to address Japan's manpower problems in both labour-intensive industries as well as higher value-added ones that require foreign talents. Japan can increase female participation in its workforce, retrain more elderly to re-enter the workforce or introduction technology to replace human manpower needs. Some popular media sources argue

[25] Nagata, Kazuaki, "With Fast-Track Permanent Residency Rule, Japan Looks to Shed Its Closed Image" dated 4 January 2018 in *Japan Times* [downloaded on 4 January 2018], available at https://www.japantimes.co.jp/news/2018/01/04/national/fast-track-permanent-residency-rule-japan-looks-shed-closed-image/#.WvtswaSFOpo.

[26] Aiyar, Pallavi, "Rhetoric and Reality of Japan's Skilled Labor Dilemma" dated 27 November 2017 in *Nikkei Asian Review* [downloaded on 27 November 2017], available at https://asia.nikkei.com/Economy/Rhetoric-and-reality-of-Japan-s-skilled-labor-dilemma2.

[27] Aiyar, Pallavi, "Rhetoric and Reality of Japan's Skilled Labor Dilemma" dated 27 November 2017 in *Nikkei Asian Review* [downloaded on 27 November 2017], available at https://asia.nikkei.com/Economy/Rhetoric-and-reality-of-Japan-s-skilled-labor-dilemma2.

that Japan is keen on preserving its cultural homogeneity and prevention of perceived crime rate spike, thus resorting to technologies like robots to meet its manpower needs. Underlying this perception is that robots and technologies are culturally neutral, therefore they cannot disrupt the social fabric of the Japanese society and they are incapable of committing crimes which conservatives are worried about when it comes to migration debates. Conservatives detect these advantages on top of the fact that robots cannot complain, do their jobs well and follow instructions to execute tasks logically and rationally.

From television broadcasting journalist Erica the robot to other androids, humanoids and artificial intelligence (A.I.) applications in hotel reception (such as the dinosaur receptionist in Henna Hotel!) and janitors,[28] Japanese robots are taking over the occupations of not just factory-based industrial robots but also jobs that require the human touch. These machines are alternatives to migrants to resolve Japan's aging population and projected impending labour shortage. Japan is the most aged population in the world where 34% of 120 million people are over the age of sixty and the percentage is expected to climb to 42% by 2050 while the overall population number will be down to 60 million by 2068, its people are not procreating and also losing interest in sex (33.3% of Japanese males going into their thirties with a sexless lifestyle).[29] In the past, financial incentives to procreate have failed.

Making up the numbers, robot production is going up, with 340,000 as at 2017 and eventually growing to more than 3 million robots by 2025.[30] This means there will be nearly twice as many robots in 2025 as there are foreigners working in Japan in 2017. There are other contraptions that have robotic parts but are not autonomous or stand-alone units. The Hybrid Assistive Limb (HAL) and other robot exoskeletons help the elderly, women, farmers, caregivers, and other jobs that need physical strength enhancement to do heavy lifting. It alleviates pressure to the backbone and overall physical conditions and can keep more elderly people in the job market by enhancing their strengths. Occupations like caregiver, farmers, logistics deliveries, nurses, and other strength-intensive jobs can make use of robotic exoskeletons to enhance human capabilities. It can also stave off retirement for a large number of silver generation citizens. It also

[28] CBS News and Adam Yamaguchi, "Replacing Humans: Robots Among Us" dated 27 April 2018 in CBS News, available at https://www.cbsnews.com/news/robots-replacing-humans-cbsn-originals/.

[29] CBS News and Adam Yamaguchi, "Replacing Humans: Robots Among Us" dated 27 April 2018 in CBS News, available at https://www.cbsnews.com/news/robots-replacing-humans-cbsn-originals/.

[30] CBS News and Adam Yamaguchi, "Replacing Humans: Robots Among Us" dated 27 April 2018 in CBS News, available at https://www.cbsnews.com/news/robots-replacing-humans-cbsn-originals/.

keep elderly farmers working in the fields, making up for the hollowing out of Japan's rural areas due to younger Japanese migrating to the cities and prevent overdependence on imported food supplies. Elderly farmers and women can benefit from backbreaking work in Japan's agricultural areas and rice growing regions.

Besides assistive robots and robotic parts like HAL, other categories of robots in Japan also help to alleviate labour pressures. Therapeutic robots like Paro which are built like infant seals can keep company with elderly and dementia patients and such robots help to replace human caregivers that are in short supply in Japan. Paro interacts with its human partners using seal-like cries and, when it is out of power, the robot seal is recharged with a contraption shaped like a baby pacifier. The design concept behind Paro is *kawaii* which is part of the cute industry in Japan, and such cute things can help regulate stress, anxiousness, pain/suffering and down mental states, according to the studies done by the team behind Paro.[31]

Another category of robots is known as social robots. Japan came up with the world's pioneering social robot that has been commercialized and made available for US$20,000. Pepper has not only been adopted by industries and service sector companies but it has also kept individual clients company. Pepper can be seen commonly in Japan's service sector providing directions and help assistance for customers. Some individual Japanese owners even take it out for a strolls and have lunch with them, forming a cognitive and emotional bonds with their robots. Such human-robot coexistence is easily implemented in Japan as the nativist religion Shinto attributes a soul to every object in the world, both living and non-living things. Therefore, even non-living things like robots are believed to possess a soul of their own.

Dr. Hiroshi Ishiguro is a well-known android scientist in Japan. He has created robotic clones of real people, including his own likeness, his daughter, a journalist with Eurasian heritage, etc. Many researchers believe that the next step is to overcome the uncanny valley and build robots so lifelike that it becomes impossible for humans to tell them apart and that will be the turning point when fear of robots begins to dissipate. When these human-like androids are paired off with complementary technologies like A.I., they can then begin to substitute for humans even in service jobs, creative industries, professional firms and programming/coding manpower that Japan is short of and finding difficulties in recruiting from the global human resource pool.

---

[31] CBS News and Adam Yamaguchi, "Replacing Humans: Robots Among Us" dated 27 April 2018 in CBS News, available at https://www.cbsnews.com/news/robots-replacing-humans-cbsn-originals/.

BIBLIOGRAPHY

Aiyar, Pallavi, "Rhetoric and Reality of Japan's Skilled Labor Dilemma" dated 27 November 2017 in *Nikkei Asian Review* [downloaded on 27 November 2017]. Available at https://asia.nikkei.com/Economy/Rhetoric-and-reality-of-Japan-s-skilled-labor-dilemma2.

CBS News and Adam Yamaguchi, "Replacing Humans: Robots Among Us" dated 27 April 2018 in CBS News. Available at https://www.cbsnews.com/news/robots-replacing-humans-cbsn-originals/.

Chandran, Nyshka, "Foreigners Could Ease Japan's Labor Shortage, but Tokyo Prefers Robots" dated 9 March 2018 in CNBC Asia [downloaded on 9 March 2018]. Available at https://www.cnbc.com/2018/03/09/foreigners-could-ease-japans-labor-shortage-but-tokyo-prefers-robots.html.

Mainichi Shimbun, "Learning to Coexist with Foreign Workers, on Whom Japan Relies Heavily" dated 28 February 2018 in *Mainichi Japan* [downloaded on 28 February 2018]. Available at https://mainichi.jp/english/articles/20180228/p2a/00m/0na/016000c.

Mehta, Dhriti, "A New Deal for Japan's Foreign Workers" dated 28 November 2017 in the *Journal of International Affairs* Columbia University website [downloaded on 28 November 2017]. Available at https://jia.sipa.columbia.edu/online-articles/new-deal-japans-foreign-workers.

Nagata, Kazuaki, "With Fast-Track Permanent Residency Rule, Japan Looks to Shed Its Closed Image" dated 4 January 2018 in *Japan Times* [downloaded on 4 January 2018]. Available at https://www.japantimes.co.jp/news/2018/01/04/national/fast-track-permanent-residency-rule-japan-looks-shed-closed-image/#.WvtswaSFOpo.

Nikkei Staff Writers, "Japan to Allow Foreign Interns to Work Five Additional Years" dated 11 April 2018 in *Nikkei Asia* website [downloaded on 11 April 2018]. Available at https://asia.nikkei.com/Politics/Japan-to-allow-foreign-interns-to-work-five-additional-years.

Sieg, Linda and Ami Miyazaki, "Japan Eyes More Foreign Workers, Stealthily Challenging Immigration Taboo" dated 26 April 2016 in Reuters [downloaded on 26 April 2018]. Available at https://www.reuters.com/article/us-japan-immigration/japan-eyes-more-foreign-workers-stealthily-challenging-immigration-taboo-idUSKCN0XN07X.

Smith, Noah, "Japan Struggles to Attract Immigrants as Shrinking Population Time Bomb Keeps on Ticking" dated 30 November 2017 in *The Independent* [downloaded on 30 November 2017]. Available at https://www.independent.co.uk/news/world/asia/japan-immigrants-migrants-worker-shortfall-shrinking-population-demography-a8084436.html.

The Asahi Shimbun, "Editorial: If Japan Wants More Foreign Workers, More Flexibility Needed" dated 26 February 2018 in *The Asahi Shimbun* website [downloaded on 26 February 2018]. Available at http://www.asahi.com/ajw/articles/AJ201802260027.html.

CHAPTER 7

Case Study 2: Service Learning

SERVICE LEARNING IN DISASTER RELIEF VOLUNTEERISM IN JAPAN: A SCOPE PAPER[1]—BACKGROUND

Conventionally, one of the motivation for instituting service learning in Japan is the perception that students there are losing civic-mindedness, a sense of morality and interest in the community. This was not a new phenomenon in the twenty-first century as the end of the bubble economy in Japan was previously cited as a causal factor for the rise of the *shinjinrui* or a "new breed" of humans. The term referred to growing numbers of Japanese youths who lost their sense of direction after the era of relative ease in getting jobs and also settling into Lifetime Employment (LTE) systems had broken down as Japanese economic growth slowed down. Japanese social trends of *ijime* (school bullying) and inability by some youths to attend school (*futouko*) showed increases in Japan. Out of this background, heading into the twenty-first century, there are therefore incentives to turn to service learning as an antidote to arrest such social trends in Japan.

This chapter's contribution to the literature on service learning in Japan is focusing on its application in the field of disaster relief and environmental protection. The idea of using service learning to manage social trends has been studied quite extensively in current literature on service learning in Japan but using service learning for creating awareness in other areas like environmental conservation and disaster relief is somewhat neglected or understudied in the existing literature. This writing is interested to pursue this line of enquiry to understand how Japan, which is well-known for

---

[1] The author thanks Dr. Jason Morris Jung (Singapore University of Social Sciences or SUSS) for his comments, suggestions and reviews.

© The Author(s) 2019   97
T. W. Lim, *Industrial Revolution 4.0, Tech Giants, and Digitized Societies*,
https://doi.org/10.1007/978-981-13-7470-8_7

its environmental management and sustainable development as well as natural disasters coping mechanism, has integrated environmental volunteerism and awareness as well as disaster relief work into its service learning curriculum for both schools and other non-governmental organizations (NGOs), e.g. non-profit organizations (NPOs).

*Thesis Statement and Methodology

Besides surveying the contemporary history of service learning in Japan, this writing is interested to examine service learning from the perspective of volunteering to do relief work with communities affected by manmade disasters that has a negative impact on the natural environment. The methodology used has a two-pronged approach. The first approach analyses primary and secondary sources of textual information. Secondary sources of information include studies done by previous service learning instructors in Japan and their written experiences and case studies. Primary sources of information include university policy statements, fieldwork reports from visiting institutions in Japan and papers from the school authorities on the state of service learning in Japan. The other approach relies on observation studies from the author's own experiences with volunteering and program planning in post-disaster relief in Japan. The author contextualized these experiences within increasing consciousness and understanding of service learning framework through accreditations and certification by attending outdoor and leadership training programs.

In other words, there is a conscious effort to re-examine volunteer experiences from the viewpoint of service learning ideas and concepts and detect the dichotomy between volunteerism and service learning so this can provide further feedback for future volunteer work in Japan and improve the coordination as well as partnership with the recipients of service learning projects. This writing will be examining the following topics in the field of service learning in Japan: (a) surveying the increasing institutionalization and networking of Japanese universities involved in service learning as a possible model for outreach; (b) comparing its curriculum with other youth leadership training programs that the author has attended and highlight idiosyncratic, unique or cultural features that stand out; (c) use service learning concepts to examine the author's past case study of environmental and natural disaster relief volunteerism in Japan and some selected concepts of youth expedition (YEP) training experiences.

*Literature review—(a) surveying the literature on increasing institutionalization of service learning in Japan.

The theoretical roots of service learning arose from John Dewey's association of epistemology and pedagogy with citizenship and democracy and the former two entities help shape and direct accumulated experiences that built on prior knowledge and experiences; and these experiences must have the positive quality of agreeableness as well as having an impact on later experiences.[2] An important element of Dewey's service learning theory is the introduction of reflective thinking and the use of observation to produce facts and ideas and all these elements are encapsulated in a project that must stimulate interest, have inherent educational value, pique curiosity, generate the demand to know more information and value-add to long-term development.[3] Dewey's philosophy, similar to some elements of groupist Japanese culture, believed in the power of communitarianism. He espoused the idea of a "Great Community" or a local community that was moral, intellectual and lasting with opportunities for face-to-face interactions, all of which are important particularly in the context of a sense of crisis due to the destruction or marginalization of the community through industrialization and the mechanization of human functions.[4] When youths are imbued with self-directed learning, a sense of identification with the community and infused with a spirit of service, Dewey believes they can become effective units that contribute to the collective whole.[5] These same Dewey-ian elements can also be found in specific literatures written on service learning in Japan related to environmental conservation and disaster relief efforts. The existing literatures in this area advocate saving lives and alleviating damage to the environment. Some of them are introduced below.

Kuramoto and Nguyen's study is probably one of the most relevant literature for this writing in terms of analysing the Minamata mercury poisoning manmade natural disaster. He examines how students are affected by the event and their reflections in volunteering to recovery work in Minamata.[6] The author worked with a Japanese Non-Government Organization (NGO)

---

[2] Giles Jr., Dwight E. and Janet Eyler, "The Theoretical Roots of Service-Learning in John Dewey: Toward a Theory of Service-Learning" dated Fall 1994 in the *Michigan Journal of Community Service Learning* Vol. 1 No. 1 [downloaded on 1 January 2017], available at https://www.american.edu/ocl/volunteer/upload/Eyler-and-Giles-1994.pdf, pp. 78–79.

[3] Giles Jr., Dwight E. and Janet Eyler, "The Theoretical Roots of Service-Learning in John Dewey: Toward a Theory of Service-Learning" dated Fall 1994 in the *Michigan Journal of Community Service Learning* Vol. 1 No. 1 [downloaded on 1 January 2017], available at https://www.american.edu/ocl/volunteer/upload/Eyler-and-Giles-1994.pdf, p. 80.

[4] Giles Jr., Dwight E. and Janet Eyler, "The Theoretical Roots of Service-Learning in John Dewey: Toward a Theory of Service-Learning" dated Fall 1994 in the *Michigan Journal of Community Service Learning* Vol. 1 No. 1 [downloaded on 1 January 2017], available at https://www.american.edu/ocl/volunteer/upload/Eyler-and-Giles-1994.pdf, p. 81.

[5] Giles Jr., Dwight E. and Janet Eyler, "The Theoretical Roots of Service-Learning in John Dewey: Toward a Theory of Service-Learning" dated Fall 1994 in the *Michigan Journal of Community Service Learning* Vol. 1 No. 1 [downloaded on 1 January 2017], available at https://www.american.edu/ocl/volunteer/upload/Eyler-and-Giles-1994.pdf, p. 82.

[6] Kuramoto, Tetsuo and Nguyen Thi Thu Huong, "Findings from Case Study of Service-Learning in Japan—From Points of 'Minamata Disease' (Mercury Pollution) Issues" dated January 2013 in the *Journal of the Faculty of Culture and Education* Vol. 17 No. 2 (Japan: Saga University), 2013, p. 92.

to reflect on his experience for a better comprehension of the needs of the local Minamata community and honed his knowledge and skills in helping out with disaster relief in that area. Using the models and templates of service learning education in existing case studies found in the literature review, this writing will draw up a proposal of how the volunteer group can reach out to non-Japanese students in the tertiary educational institutions and these students can work with the NGO with the additional rigour of service learning concepts. This proposal builds on the work that the author has previously carried out with a non-profit organization in Minamata (Japan).

Service learning in Japan has gone beyond an educational venture and developed into a possible career option, including work related to disaster relief. Yutaka Sato and his team's writing even suggests that there is growing recognition of an expanding NGO sector in Japan where one could opt for professional career.[7] Sato's observation is compatible with trend of growing civil society-local government collaboration in Japan, especially after the 1995 Great Hanshin Earthquake (also known popularly as Kobe Earthquake) where the first groups to arrive at the disaster sites were volunteers from religious groups, NGOs and even the yakuza gangs before the arrival of official teams. There was growing recognition that NGOs can partner with local authorities because of the former's knowledge in local conditions, the potential for government to conserve resources by farming out functions that can be better performed by the civil society groups and incentivize non-profit groups by putting in place strict accounting and governance practices while allowing these groups to perform what they do best in local communities. Due to the possibility of developing the learning process as a career and genuine need for manpower in the field of disaster relief, accredited leadership and outdoor skills can also be integrated as part of the service learning program.

Another important and relevant writing is Sescon and Tuano's case study of service learning application in natural disasters. Although this article is written on the case study of the Philippines, it cites Japan as a case study and possible model for coping with natural disasters. The writing cited the existence of a massive Japan Civil Network for Disaster made up of 500 organizations mobilized after the Great East Japan Earthquake (popularly known as "311") to help with relief and recovery efforts where 400,000 volunteers helped out.[8] Sescon and Tuano highlighted the scale of disaster relief efforts

---

[7] Sato, Yutaka, Florence McCarthy, Mutsuko Murakami, Takashi Nishio, and Kano Yamamoto, "An Appreciation of Cross-Cultural Differences Through International Service-Learning at International Christian University, Japan" in *Service-Learning in Asia Curricular Models and Practices* (Hong Kong: Hong Kong University Press), 2010, p. 33.

[8] Sescon, Joselito and Philip Tuano, "Service Learning as a Response to Disasters and Social Development: A Philippine Experience" dated 2012 in *Japan Social Innovation Journal* Vol. 2 No. 1 (Japan: Japan Social Innovation Journal) in the Japan Science and Technology Information Aggregator, Electronic (J-Stage) website [downloaded on 1 January 2017], available at https://www.jstage.jst.go.jp/browse, p. 64.

in Japan and implied the necessity to maintain a level of voluntary relief help and volunteerism by school-going youths by integrating community development curriculum into the syllabuses of schools in the Philippines. Southeast Asia has its fair share of natural and manmade disasters that makes an impact on the natural environment as well. Organizations and educational institutions in countries affected by these natural disaster can coordinate with non-affected countries within the region in terms of relief work. Such multilateral cooperation can also foster the Association of Southeast Asian Nations (ASEAN) regional spirit as the region integrates closer into a community.

Miyazaki Takeshi's study is probably one of the most extensive on the curriculum of Service Learning in Japan, including the highest six ranking universities in Japan. He mentions several features of Service Learning in the Top Six Japanese Universities, including: emphasis on compatibility with local community needs; outreach to receiving parties of service learning project for dialogue at the university; faculty members of the university have meetings with the receiving audiences of service learning projects every fortnightly, etc.[9] The mechanics of how service learning is designed in tertiary institutions' curriculum can be discerned from his writing. They serve as additional templates for examining the author's service learning experiences related to the natural environment in Japan.

Significance and Importance of Disaster Relief and Environmental Conservation Volunteerism

Teaching service learning, encouraging community-based research and leading volunteer groups for missions related to environmental conservation and disaster relief efforts are important because the impacts of environmental damage and natural disasters tend to be long-term. In particular, teaching the future generation to tackle these issues is crucial to managing the problems longitudinally. Sustainable community-based research also helps to understand the problems better to cope with their long-term impact. With urbanization and economic development in East Asia, many youths have become disconnected and disengaged with the environment and live in temperature/climate-controlled urban environments with little contact with nature and are only aware of Mother Nature's fury when there is a natural disaster (manmade or otherwise). As youths increasingly engage in the virtual world, immerse in social media communications, they have become removed from physical contact with the natural environment. Without opportunities to engage in environmental conservation work, there are no meaningful opportunities for many of them to contribute to improving the natural

---

[9] Miyazaki, Takeshi, "How Schools Measure the Impact of Service Learning on Communities: Through the Investigation of Higher Education Institutions in Japan and the US" dated 6 June 2013 in the Lingnan University website featuring a Soka University presenter (Hong Kong: Lingnan University), 2013, pp. 17–18.

environment, therein lies the importance of environmental volunteerism. Service learning and YEP leadership programs help to led youths outside the confines of their classrooms and the comfort of their homes to learn more about the environment. An integrated environment lesson plan and outdoor experiential learning provide professional training and coaching for students before they embark on their outdoor experiential learning.

In conceptualizing service learning assignments related to the environment, it may be useful to distinguish service learning from basic volunteerism and community work. Volunteerism alone may not be enough to make the students' learning experiences a fruitful one. Andrew Furco's model in differentiating service learning, community service and volunteerism is instructive here. He argues that community service and volunteerism aims to benefit the organizations served and the former is characterized as charity carried out in a top-down approach (sometimes with self-satisfaction in mind) and may led to status quo dependency with the transfer of benefits one-directionally from the giver to the taker.[10] Community service on the other hand has a more systematic framework that sustains the activities over a longer-term for the participants but generally does not include reflective learning and/or academic contents.[11] Service learning attempts to reach an equilibrium between the goals of student education and serving the community, contribute to both ends, seeks to have a transformative impact and eventually, in the process, knowledge is gained not only by experience but also through systematic self-reflections.[12] The relationship between the community served and the server is based on reciprocity as dividing lines between both roles are amorphous, even as youths/students' assignments and research tasks are formulated together with the community prioritized according to their needs.[13]

[10] Jacoby, Barbara and Jeffrey Howard, "Introduction to Service Learning" dated October 2014 in *Service-Learning Essentials: Questions, Answers, and Lessons Learned* hosted on The University of Vermont website [downloaded on 1 January 2017], available at http://www.uvm. edu/rsenr/rm230/costarica/Service%20Learning%20Readings/Jacoby_Intro%20to%20SL_ Ch1.pdf (San Francisco, CA: Wiley), 2014, p. 2.

[11] Jacoby, Barbara and Jeffrey Howard, "Introduction to Service Learning" dated October 2014 in *Service-Learning Essentials: Questions, Answers, and Lessons Learned* hosted on The University of Vermont website [downloaded on 1 January 2017], available at http://www.uvm. edu/rsenr/rm230/costarica/Service%20Learning%20Readings/Jacoby_Intro%20to%20SL_ Ch1.pdf (San Francisco, CA: Wiley), 2014, pp. 2–3.

[12] Jacoby, Barbara and Jeffrey Howard, "Introduction to Service Learning" dated October 2014 in *Service-Learning Essentials: Questions, Answers, and Lessons Learned* hosted on The University of Vermont website [downloaded on 1 January 2017], available at http://www.uvm. edu/rsenr/rm230/costarica/Service%20Learning%20Readings/Jacoby_Intro%20to%20SL_ Ch1.pdf (San Francisco, CA: Wiley), 2014, p. 3.

[13] Jacoby, Barbara and Jeffrey Howard, "Introduction to Service Learning" dated October 2014 in *Service-Learning Essentials: Questions, Answers, and Lessons Learned* hosted on The University of Vermont website [downloaded on 1 January 2017], available at http://www.uvm. edu/rsenr/rm230/costarica/Service%20Learning%20Readings/Jacoby_Intro%20to%20SL_ Ch1.pdf (San Francisco, CA: Wiley), 2014, p. 4.

Outreach

Besides local area communities, service learning in Japan also has an external orientation. Sending university students to remote or agricultural areas outside Japan and in the East Asian region is also a form of Track II diplomacy with people to people exchanges. This has the potential to enhance grassroots contact or exchanges between youths with the functionalist belief that greater exchanges can minimize misunderstandings between peoples of different countries. Functionalism in international relations present another aspect of relationships between peoples, societies and groups/organizations. It is based on the idea of cooperation between different groups of people based on enhancing mutual interests, detecting common needs, sharing public goods and such cooperation need not necessarily be predicated upon state structures.

People to people exchanges is a liberal worldview that sees the global community as a platform for reducing tensions, preventing conflicts, promoting dialogues and capacity-building exchanges between groups of people (and not necessarily involving the state). Functionalism which believes in the potential of non-state group to promote greater understanding of different countries, societies and youths/peoples is also compatible with the ideas of globalization, transnationality and cosmopolitanism. Cooperation would not be possible if members of a functionalist community did not come together through consensus, the phenomenon of globalization and acceptance of multiculturalism and respect for diversity and differences between different groups of people leading to a cosmopolitan worldview.

Functionalism is built on consensus, a desire for greater understanding, expertise by specialists shared with others in the interest of public good, and the idea of collective governance or mutual self-help and brotherhood for all. Consequently, there is an accent on capacity-building and learning from each other through state and non-state approaches and institutions. Volunteerism and service learning are one aspect of such capacity-building exchanges. The difference between the two is that service learning is a two-way process in that those in service learn and benefit from the community as much as the community teaches and learn from the volunteers. Both capacity building and learning from each other are characteristics found in service learning practiced by NGOs and educational institutional. Cooperation between such groups can be classified as a form of Track II diplomacy, with people to people exchanges, fostering understanding between youths and even cultivating young leaders in the next generation who develop their own networks of friendship and stronger understanding of their youth counterparts in other countries. These end results are collateral spillovers from service learning expedition teams sent to work on projects in other countries. When youth groups, NGOs, NPOs, civil society groups, local communities, volunteer organizations and service learning groups meet and build up networks with one another, they become enmeshed in a matrix of cooperation.

Consequently, this contributes to regional integration. The more a region is integrated and enmeshed within a network of capacity-building and volunteerism, the greater the incentives for cooperation between peoples rather than resort to conflicts and disagreements. When institutions and networks are set up for volunteerism, they lead to more entrenchment of exchange platforms and expansion of channels for exchanges and mutual learning. These are no-detriment items that can only lead to positive outcomes. In some cases, service learning expeditions and volunteerism can resolve a local community problem much earlier, more efficiently and/or at lower costs compared to political authorities. There are also spillover benefits, e.g. volunteers or service learning teams building infrastructures for the local community while experiencing and learning about local cultures can motivate economic development of that area and/or improve the basic rights of that community. Expertise are shared, local cultures are learnt and knowledge is exchanged. The exchange of expertise and knowledge lies at the heart of neo-liberal thinking and functionalism.

The writing will examine case studies in this area and analyse its implications for improving the environments of regional countries and enhance good will through such exchanges in the case of Japan. Interestingly, there are programs in Japan that are solely externally-oriented. The Middlebury Campus report on service learning in Japan noted that "service learning center at ICU [International Christian University] in Japan allowed students to participate in service learning projects in countries throughout Asia and Southeast Asia, but not in Japan".[14] Sato, McCarthy, Murakami, Nishio and Yamamoto's important case study of service learning in ICU reveals that there are three types of international service learning programs on campus, including (1) despatching students to other institutions or agencies; (2) hosting students from other Asian institutions, and (3) selecting a single one-stop location and gathering students from Asia and/or Africa for collective interaction in a multicultural setting.[15]

ICU also started a service learning summer program in 2006 (the International Service-Learning Model Program or ISLMP) centred on the idea of *kyosei* (multicultural symbiosis) derived from a grant funded by Japan's Ministry of Education, Culture, Sports, Science and Technology with the specific goal of enhancing the international makeup of staff and students

---

[14]Mueller, Tabitha, "Students Participate in Service-Learning Program in Japan" dated 21 September 2016 in The Middlebury Campus website [downloaded on 1 January 2017], available at https://middleburycampus.com/article/students-participate-in-service-learning-program-in-japan/.

[15]Sato, Yutaka, Florence McCarthy, Mutsuko Murakami, Takashi Nishio, and Kano Yamamoto, "An Appreciation of Cross-Cultural Differences Through International Service-Learning at International Christian University, Japan" in *Service-Learning in Asia Curricular Models and Practices* (Hong Kong: Hong Kong University Press), 2010, p. 38.

in ICU.[16] Besides providing exciting cultural experiences and networking with students from other cultures, participants of the program also learn to adapt to a new environment, linguistic exposure, culinary habits, local community practices and customs as well as coordinating with a local NGO.[17]

In the Japanese context, another example of regional outreach is the "Re-inventing Japan Project" administered by Ehime University and also featured on the website of the Japan Society for the Promotion of Science. It consists of a partnership between Japan and Indonesia where Japanese and ASEAN university students are able to engage in community work from a period of 7 days to three months in the area of thematic service learning that leads to graduate degrees in agriculture.[18] An interesting feature of this program is that social media tools like Facebook is utilized to disseminate the outcome of the project to audiences and highlight the achievements while a documentary video is made before and after the experience in Indonesia.[19] In fact, Yutaka Sato and his team argue that service learning in Asia is influenced by the International Christian University (ICU) Japanese model in that networking amongst universities and global multiculturalism were emphasized in addition to personal and career development.[20]

Policy and curriculum—(b) comparing its curriculum with other youth leadership training programs that the author has attended.

In terms of policy, the Japanese government, through its Ministry of Education, Culture, Sports, Science, and Technology (MEXT), instituted the "Rainbow Plan" (Full name: "The Education Reform Plan for the Twenty-First century") to educate young people to be "open and warm-hearted... through participating in community service and various programs" and made

---

[16]Sato, Yutaka, Florence McCarthy, Mutsuko Murakami, Takashi Nishio, and Kano Yamamoto, "An Appreciation of Cross-Cultural Differences Through International Service-Learning at International Christian University, Japan" in *Service-Learning in Asia Curricular Models and Practices* (Hong Kong: Hong Kong University Press), 2010, p. 42.

[17]Sato, Yutaka, Florence McCarthy, Mutsuko Murakami, Takashi Nishio, and Kano Yamamoto, "An Appreciation of Cross-Cultural Differences Through International Service-Learning at International Christian University, Japan" in *Service-Learning in Asia Curricular Models and Practices* (Hong Kong: Hong Kong University Press), 2010, p. 43.

[18]Ehime University, "Re-inventing Japan Project" dated FY2014 in the Japan Society for the Promotion of Science website [downloaded on 1 January 2017], available at https://www.jsps.go.jp/.

[19]Ehime University, "Re-inventing Japan Project" dated FY2014 in the Japan Society for the Promotion of Science website [downloaded on 1 January 2017], available at https://www.jsps.go.jp/.

[20]Sato, Yutaka, Florence McCarthy, Mutsuko Murakami, Takashi Nishio, and Kano Yamamoto, "An Appreciation of Cross-Cultural Differences Through International Service-Learning at International Christian University, Japan" in *Service-Learning in Asia Curricular Models and Practices* (Hong Kong: Hong Kong University Press), 2010, p. 31.

it mandatory for all students to perform community service.[21] Kamakura Junior High School started experimentally with service learning course that congregate a single session or period weekly over an overall 25 periods (50 hours per semester) and it is uniquely organized by the students themselves with minimal supervisory inputs from the teaching staff.[22] There was resonance between the activities of Kamakura Junior High School with Japan's major social trends such as visiting elderly hospices in the context of a rapidly aging population.[23] Besides secondary schools, pioneering curriculum on service learning integrated into sociological courses at the tertiary education level had begun as early as the 1990s. For example, Tokyo International University (TIU) from Kawagoe Japan founded an external campus with Willamette University of Salem Oregon which became the Tokyo International University of America (TIUA). They co-designed a course related to global education in 1989 that featured concepts and ideas of poverty, homelessness, preparing food for young street urchins, sharing written notes on their exposure to poverty in Japan and the US.[24]

Thus far, the emphasis has been on youth issues with less emphasis on environmental conservation or voluntary clean-up activities. Through the author's previous observation, experience and fieldwork, the writing will look at how volunteering to work with the environment can possibly encourage social consciousness amongst Japan's youths/student by adopting a service learning approach. Besides the epistemological aspects of service learning and developing cultural understanding, there is also potential for students to hone their leadership skills. Unlike traditional Japanese service learning emphases on encouraging youths to engage with social problems, societal trends and socioeconomic challenges, service learning and volunteerism in the fields of disaster relief requires some form of physical fitness and resilience. Accreditation by professional bodies for skills picked up in the service learning program is a useful feature for consideration in Japanese service learning

---

[21]Feinburg, Joseph R., "Service Learning in Contemporary Japan and America" dated October 2002 in University of Nebraska Omaha DigitalCommons@UNO website [downloaded on 1 March 2017], available at http://digitalcommons.unomaha.edu/cgi/viewcontent.cgi?article=1000&context=slceinternational, p. 369.

[22]Feinburg, Joseph R., "Service Learning in Contemporary Japan and America" dated October 2002 in University of Nebraska Omaha DigitalCommons@UNO website [downloaded on 1 March 2017], available at http://digitalcommons.unomaha.edu/cgi/viewcontent.cgi?article=1000&context=slceinternational, p. 369.

[23]Feinburg, Joseph R., "Service Learning in Contemporary Japan and America" dated October 2002 in University of Nebraska Omaha DigitalCommons@UNO website [downloaded on 1 March 2017], available at http://digitalcommons.unomaha.edu/cgi/viewcontent.cgi?article=1000&context=slceinternational, p. 369.

[24]Heuser, Linda, "Service-Learning as a Pedagogy to Promote the Content, Cross-Cultural, and Language-Learning of ESL Students" dated Winter 1999 in *Teaching English as a Second Language (TESL) Canada Journal/Revue TESL Du Canada* (Canada), 1999, p. 59.

programs and this is not found in the current literature on service learning in Japan. Professionalization in imparting these skillsets by different accreditation bodies and also incorporating elements of a leadership training program are possible features for consideration in tertiary-level service learning programs in Japan.

*Case study—(c) using service learning concepts to examine environmental and natural disaster relief volunteerism in Japan with references to YEP training.

In the university where the author was working in 2011, he represented his department to work with a Non-Profit Organization (NPO, hereby kept anonymous with the acronym "KS") at the Minamata mercury poisoning disaster site in 2011. It was a community voluntary work program designed by an NPO for non-Japanese students to visit Minamata, the purpose was to evaluate the potential of the program for a study trip, community exchanges and carry out some short-term volunteer work. KS is one of the major disaster relief NGO working with Minamata mercury poisoning victims since the Minamata disease was discovered in 1956. Minamata has since become a case study of environmental disaster and post-disaster relief in Japanese school textbooks. It is also a case study of the excess of accelerated economic development without due regard for the environment or environmental regulations. Minamata resulted from the decision of a major Japanese plastic manufacturer Chisso's decision to dump its mercury by-products into the Shiranui sea. Mercury was consumed by the fishes and then traces found its way into cats that consumed those fishes. For urban youths who do not have substantial access to nature and/or understand human dependence on the natural environment for food sources (e.g. Minamata's fishing industry), a trip to study the mercury poisoning incident can highlight the importance of environmental protection for them. It is not a service learning study trip to do charity but to learn from and work with the community within a framework that combines academic requirements, self-reflection opportunities and making a real impact on the environment through contributing to enhancing awareness of the incident and working with local civil society in persistent post-disaster follow-up work, e.g. organizing talks by victims and also assisting individual victims who are still facing other challenges in their old age.

Left caption: the field that sits on top of the containment vessel built to hold the sludge contaminated by mercury. Photo by author, taken during fieldwork. This is a useful site to curate for service learning students. They can observe the result of the clean-up that followed the containment and also look at how the local community use such spaces for school, leisure and sports activities. Former contaminated areas need not be permanently stigmatized with environmental pollution. Service learning programs can learn how such spaces were reconfigured as environmentally-clean areas and learn how the local community take care of such green spaces.

Right caption: glassware works made by the victims of Minamata poisoning for sale at the NPO facilities that is rented out as a form of social enterprise to raise funds for the victims and the NPO, photo taken by author during fieldwork. This is an opportunity for volunteers to learn from the local community the skills to make traditional Japanese glassware (known as *kiriko*) and produce them through acquired skills for retailing to donors.

Left caption: the now-pristine Shiranui Sea that was once contaminated by mercury. The author was offered and consumed turban shellfish caught in this area during his fieldwork. Service learning volunteers can contribute to the maintenance of this clean environment by picking up any washed-up seaweed, fallen leaves and other natural debris. In the top left hand corner of this photo, there is a fishing vessel out to net squids that were in season during the author's visit. Photo taken by the author.

Right caption: the canal where the author spotted dragonflies and was told by the local guides that dragonflies can only be found in areas with pristine water sources. Volunteers can help document the wildlife at these rejuvenated areas and create a guidebook written in English for future visitors. Photo taken by author.

Left caption: the Shiranui Sea is now a site for water sports such as canoeing. Volunteers on service learning programs can take this opportunity to experience marine-based outdoor activities as part of their bonding and networking interactive sessions with the local community. Photo taken by author during fieldwork.

Right caption: the rejuvenated Minamata area is now the site of agricultural activities. Water from the padi fields are drained off to the Shiranui sea through conduits. Photo taken by author during fieldwork.

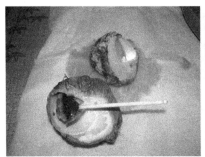

Left and right photo captions: the shells that were caught from the Shiranui Sea is barbequed by locals to welcome the author's arrival. Service learning volunteers can attend such BBQ parties and network with local community members. They can also document the rich marine life (including those that are edible) in this region in the guidebook based on their experience. Photo taken by author during fieldwork. The photo on the right likewise shows cooked squids that were caught in the Shiranui Sea, along with locally-grown vegetables.

Soon after, humans who consumed seafood in that region also had mercury entering their bodies and interfering with their central nervous system and brain functions. The victims led a painful life losing control over their muscles and mothers that consumed the mercury-tainted seafood gave birth to baby with defects. Some perished in the process. Eventually, the authorities contained all the mercury-tainted mud and water in a gigantic large basin capped off with a green park space on top of the containment vessel. Socially, victims of Minamata poisoning experienced social stigma, threats and even marginalization from mainstream society, preventing a large number from stepping forward to claim compensation. KS was a citizen action body formed to advocate compensation and recognition for the victims, many of whom were hidden from public view. KS also worked with the local museums to strengthen environmental awareness in the region. KS has networked with international partners to outreach to other countries and share their community's experience with manmade environmental disaster. In other words, KS was the ideal partner for future assignments involving students/youths since it was in the best position to articulate local community priorities and needs, a feature of service learning and YEP program design with the community and by the community.

The concept of service learning was not a major intention of the program in the author's scoping trip to Minamata. It would be interesting to implement a service learning program for international student volunteers in an internationally well-known site for disaster relief and environmental clean-up. On hindsight, the author argues that, if the concept of service learning was adopted at that point of time, a possible conceptual model in terms of designing the flow of the learning progress and syllabus might be the pioneering ICU model for service learning courses in the following:

Flow of the learning progress and syllabus for service learning

Introduction to service learning → International and Community Service Learning → Reflection on Service Experiences

Preparation for Service-Learning Field study

(*Source* Sato, Yutaka, Florence McCarthy, Mutsuko Murakami, Takashi Nishio, and Kano Yamamoto, "An Appreciation of Cross-Cultural Differences Through International Service-Learning at International Christian University, Japan" in *Service-Learning in Asia Curricular Models and Practices* [Hong Kong: Hong Kong University Press], 2010, p. 35.)

The components of "Introduction to Service Learning" and "Preparation for Service-Learning Field Study" were not introduced on the author's own study trip to Minamata. On hindsight, they would have been helpful for the following reasons. At the preparation stage, it would have been useful to go through a number of personality tests, cognitive reasoning and bonding sessions before embarking on the expedition itself in order to assess the aptitude for participating in the expedition itself. Conceptually, on hindsight, it is also useful to integrate the goals of the program that combines the features of scholastic progression and requirement, syllabus design according to the guidelines by professional bodies in service learning coaching and outdoor training, cultivating leadership skills and teamwork as well as enhancing self-motivated and self-driven learning process of the students.

Service learning objectives and goals

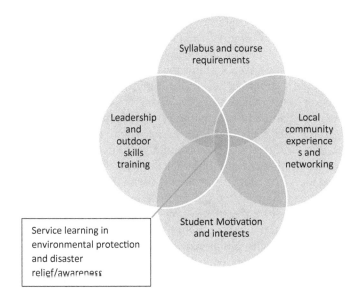

Achievements by the students in picking up local knowledge and understanding of an environmental disaster and its recovery during the Minamata trip can be better evaluated. Student participants can evaluate their experiential learning in terms of preparedness for handling future expeditions, as what a YEP leader would expect. Students can better articulate their takeaways from the study mission. They can also keep folders and portfolios of their contribution to their departments that can include visual materials, fieldwork notes, reports and other paraphernalia that can effectively textualize and capture their extensive experience. Students can be encouraged to archive and record down memories through writing case studies of scenarios they encountered. Recording down events created case precedents that allow students to have constant and gradual self-improvement and they also had a textual reference when it comes to applications of knowledge and skills that were acquired instinctively when coping with dynamic unpredictable situations or through theoretical courses and then applied practically in real-life circumstances.

Reflective paper writing allows students to keep records of each expedition and they became useful resources that they could use to share with their peers. When reading the accounts and discussing with fellow teammates and other stakeholders in future expeditions, students could be critical of past experiences and understand that no single coping mechanism is perfect. For personal development, the importance of learning through reflection, especially in the aftermath of rigorous and physically-demanding activities, the importance of scribing, archiving and recording the events and memories of these events for a multitude of purposes, including records of official history are particularly useful when memories dim with time. Keeping a logbook for extraordinary events and emergencies like medical evacuation and learning and reflecting on past experiences to enrich existing knowledge base in preparation for future experiential learning trips are useful.

Going through a course in service learning concepts is helpful to understand the process as one where students learn from the community as much as the community benefit from their presence and assistance. They can become a student of people they serve and learning about the needs of the community through the residents, denizens or stakeholders in that community well-being. This was something that the author learnt through the YEP Leaders' Training course in Singapore. In the YEP program, participants were taught to habitualize self-reflections and sat around in circle on the last day of the program to discuss about the mistakes made as a team. The camaraderie developed between participants and archived memories related to the outings or tasks in the program became collective memories. These were one-off reflection sessions and it was up to the individual participant to record down the lessons learnt for future expeditions. For the student participants, they had to apply it almost immediately as they were student leaders who were on the verge of leading their teammates into rural areas in Asia for volunteer work.

Finally, when service learning concepts are implemented, networking with their counterparts in Minamata can take place within a conceptual framework rather than ad hoc contact between a homestay guest and a university student on a study mission. A service learning network can look like the following structure that embeds all stakeholders. In this aspect, critical reflective sessions help when assessing inter-cultural interactions, such as interpreting the importance of symbolic signifiers in local community cultures. Symbolic and affective meanings may be interpreted subjectively by individuals rather than understood as a collective universal symbol by all participants and members of a trekking expedition. This is important as interpretations of symbolic meaning require consultation and consensual-seeking sessions to reach a common understanding of something encountered in the expedition or in the preparation stages before the expedition. Critical readings of archived memories allow them to enter each new expedition with a blank mental canvas and an open mind. They could also fully grasp the complexity and perplexity of any outdoor activities which carried them their own level of risks, challenges and rewards. The accumulation of the above experiences help students do scenario planning when organizing future sustainable community activities outside their own countries.

A possible service learning network for designing a service learning study mission to Minamata

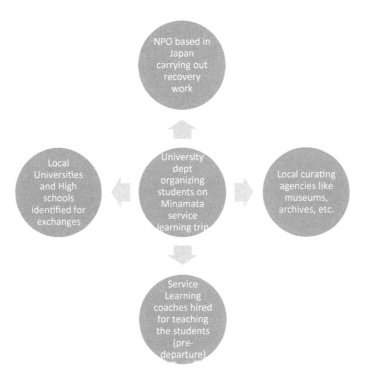

University department and students interested in a Minamata service learning program can benefit from such networks that can sustain contact between students and teaching staff. It makes the students' trip more meaningful and they can also apply service learning concepts to maintain the links beyond personal contact.

CONCLUDING REMARKS

In designing this service learning program to learn about the Minamata mercury poisoning history and the relief efforts thereafter, there are elements in the abovementioned programs that can be adapted and integrated into the Minamata case study of a service learning expedition to learn about disaster relief efforts and environmental clean-up. The program was originally designed as an observation-based, experiential learning program. The integration of self-reflective essays, quizzes testing the students' knowledge of local culture and also pre-departure accreditation and certification for expedition participation are all potentially value-added features for improving the program. The next step for this project is to work with the NGO partner in Japan to develop a program that integrates service learning feature.

It would consist of three components: (1) the students' diachronic observation of activities carried out by the NGO and systematic recording, archiving and curating their experiences for self-reflective sessions; (2) leadership and outdoor training offered by professional bodies to give accreditations to pre-departure service learning program sessions; (3) forming networks with KS and other stakeholders in the Minamata region. In the same way that environmental issues and disaster relief efforts can be studied as part of service learning and expedition (and leadership) programs, another related topic associated with the environment where the above points about program design is applicable is in the area of working with local communities affected by the natural resource extractive sector. This could also be a future extension of this project and writing.

BIBLIOGRAPHY

Ehime University, "Re-inventing Japan Project" dated FY2014 in the Japan Society for the Promotion of Science website [downloaded on 1 January 2017]. Available at https://www.jsps.go.jp/.

Feinburg, Joseph R., "Service Learning in Contemporary Japan and America" dated October 2002 in University of Nebraska Omaha DigitalCommons@UNO website [downloaded on 1 March 2017]. Available at http://digitalcommons.unomaha.edu/cgi/viewcontent.cgi?article=1000&context=slceinternational, p. 369.

Giles Jr., Dwight E., and Janet Eyler, "The Theoretical Roots of Service-Learning in John Dewey: Toward a Theory of Service-Learning" dated Fall 1994 in the *Michigan Journal of Community Service Learning* Vol. 1 No. 1 [downloaded on 1 January 2017] Available at https://www.american.edu/ocl/volunteer/upload/Eyler-and-Giles-1994.pdf, pp. 78–79.

Heuser, Linda, "Service-Learning as a Pedagogy to Promote the Content, Cross-Cultural, and Language-Learning of ESL Students" dated Winter 1999 in *Teaching English as a Second Language (TESL) Canada Journal/Revue TESL Du Canada* (Canada), 1999, p. 59.

Jacoby, Barbara and Jeffrey Howard, "Introduction to Service Learning" dated October 2014 in *Service-Learning Essentials: Questions, Answers, and Lessons Learned* hosted on The University of Vermont website [downloaded on 1 January 2017]. Available at http://www.uvm.edu/rscnr/rm230/costarica/Service%20Learning%20Readings/Jacoby_Intro%20to%20SL_Ch1.pdf (San Francisco, CA: Wiley), 2014, p. 2.

Kuramoto, Tetsuo and Nguyen Thi Thu Huong, "Findings from Case Study of Service-Learning in Japan—From Points of 'Minamata Disease' (Mercury Pollution) Issues" dated January 2013 in the *Journal of the Faculty of Culture and Education* Vol. 17 No. 2 (Japan: Saga University), 2013, p. 92.

Miyazaki, Takeshi, "How Schools Measure the Impact of Service Learning on Communities: Through the Investigation of Higher Education Institutions in Japan and the US" dated 6 June 2013 in the Lingnan University website featuring a Soka University presenter (Hong Kong: Lingnan University), 2013, pp. 17–18.

Mueller, Tabitha, "Students Participate in Service-Learning Program in Japan" dated 21 September 2016 in The Middlebury Campus website [downloaded on 1 January 2017]. Available at https://middleburycampus.com/article/students-participate-in-service-learning-program-in-japan/.

Sato, Yutaka, Florence McCarthy, Mutsuko Murakami, Takashi Nishio, and Kano Yamamoto, "An Appreciation of Cross-Cultural Differences Through International Service-Learning at International Christian University, Japan" in *Service-Learning in Asia Curricular Models and Practices* (Hong Kong: Hong Kong University Press), 2010, p. 38.

Sescon, Joselito and Philip Tuano, "Service Learning as a Response to Disasters and Social Development: A Philippine Experience" dated 2012 in *Japan Social Innovation Journal* Vol. 2 No. 1 (Japan: Japan Social Innovation Journal) in the Japan Science and Technology Information Aggregator, Electronic (J-Stage) website [downloaded on 1 January 2017]. Available at https://www.jstage.jst.go.jp/browse, p. 64.

CHAPTER 8

Case Study 3: The Rise of Smart Cities in China—Domestic Development and Comparative Perspectives

BACKGROUND TO CHINESE SMART CITIES CONSTRUCTION

Smart cities (*Zhihui chengshi* in Chinese Hanyu Pinyin) is now a mainstay feature of urban construction and management in Northeast Asia and beyond. Smart cities rationalizes megacities growth by making it more sustainable and friendlier to the green environment. The University of California study indicated that approximately 1.6 million individuals in China perish annually from heart, lung and stroke brought about by air pollution so environmental management will be very crucial as Chinese cities growth into smart megacities.[1] China is approaching the smart cities projects using the Special Economic Zones (SEZs) model in the late 1970s when China opened up. Reputable international consulting company Deloitte reported that, out of 1000 smart cities projects underway globally, China makes up approximately 500 of them.[2] The authorities designated a number of cities for smart cities capabilities and then use a gradual approach in constructing smart cities

---

[1] Tabbitt, Sue, "Could China's Cities Outsmart the West?" dated 2 February 2016 in The Network Cisco's Technology News Site [downloaded on 1 January 2018], available at https://newsroom.cisco.com/feature-content?type=webcontent&articleId=1735469.

[2] *The Straits Times*, "China Outnumbers Other Countries in Smart City Pilots: Report" dated 20 February 2018 in *The Straits Times* [downloaded on 20 February 2018], available at https://www.straitstimes.com/asia/east-asia/china-outnumbers-other-countries-in-smart-city-pilots-report.

This case study is derived from a limited circulation background brief working paper for National University of Singapore (NUS EAI): Lim, Tai Wei, EAI Background Brief No. 1365—The Rise of Smart Cities in China: Domestic Development and Comparative Perspectives (Singapore: National University of Singapore), 2018.

© The Author(s) 2019
T. W. Lim, *Industrial Revolution 4.0, Tech Giants, and Digitized Societies*,
https://doi.org/10.1007/978-981-13-7470-8_8

and build up model best practices showcases before asking other lower tiered cities to imitate the forerunners. In terms of cities with demonstrative power and best practices, China identified 100 new smart cities from 2016 to 2020 to showcase urban management, planning and development.[3]

Chinese companies are also studying technologies developed in the West, Japan and the four tiger economies for suitability and possible implementation. China selects solutions that have proven to work in other countries, indigenize them and then adapt those solutions to fit local conditions. Applying digital smart cities solutions from other countries is challenging as China has installed a Great Firewall so consumers and retailers have to use a cloud-based system for their products and services or a proprietary system to overcome this issue. Vice General Manager (GM) Guo Huiming from Beijing Aerospace Changfeng Science Technology Industry Group Co. Ltd. of CASIC whose company won a bid to develop the Wuhan smart city in the province of Hubei defined a smart city with three points. First, he argues urban residents will have a more comfortable and harmonious life; Second, enterprises will have a more optimal environment for doing business and, lastly, urban services and functions related to the city's daily operations will be more productive.[4]

China's concern with a harmonious society (*xiaokang shehui*) is reflected in this definition. Most Northeast Asian societies are high context cultures and look towards collectivism, groupism and communitarian goals for progress and maintaining societal coherence while staving off conflicts and social tensions. The concept of comfort is in fact universal to all plans to construct smart cities. Most smart cities want to bring about convenient lifestyles and make it easier for urban residents to perform their daily functions. The second criteria of business environment enhancements is also universal to all smart cities. Many smart city plans to have efficient systems to maximize productivity and output from its worker residents. Smart cities also tend to be attractors of global business, investments and finances, so they are sensitive to global capital flows looking for a place to park or desire to attract entrepreneurs, investors and industries looking to set up industrial parks and factories.

China's ultimate goal for smart cities is a modernized socialist economy that has put in place high tech applications like Artificial Intelligence (A.I.), Internet of Things (IoT), use of big data and robotics. These plans were made known publicly in 2012 after the Chinese government gave their official approval. The accent was on studying implementation of such

---

[3] *The Straits Times*, "China Outnumbers Other Countries in Smart City Pilots: Report" dated 20 February 2018 in *The Straits Times* [downloaded on 20 February 2018], available at https://www.straitstimes.com/asia/east-asia/china-outnumbers-other-countries-in-smart-city-pilots-report.

[4] Hu, Yang, "CASIC Helps Chinese Cities Get Smart" dated 14 November 2012 in *China Daily* [downloaded on 1 January 2018], available at http://www.chinadaily.com.cn/business/greenchina/2012-11/14/content_15927027.htm.

technologies in the living labs of selected pioneering smart cities. The Chinese developmental model is typically regarded as top-down so some believe that if the government put resources into their plans, they will generally drive it to fruition and completion. The same strategy is now applied to smart cities schemes. Intelligent systems will complement connectivity infrastructures in China. For example, they are applied in the Beijing megacity area (a hyper-connected conurbation) known as the Jing-Jin-Ji (Beijing-Tianjin-Hebei) stretching out over 82,000 square miles to manage the highways and bridges that link up this large area.[5] Another conurbation eyed for implementation of smart technologies is Chongqing in Sichuan. Incidentally, this is where Singapore is working with China to construct the third government to government known as Chongqing Connectivity Initiative (CCI).

There is a private sector component to this initiative too because the authorities hope to lure companies to become solutions providers and they can use Chinese designated smart cities to implement and experiment with their technologies. When these companies have successfully provided their solutions and overcome challenges, their systems will become entrenched in the smart cities, so they would only need to provide upgrades, patches and further modifications to the basic systemic features to ensure its relevance to the city's constantly evolving development. Local companies are preferred because one of the major challenges of constructing smart cities is the idiosyncrasies of local conditions. Therefore, companies that are originally located in the smart cities are most well-placed to recognize these local features and develop solutions for them. There is a sense of embeddedness when local companies are heavily involved in the projects. In addition, when the local companies are successful in one Chinese city, they can effectively market their track record and past achievements to other Chinese cities, given that China is such a large market and represent the largest national network of smart cities in the world. With a strong relationships forged in a particular smart city amongst its local companies working together to provide solutions to the city's development, these companies may cooperate and export the same jointly-developed solutions to other economies.

Because China's cities are divided unofficially into tiers based on level of economic development, importance to provincial and central governments, solutions developed for the first-tier cities can be used in other leading global cities while those developed for third tier cities may be more cost-effective systems, suitable for developing economies' needs and state budgets. If Chinese technologies turn out to be successful in the first city

---

[5] Tabbitt, Sue, "Could China's Cities Outsmart the West?" dated 2 February 2016 in The Network Cisco's Technology News Site [downloaded on 1 January 2018], available at https://newsroom.cisco.com/feature-content?type=webcontent&articleId=1735469.

of implementation, they can then be exported to other countries, including ASEAN or Association of Southeast Asian Nations which has Singapore-led aspirations to link up all smart cities in the region. The state benefits from such investments after the private sector has installed technologies that can help the authorities with governance and urban management.

Eventually ASEAN economies will become very important in China's Belt and Road Initiative (BRI) regional map so it helps to be a forerunner to leapfrog over competition from companies in other countries. China is already helping to install High Speed Railway (HSR) systems in Laos, Thailand, Indonesia and Cambodia so smart systems that work for China's domestic public transportation needs may be helpful for the Southeast Asian context as well. Such technologies may be related to public transportation systems like sensors to detect and direct traffic, electronic boards at bus stops, traffic obstruction management/resolution, big data utilization with predictive and extrapolation capabilities (analytics), etc. Beijing the capital city for example is especially vulnerable to traffic jams. Sensors provide real-time data to commuters. Data from sensors can also be fed into intelligent controls for managing city infrastructural needs.

The data collection and management technologies may also be related to national economic management with trackers on vital statistics and data, including employment figures, social stability benchmarks, skills and education-related numbers, etc. The data gathered by the private sector firms working on smart cities projects may become valuable to the Chinese local governments for their use in maintaining social controls, monitoring urban developmental needs and smooth running of day to day operations. This aspect is especially relevant to tech giants like Alibaba as they obtained data from both customers well as retailers in China. Their data collection and analytical abilities can scan entire economies or markets in an instant. Information and Community Technologies (ICT) infrastructure within the rubric of smart cities are equally important. These communication devices can be used for mass mobilization, social events organization, and even connectivity with other economies within China's ambitious Belt and Road Initiative (BRI, formerly known as the One Belt One Road OBOR initiative).

At a higher level of conceptualization, smart cities may provide solutions that can help to save labour or working time for human workers as well, releasing them to work on higher value-added activities that are not manpower-intensive. This is probably the most compelling argument made in favour of technological use, even if it displaces some human jobs. Saving labour also means that the same technologies can increase convenience for smart city residents and this feature can attract global talents to work, reside or migrate to the smart cities. China actually has the largest number of smart cities projects in the world. Like other major IT powers in the world, the country hopes to tap into the IoT. Its national master plan for building a nationwide network of smart cities originated from 2012.

Because of China's unique political-economic system that combines a centralized economy with a proactive developmental state and a market economy that responds to demand and supply, when the authorities focus on a particular project or initiative, the resources channelled to driving it as well as the determination to make that initiative a success tends to be very high. When developing smart cities, China has certain pre-existing advantages over other countries with their high mobile penetration, large existing consumer base for Chinese tech giants like Tencent (which owns WeChat), Alibaba (including the cashless payment system Alipay) and Baidu.

2017 appears to be a milestone date in the formation of Chinese smart cities as the country designated the target number of smart cities construction at 500 beginning that year. The chosen ones to become smart cities include 95% of provincial capital cities and 83% of prefecture cities.[6] This effectively makes China the largest smart cities market in the world. Most Chinese smart cities-designate start off with being pilot projects while others tie up with Information Technology (IT) companies like Tencent. Many factors foster or encourage the growth of smart cities. The momentum of growth is pulled along by the very fact that China is urbanizing fast and its population is moving in large numbers to the urban areas, thus complementing the expansion of cities. To manage this population boom, smart cities help to create optimal interactive infrastructures to handle large numbers of people living in close proximity with one another.

Because the project involves a large number of city folks and urban denizens, smart cities project are by nature required to be inclusive and involve a large number of stakeholders including ordinary citizens and private enterprises. Inclusivity also ensures that local and national governments can understand local concerns and issues from native voices rather than plan from afar without paying attention to local needs. The emotive aspects of urban construction, infrastructure provision and people's needs are of utmost importance to the success of smart cities. In China and most of Northeast Asia, harmony in a collective society as well as a comfortable business environment is significant. Even individuals who are incapacitated in some ways like handicapped residents of smart cities can rely on technologies to navigate through their daily needs without insurmountable obstacles. Essentially, no one is really left behind in the smart city with technological solutions reaching out to a pluralistic diversity of human needs in those cities. Eventually, smart cities technology will even penetrate rural areas.

In this sense, private sector companies are no longer operating purely in terms of profit orientation, but there is also a sense of empathy, emotive attachment and sensitivity to the needs of the smart city's denizens. When this happens, private companies involved in smart city projects become

---

[6] *People's Daily Online*, "China's 'Smart Cities' to Number 500 Before End of 2017" dated 21 April 2017 in *China Daily* Online [downloaded on 21 April 2017], available at http://www.chinadaily.com.cn/china/2017-04/21/content_29024793.htm.

a bridge between the people and society with the local authorities, solving problems that pop up in the official master plan of development and responding to complaints by residents who use the city's infrastructural facilities. Infrastructures can become wheel chair friendly. Individuals with declining physical strengths can put on a robotic suit or exoskeleton to enhance their strengths and carry on with daily lives. Assistive robots can take care of patients with Alzheimer's disease or dementia. Automated bathtubs can wash patients who are immobile. Bionic limbs can replace human stumps and facilitate wearers to lead normal lives. The possibilities are endless.

The state then plays the role of an overall system integrator, something China has done very successfully in the cashless payment sector for example. As a centralized systems integrator, the state can then centripetally pull in private sector stakeholders to become permanent fixtures in providing smart cities solutions competitively with all other solution providers to constantly upgrade the cities' infrastructural capabilities rather than the traditional contractor of providing one-off services for tender and then leave the projects after making a profit.

Transportation Infrastructure

During the 32nd ASEAN Summit (25 April 2018–26 April 2018), the chair of the summit Singapore initiated the idea of linking up a network of smart cities in Southeast Asia. If China is able to leapfrog the advanced cities in the West and Japan and develop its own national network of smart cities, it can have a head-start in constructing smart cities or specific solutions for those cities. An early head-start is important because South Korea, Hong Kong, Taiwan and Japan all have ambitions to build their own smart cities. In China, State-Owned Enterprises (SOEs) are also in the running to become smart cities solutions providers. For example, SOE China Aerospace Science and Industry Corporation (CASIC) has projects in China, Pakistan and Myanmar in dual use technologies that can benefit security systems and the company has also looked into entering public transportation, healthcare and public infrastructure sectors.[7]

Security systems solution are likely to be dual use technologies that have potential for both military and public order applications. They can be used for managing security needs for the Olympics or other large-scale sports games. At the same time, the same systems can be installed in the battlefields for identifying genuine refugees through facial recognition technologies. Observers have noted that Chinese smart cities are particularly interested in the control management aspects. Therefore, CCTVs and surveillance

[7] Hu, Yang, "Smart City: Opportunity and Challenge for Enterprises" dated 15 November 2012 in *China Daily* [downloaded on 1 January 2018], available at http://www.chinadaily.com.cn/business/2012-11/15/content_15935688.htm.

technologies for monitoring, traffic management and people flow in smart cities are a growth area in China. Other than SOEs, private sector enterprises are also going into the lucrative public transportation sector. Profit orientation appears to be high on the list of Chinese companies keen to cash in on public transportation infrastructure construction. For example, the Shanghai-Hangzhou-Ningbo Highway worked with cashless mobile payment providers Alipay and China Guangfa Bank to enable 40,000 vehicles plying the highway daily to pay tolls through mobile payments.[8]

C<small>HALLENGES</small>

Wang Yanjing is the Executive Vice Director of the IoT under the China Communications Industry Association (CCIA) which is a foremost organization pushing and advocating smart cities in China. He argued that the main challenge in constructing Chinese smart cities is the financing and apportionment of assignments between state agencies and firms, compounded by local area government's caution about dispensing state funds before seeing a profit-making project.[9] This sometimes manifests itself as a waiting game as private sector firms or enterprises wait for the state to make the first move in guaranteeing smart cities investments as long term projects backed up by the government before the private sector moves into invest in those cities. Therefore, smart cities aspirants may need to set up multi-stakeholder institutions and meetings to come up with social consensus on how to approach large-scale projects so that both the state and private sector are willing to combine resources to construct smart city projects This can kick-start the process of initial investments. The tripartite of state officials and bureaucrats, scientists and researchers and entrepreneurs and private sector entities therefore are extremely important to come up with technologies that are useful and suited to local conditions.

China is strong in indigenous technologies when it comes to hardware (after all, it is nicknamed the world's factory) but it is comparatively weaker in software with only 30% of its start-ups software-based compared to 90% in Silicon Valley.[10] In addition, applying digital smart cities solutions from other countries is challenging as China has installed a Great Firewall so consumers and retailers have to use a cloud-based system for their products and services

[8] *People's Daily Online*, "China's 'Smart Cities' to Number 500 Before End of 2017" dated 21 April 2017 in *China Daily* Online [downloaded on 21 April 2017], available at http://www.chinadaily.com.cn/china/2017-04/21/content_29024793.htm.

[9] Hu, Yang, "Smart City: Opportunity and Challenge for Enterprises" dated 15 November 2012 in *China Daily* [downloaded on 1 January 2018], available at http://www.chinadaily.com.cn/business/2012-11/15/content_15935688.htm.

[10] Tabbitt, Sue, "Could China's Cities Outsmart the West?" dated 2 February 2016 in The Network Cisco's Technology News Site [downloaded on 1 January 2018], available at https://newsroom.cisco.com/feature-content?type=webcontent&articleId=1735469.

or a proprietary system to overcome this issue. Therefore, Chinese companies are keen to hire and employ Silicon Valley coders, programmers and ICT specialists to come up with apps, software and algorithms to operate their hardware devices. Sometimes, China's strengths in manufacturing is combined with foreign companies like Kii which are strong in software to manufacture innovative products. Kii is working with Chinese LED manufacturer Yankon to design cheap energy conserving IoT smart lighting solutions that can be turned on and off using a smartphone.[11]

Near Future

In the near future, constructing smart cities may no longer be a choice and become a necessity as urbanization proceeds exponentially and cities grow into megacities (defined as cities with ten million population or more) with exploding populations, overcrowded public transportation systems and the need to manage healthcare of large numbers of people living in close proximity. By the year 2030, China's urbanized population may cross the one billion people threshold as it has already grown exponentially by 500 million people in the last 30–35 years.[12] Contemporary dense cities will become even denser. There are plans to combine cities together to form a mega conurbation of more than 100 million strong population. There are plans for the capital city of Beijing (current population 20 million) to combine with peripheral regions to become a 130 million strong "super-megacity" (six times larger than New York City and larger than the entire population of Japan).[13] When that happens, almost every aspect of urban management will be impacted severely, including communications, transportation, education, housing, etc.

Diseases are also likely to spread faster, resources will become scarcer to cater to a much larger population base. Many first-tier global cities also have aging population or have increasing numbers of elderly to look after. China has another unique problem. Its one child policy was so successful that younger Chinese now have to support a larger number of elderly whose lifespans are extending due to better medical technologies. There is also a large migration of younger Chinese to the urban areas, leaving their elderly family members and relatives in the countryside. This results in the hollowing out of the countryside.

[11] Tabbitt, Sue, "Could China's Cities Outsmart the West?" dated 2 February 2016 in The Network Cisco's Technology News Site [downloaded on 1 January 2018], available at https://newsroom.cisco.com/feature-content?type=webcontent&articleId=1735469.

[12] Tabbitt, Sue, "Could China's Cities Outsmart the West?" dated 2 February 2016 in The Network Cisco's Technology News Site [downloaded on 1 January 2018], available at https://newsroom.cisco.com/feature-content?type=webcontent&articleId=1735469.

[13] Tabbitt, Sue, "Could China's Cities Outsmart the West?" dated 2 February 2016 in The Network Cisco's Technology News Site [downloaded on 1 January 2018], available at https://newsroom.cisco.com/feature-content?type=webcontent&articleId=1735469.

Therefore, smart cities can be designed to cope with eldercare for such elderly parents (left behind by their children) through the use of smart technologies. Reliance on technologies then becomes a reality for these cities and their healthcare sectors. As the Chinese economy prosper and grow, obesity as a disease is increasing and there are more than 100 million people with diabetes. This is a ready market of patients who need health tracking devices and health monitoring kits.[14] The application of infrastructure technologies will be extensively applied to all sectors including healthcare to enhance hospital capabilities. Due to the extensive and highly versatile nature of technological applications, the systems that are developed are likely to have multipurpose utilization in different areas of applications.

BIBLIOGRAPHY

Hu, Yang, "CASIC Helps Chinese Cities Get Smart" dated 14 November 2012 in *China Daily* [downloaded on 1 January 2018]. Available at http://www.chinadaily.com.cn/business/greenchina/2012-11/14/content_15927027.htm.

Hu, Yang, "Smart City: Opportunity and Challenge for Enterprises" dated 15 November 2012 in *China Daily* [downloaded on 1 January 2018]. Available at http://www.chinadaily.com.cn/business/2012-11/15/content_15935688.htm.

People's Daily Online, "China's 'Smart Cities' to Number 500 Before End of 2017" dated 21 April 2017 in *China Daily* Online [downloaded on 21 April 2017]. Available at http://www.chinadaily.com.cn/china/2017-04/21/content_29024793.htm.

Tabbitt, Sue, "Could China's Cities Outsmart the West?" dated 2 February 2016 in The Network Cisco's Technology News Site [downloaded on 1 January 2018]. Available at https://newsroom.cisco.com/feature-content?type=webcontent&articleId=1735469.

The Straits Times, "China Outnumbers Other Countries in Smart City Pilots: Report" dated 20 Feb 2018 in *The Straits Times* [downloaded on 20 February 2018]. Available at https://www.straitstimes.com/asia/east-asia/china-outnumbers-other-countries-in-smart-city-pilots-report.

---

[14]Tabbitt, Sue, "Could China's Cities Outsmart the West?" dated 2 February 2016 in The Network Cisco's Technology News Site [downloaded on 1 January 2018], available at https://newsroom.cisco.com/feature-content?type=webcontent&articleId=1735469.

CHAPTER 9

Case Study 4: "Active Aging" and "Healthy Aging"—A Comparative Survey of Coping Mechanisms for Greying Populations in Japan and Hong Kong

Introduction and Background

Many economies in East Asia, especially the advanced developing as well as developed economies, exhibit signs of an aging population. Within these Northeast Asian societies, two in particular (Hong Kong and Japan) stand out as they confront the challenges of an aging population economically, politically and socially. They have become natural case studies of the impact of an aging population on socioeconomic development. Between the two, Hong Kong is well-known as a migrant society (especially internal migration from China) while Japan is generally conceptualized as a homogenous population, an island nation where many of its national consider themselves as Japanese culturally and nationality-wise. Therefore, for Hong Kong, replenishing their stock with migrants has always been a solution for their aging populations with low replacement rates. But, at the same time, against the backdrop of a global anti-immigration wave like Brexit and backlash against globalization, post-Occupy Central Hong Kong society have expressed a desire to maintain local population stocks and reduce overreliance on migrants. Japanese conservatives and some bureaucratic factions in government departments like the Ministry of Justice have consistently maintained their resistance to indiscriminately accepting migrants, particularly illegal migrants. They advocate careful procedure for legal immigration and select individuals with skills in short supply (many immigrants to Japan end up working in jobs that are *kitanai* (dirty), *kitsui* (demanding) and *kiken* (dangerous). In the past, illegal migrants in Japan were involved in some high profile criminal activities that was repeatedly broadcasted in the media: from Iranian fake phone card gangs in the 1990s to Asian over-stayers in the twenty-first century.

© The Author(s) 2019
T. W. Lim, *Industrial Revolution 4.0, Tech Giants, and Digitized Societies*,
https://doi.org/10.1007/978-981-13-7470-8_9

In Hong Kong, the expression and desire to put Hong Kong interests first is manifested through social movements, the most prominent of which was the Occupy Central Movement. The major reasons for the protests was a perceived reluctance on the part of the Chinese authorities to grant Hong Kong a universal suffrage system. There was also expressed unhappiness over the additional condition of having a Chief Executive that is required to show his/her love to the motherland, to Hong Kong and not be at odds with Beijing and the Chinese Communist Party (CCP). However, bread and butter issues were also very much underlining the protests. Occupy Central protestors did not like the keen competition for jobs brought about by migrants while young university graduates were resentful of high property prices caused by an influx of mainland Chinese investments in Hong Kong's property scene. All these added to sentiments for a Hong Kong first policy and governance. It was believed that the election of a Hong Kong Chief Executive through universal suffrage is able to optimize and maximize domestic Hong Kong interests, especially for its native born.

In Japan, which is a liberal democracy, political conservatives have been quite consistent in maintaining a prudent attitude towards incoming migrants. Much of these efforts is carried out through democratic means to convince the political elites to be more selective about migration. For most of the past half a century, Japan had been ruled by a conservative party, the Liberal Democratic Party (LDP). Only on two occasions were the LDP defeated by the opposition parties, for a few months in the 1990s and between 2010 and 2013. However, at the same time, Japan is welcoming of talented migrants (See Chapter 6 [Case Study 1] for more details on this). In fact, both cities, Hong Kong and Tokyo (and the rest of Japan) continue to express a strong desire to attract high quality migrants and foreign talents as well as migrants who are willing to work in jobs shunned by locals or in highly skilled jobs that are in great demand but faces shortages of human resource. Therefore, in this context, the migration policy is fine-tuned rather than mothballed. Both cities continue to be very attractive places for new migrants in search of better working conditions and standards of living. In fact, in the case of Japan, the current conservative government of Japanese Prime Minister Shinzo Abe is keen to relax visa and migration requirements for top talents in crucial fields like STEM (Science, Technology, Engineering and Mathematics) to migrate to Japan and work or/and settle there.

Given this scenario, with greater resistance to migration, especially towards unskilled and/or illegal migrants, there is now a greater call to rely more on domestic human resource and maximize their productivities and also offer greater economic and job opportunities for formerly marginalized groups. The policies in Japan and Hong Kong designed to alleviate the negative effects of an aging population are of great interest to demographics, aging and social welfare research. The two societies show a significant contrast in their approach towards coping with an aging population. Hong Kong has spawned an Non-Profit Organization (NPO) sector working with the bureaucracy, volunteers, social workers, community groups to look after the needs of the elderly. It is a laissez-faire approach dependent on community groups and volunteers with shared resources from the government. Japan's approach contrasts with Hong Kong in the sense that it too has a highly active NPO sector but the NPO sector works closely with the government in a civil society-state partnership with the state providing resources to local groups to manage certain programs while steering the NPO towards professionalization. This arose out of the Japanese society's strong trust in the competency of its public sector and liberal democratic instincts as well as cultural affinity towards harmony, collectivism and consultation/consensus. Culturally, consensus rather than a top-down approach is needed to bring all stakeholders together to carry out initiatives.

In addition to a unique civil society-state partnership, Japan also adopts a technological approach to mitigating the aging challenge. At the forefront of research and technological capabilities for assistive, therapeutic and android robots, Japan has deployed robots to assist with elderly care. It is fine-tuning the robotic solution to relieve the country's shortage of elderly care and healthcare workers. Its technological solution also arises from some reluctance by the conservative segments of the population to opening up the floodgate for more migration and fears of illegal migrant disrupting social harmony. This writing has a comparative perspective that examines policies related to the coping mechanisms of the two Asian societies when it comes to managing the aging population. It adopts a unique multidisciplinary approach in drawing from political science/public administration, gerontology, area studies and history to examine the following two issues:

1. What are the historical, current and future scenarios/prospects for civil society-state collaboration in managing an aging population in Hong Kong and Japan?
2. What are the technologies available to both societies in managing an aging population and issues in implementing them?

LITERATURE REVIEW AND RESEARCH PARADIGM

In answering the above research questions, the writing will adopt the paradigm of "active aging" (now known officially as healthy aging by World Health Organization or WHO) to analyze how civil society-state collaboration, technological progress and government policies can help to assist elderly people in living a long *and* healthy life. The World Health Organization (WHO) is probably the organization at the forefront of this revolution. WHO assumes that living long and healthy is an entitlement and a right but it is subjected to the living conditions of each individual, including issues and factors like environmental pollution, socioeconomic access to healthcare and social welfare and economic options like working. "Active aging" (circa 2002) which is revised by WHO to become "healthy aging" concerns the potential of letting people do what they like and value in their lifetimes, even with a pre-existing health issue or condition. WHO defines Healthy Ageing "as the process of developing and maintaining the functional ability that enables well-being in older age".[1] The concept of "functional ability" is having capabilities (the convergence of individual capabilities/intrinsic capacities, environmental factors and the dynamics between these two) to enable all people to be and do what they have reason to value.[2] These functional activities including taking care of their basic needs, the ability carry out daily decisions, be able to get to places, to have and keep up relationships and to be useful to society.[3]

Behind the idea of active aging is a reliance on the thinking that contemporary pharmaceuticals, medicine and lifestyles are now making it possible for humans to be productive, healthy and even fit work schedules into their advanced ages (some believe right up to the age of 80s). The idea and concept of intrinsic mental and physical capacities to:

1. carry out daily activities and exercise one's cognitive faculties in interacting with one's family members, local community, society in general, the physical environment;
2. remain fully engaged in attitudes/beliefs/value systems when interacting with others;
3. respond to social/state policies is an important feature of healthy ageing.

An important point is to distinguish between individual needs and the elderly's level of fitness and the strength of one's state of health (i.e. whether they are strong, dependent on elderly care or mobile but needs some form of medical attention). In the literature review, the European Union's (EU) status report of their active ageing scenario stated the challenge of providing comprehensive social welfare and protection in the context of globally economically weaker low-growth conditions and with increasing numbers of elderly.[4] Even though Hong Kong and Japan are comparatively wealthy societies, they have not opted for social welfare and free medical benefits. Therefore encouraging active ageing through various means/methodologies studied in this writing is crucial.

---

[1] World Health Organization (WHO), "What Is Healthy Ageing?" in WHO website [downloaded on 1 March 2018], available at http://www.who.int/ageing/healthy-ageing/en/.

[2] Ibid.

[3] Ibid.

[4] European Commission Directorate-General for Employment, Social Affairs and Inclusion, "Active Ageing Report" dated January 2012 in Special Eurobarometer 378 (EU: Directorate-General for Communication [DG COMM] "Research and Speechwriting" Unit), available at http://ec.europa.eu/commfrontoffice/publicopinion/archives/ebs/ebs_378_en.pdf.

SCENARIOS/PROSPECTS FOR CIVIL SOCIETY-STATE COLLABORATION

In studying this aspect, it is helpful to turn back the clock a little to look at the recent historical origins of active aging in terms of public policy in both Hong Kong and Japan. Hong Kong's experience with managing civil society-state collaboration has an element of self-reliance and economic priority in not burdening the state coffers for social welfare. It also has a case of subcontracting elderly care to the hinterland, something discussed later in the section below. Since at least 2014, Hong Kong's government has made "active ageing" a policy mantra for managing the territory's aging and greying population. An official interpretation of active ageing from Hong Kong's official circle was articulated by the former Secretary for Labour and Welfare Matthew Cheung. Cheung noted that "active ageing" is crucial since the life expectancy in Hong Kong will rise to 85 years for men and 91 years for women in 2041 and his government defined active ageing as:

> ...optimising opportunities for health, participation and security in order to enhance the quality of life as people age...about how to enable the elderly to stay active, remain healthy, keep fit and more importantly to think positively.[5]

Hong Kong's definition appears to go beyond just functionality and well-being in the WHO version, with additional emphasis on quality of life, positive thinking and Cheung's narrative added additional elements below with a pragmatic element in Hong Kong's approach towards active ageing:

> We believe that enabling more of our elderly to stay active and healthy is the key to the future sustainability of the healthcare and social welfare systems...more independent in planning and taking care of their needs...In fact, most of the elderly in Hong Kong are self-reliant, with less than 7% of them requiring assistance at different levels in performing activities of daily living.

The narrative indicated a clear shift away from social welfare policies. It also appears that the Hong Kong authorities seems to couch self-reliance and self-dependence in economic terms, touting the low percentage of needy elderly requiring assistance. This is different from the Japanese case study where the cultural element play a bigger role in accentuating self-reliance. Culturally, Japanese people have a tendency to avoid dependence on others. Dependence is a form of cultural dissonance by Japanese society

---

[5] Cheung, Matthew, "Gov't Committed to Active Ageing" dated 28 February 2014 in the Hong Kong Information Service Department of the Hong Kong government [downloaded on 1 January 2018], available at http://www.news.gov.hk/en/record/html/2014/02/20140228_140050.shtml.

that prioritizes collective needs over the individual (leading to high context culture). Therefore, this leads to the social phenomenon of some elderly individuals in Japan actually perishing in their homes due to the cultural dis-inclination to seek help from others. They were discovered only by neighbours alerting the authorities due to smell reeking from the homes. Another example are elderly individuals committing petty crimes deliberately so that they are incarcerated in public prisons where they are able to get access to free food and sleeping space. Seeking welfare handout is still culturally perceived as a form of individualistic behaviour (particularly for the senior generations), something that is frowned upon in a society that invented the phrase "the nail that sticks out must be hammered down". While the above is manifested in Japanese society, one must not overstate the marginalization of help in Japan. In fact, reality is quite the opposite. Self-reliance in Japan has the strong support of Japanese civil society, volunteer, grassroots and NPOs. Community-based help is forthcoming in a communitarian society like Japan.

Lacking the cultural communitarian spirit of the Japanese (at least not to the same extent), Hong Kongers used to laissez-faire capitalism and a high degree of individualism, Cheung reveals that the Special Administration Region (SAR) territory banks on:

> Our heavily subsidised health-care system provides affordable and comprehensive healthcare services through public hospitals and clinics for our seniors.[6]

Even courses offered under the rubric of lifelong learning included investment/financial management seminars for the elderly offered by the Elder Academy Scheme, launched in 2007 together with the Elderly Commission, which enables the elderly to pursue continued learning in a school setting in the 108 Elder Academies providing more than 10,000 learning enrolment spaces annually.[7]

Interestingly, Hong Kong offers an option that is not available to the elderly in Japan. Hong Kong considers Guangdong to be a large and less expensive hinterland to retire and therefore it instituted the Guangdong Scheme in 2013 that allows HKers to receive a Hong Kong government allowance while residing in mainland China. The government works with the non-governmental organization (NGO) to purchase properties in Shenzhen and Zhaoqing and then leave their management to the Hong Kong-based NGO.[8] This is probably the most innovative feature of civil society-state relations in the Hong Kong case study. It is a means to subcontract elderly care to a more affordable location while letting the NGO sector run them. The

[6] Ibid.
[7] Ibid.
[8] Ibid.

net effect is lower burdens on the government since the elderly are physically located away from Hong Kong and the bureaucracy is not needed for day-to-day running of these elderly homes in mainland China.

Japan's experience with managing elderly population and an aging society is even older than Hong Kong. Japan was the first economy to develop in the modern era and in the postwar era, it was also the first to recover economically and became an Organization of Economic Cooperation and Development (OECD) member in the 1960s. Japan was also the first country to undergo the nuclearization of the family households, experience large numbers of women joining the workforce during the 1970s oil crisis, and a national contraception campaign in connection with the nuclear family. Consequently, it is also the first country in East Asia to experience the aging phenomenon, something visible to researchers, policymakers and academia by the 1980s. Therefore, policy measures were instituted as early as the 1990s. One of the landmark legislations in this aspect is The Basic Law on Measures for the Aged Society (Law No. 129, 1995) with the following major stipulations:

i. A fair and energetic society where people can be ensured that they have the opportunity of participating in diverse social activities or working throughout their lives.
ii. A society where people are respected as important members throughout their lives where local communities are formed based on the spirit of independence and solidarity.
iii. An affluent society where people can live peacefully and with fulfilment throughout their lives.

In this 1995 legislation, there is no explicit mention of the priority of lessening dependence on welfare payments as seen in the Hong Kong case. The accent appears to be place on social egalitarianism, something not unexpected for a high-context communitarian culture like Japan. There is also emphasis on social equity, allowing the elderly to have meritocratic fair access to job opportunities and other social activities. Amendment to the Act on Stabilization of Employment of Elderly Persons in 2004 and 2012 allows elderly to get employment from firms if they chose to work after the 60 years old age of retirement. As a society, the legislation hopes Japan's economy can remain at a certain income level that is considered affluent but the accent is placed on peaceful and fulfilling lives. There is no large hinterland for Japanese elderly seeking more affordable lifestyles as in the case of Hong Kong, although Japan's rural areas may offer that possibility. There are also no investment seminars built into lifelong learning, like those found in Hong Kong which is also a leading financial centre of the world. The accent on financial well-being is not emphasized as much as the Hong Kong case study, at least not in these legislation or the latter two amended Acts.

TECHNOLOGIES IN MANAGING AN AGING POPULATION

In this area, as a manufacturing powerhouse, Japan is far more advanced than Hong Kong. Japan has some of the world's most advanced technologies in robotics designed to help with managing elderly care. (Refer to Chapter 6 [Case Study 1] for more details.) They include assistive and therapeutic robots. In the assistive robot category, technologies have been developed to design and built robots that can help caregivers cope with the fast-aging population in Japan. These technologies include robotic nurses like Robot Kenji of the RI-MAN that can smell, scan and identity, process and obey commands as well as use robotic hydraulic strength to pick up patients. Such robots are likely to contribute substantially to elderly care because they can replace humans who may not possess such great strength in picking up whole patients by simply lifting them while they are lying horizontally. While the assistive robots contribute to elderly care, there are Japanese robotic technologies that can help elderly lead a better lifestyle or continue to exhibit productivity in accordance with the thinking behind active aging.

A good example are robotic suits that enhance human strength, like the Cyberdyne Corporation of Japan's Hybrid Assistive Limb (HAL) robotic exoskeleton. A consequence of Japan's aging population is that the rural countryside is being hollowed out as young Japanese seeking better jobs, pay and lifestyles leave the rural areas for the metropolitan cities in search of work. Consequently, the individuals left behind in the countryside are the elderly folks. But the countryside is highly significant to Japan's partial self-reliance factor in agricultural products even as they import food to make up for domestic deficiency. Therefore, elderly farmers are left behind to carry on with the job of tending to farmlands which involves backbreaking physical work. The HAL offers them a technological solution as the elderly can put on robot exoskeletons to enhance their physical strengths and continue with brute strength and labour necessary for farm work. This is completely in line with the philosophy of active aging, extending the productivity of Japanese elderly farmers for the workforce, should they choose to continue with agricultural work.

While it does not possess the manufacturing prowess of its Japanese counterpart, Hong Kong is also keen to tap into technology to support its aging population and active aging narrative. In mid-2017, Hong Kong started looking into the idea of "gerontechnology" defined as the "use of technology to meet the needs of the elderly".[9] The 2017 Gerontech and Innovation

---

[9] Chan, Bernard, "Hong Kong Must Not Miss Out on Tech Revolution for the Elderly" dated 22 June 2017 in the South China Morning Post (SCMP) [downloaded on 22 June 2017], available at http://www.scmp.com/comment/insight-opinion/article/2099460/hong-kong-must-not-miss-out-tech-revolution-elderly.

Expo in Wan Chai Hong Kong has already showcased some technologies of the future: a robotic lead conducting exercises for human participants; robots that carry elderly individual to and fro the bed; a mechanized bed that transform into a wheelchair; automated walkers that move the elderly upslope while adjusting for speed when it heads downslope. Hong Kong is also picking up tips from Japan in this field as it sees the advantage of having the private sector, especially its research and development (R&D) industries, come up with devices and robots according to the needs of the market so that the government is not burdened with subsidies. This is something easy for Hong Kong's government, private sector and entrepreneurs as it has always had a laissez-faire towards capitalism, one of the leading places to do business in the world and a destination for the operational headquarters (OHQ) for tech multinationals keen to tap into the China market.

CONCLUSION

Japan and Hong Kong are coming up with innovative solutions for managing the aging population and enhancing the doctrine and idea of active or healthy aging. Japan is leading in terms of robotic technologies to assist with the elderly while Hong Kong is keen to promote lifelong learning even in skills that can augment and enhance the elderly's financial well-being and investment savviness. These are all cutting-edge solutions for other East Asian societies (and ultimately the world) that are also aging to follow. But they do come with their own set of challenges. First, the accent on technologies appears to be on the need to enhance productivity and save manpower for higher value added activities but they come with a cost. Much of the technologies remain expensive and perhaps affordable only to institutional clients. Eventually the challenge for technopreneurs is to bring down the prices of these technologies and align them closer to the middle income/middle class range of individual consumers. The other challenge is making them ergonomically friendlier and easier to use for the individual consumer since many of these technologies will eventually be operated by the elderly themselves so that they can be autonomous of caregivers. The elderly users of such technologies may not be technologically savvy or well-acquainted, thus there is a need to simplify the multiplicities of functions for them.

But there is a silver lining if these challenges are met. Ultimately, the successful tech firms and technopreneurs can export these technologies overseas if proven to be successful, especially the East Asian market which alone will have enough demand to absorb the sales of such technologies. Other than the Philippines and Vietnam, all of the four tiger economies (Hong Kong, Taiwan, Singapore and South Korea, first to develop economically after Japan) as well as the large developing economy of China and some Southeast Asian states are confronting aging population (some like Singapore are already in advanced aging mode). Therefore, a rapid and efficient solution is welcomed by many stakeholders in the region and can generate income and revenue for tech companies that meet their needs. The other advantage of developing these technological solutions is that companies in the aging societies which are facing lower demand for consumption can find new markets overseas, especially since aging population is fast becoming a regional challenge.

BIBLIOGRAPHY

Chan, Bernard, "Hong Kong Must Not Miss Out on Tech Revolution for the Elderly" dated 22 June 2017 in the South China Morning Post (SCMP) [downloaded on 22 June 2017]. Available at http://www.scmp.com/comment/insight-opinion/article/2099460/hong-kong-must-not-miss-out-tech-revolution-elderly.

Cheung, Matthew, "Gov't Committed to Active Ageing" dated 28 February 2014 in the Hong Kong Information Service Department of the Hong Kong government [downloaded on 1 January 2018]. Available at http://www.news.gov.hk/en/record/html/2014/02/20140228_140050.shtml.

European Commission Directorate-General for Employment, Social Affairs and Inclusion, "Active Ageing Report" dated January 2012 in Special Eurobarometer 378 (EU: Directorate-General for Communication [DG COMM] "Research and Speechwriting" Unit). Available at http://ec.europa.eu/commfrontoffice/publicopinion/archives/ebs/ebs_378_en.pdf.

World Health Organization (WHO), "What Is Healthy Ageing?" in WHO website [downloaded on 1 March 2018]. Available at http://www.who.int/ageing/healthy-ageing/en/.

CHAPTER 10

Case Study 5: Cashless Convenience in China—A Survey of Its Development and a Case Study of the Political Economics Behind the Mechanism

Historically, financial innovation in the area of payment systems is not new in the long history of Chinese civilization. The Chinese were the first historically to introduce paper money. But modernization came late in contemporary Chinese history due to a difficult process of catching up with the West, world and civil wars and revolutions. The Chinese state was also late in integrating with the world economy due to experimentation with communism, socialism and central planning. But latecomers do have their own advantages. China made the transition to a cashless society easily leapfrogging over the credit card phase. Credit card did not take off in China as the domestic banking system was relatively less developed compared to those of the developed economies. In fact, debit cards are more common than credit cards in China. China's first credit card only arrived in 1985. Even then, the concept was not as popular. As a latecomer to the market-based capitalist system, China's conspicuous consumption was also a relatively recent phenomenon. All these factors were favourable for China's cashless revolution to take off.

Starting with China's coastal cities with high levels of smartphone connectivity, the cashless revolution gradually swept the country. Its attraction for Chinese consumers is very simple. With a swipe of a code, Chinese consumer can now make payments for just about anything. The scanning process is based mainly on a Quick Response (QR) Code designed by Japan's

This case study is derived from a limited circulation background brief working paper for National University of Singapore (NUS EAI): Lim, Tai Wei, "Cashless Convenience in China: Development and Political Economics" dated 16 August 2018 in EAI Background Brief No. 1376 (Singapore: National University of Singapore East Asian Institute NUS EAI), 2018.

Denso Corp in the 1990s for storing more data than the traditional bar code. QR code was adapted by China's cashless mobile payment systems for electronic transactions. Convenience is also enhanced by the fact that consumers can now make payments on the move. They can pay for acquisitions in advance anywhere in China or clear their loan payments on the move. Only a simple scan of QR code or other forms of product identification is needed. For drivers literally on the move, they can use cashless payment mechanisms to check toll booth charges and pay them through the phone. Another form of convenience is found in the fact that, when consumers pay for their purchases using cashless digital platforms, they can also track their consumption digitally for budgeting purposes. Electronic tracking and budgeting also act as a form of wealth manager for the user, and can instantaneously inform users of the amount of usable funds they have for making investments, e.g. investing in stocks and shares.

The cashless payment mechanism is modifying how the public consumes. WeChat Pay has become a payment mechanism of choice in China. The revolution really takes place in the areas of micro-payments, daily transactions and minor loans. In fact, the tech giants are eating into the bank profits and shaving off profits for bank services and transaction charges. Cash by comparison appears primitive and slow in Chinese payment modes. It takes only seconds to swipe and scan codes, much faster than taking out coins and paper notes. Carrying vast amounts of cash is somewhat dangerous in case of robbery and/or forgetfulness in leaving the cash at a public space. Apparently, the international media has even reported beggars in China soliciting electronic payments rather than cash.

Of course, electronic cash also means that the state is able to track monetary flows and stop transactions if necessary. This will make it difficult for money laundering or unaccountability of cash inflows to occur. (Cash, on the other hand, is more difficult to track and accounted for.) These features can assist the Chinese Xi Jinping administration with its campaign to end corruption. China wants to stem out internal corruption and also restrict the outflow of funds outside China, whether in terms of individual outflows for safer havens (locations regulated by the rule of law) or as backup alternatives to hedge against political economic risks in China. Similarly, from an official perspective, it does not want outflow of funds to deplete its foreign reserves.

Speed and convenience have also created more incentives for Chinese consumers to borrow more small loans. Alibaba looked around and was inspired by US PayPal to enable online payment, eventually overtaking the US cashless system in sheer volume of payment. (The PayPal system was the first major system to allow Palm Pilot hardware to transfer funds electronically in the 1990s.) Tencent linked Chinese consumers' social media accounts to their bank accounts, facilitating payments. In this way, the cashless mobile payment platforms have become de facto banks, giving out small loans and microfinancing to small and medium sized enterprises (SMEs) on top of individuals. The offer of hassle-free loans is seen as an advantage to SMEs hitherto constrained by traditional banks that have red tape and bureaucracy hindering faster loans. The Chinese also did not develop consumption habits like their American counterparts. There was no habit of buying on credit and then paying off for the purchases like their American counterparts. Chinese people were also hoarders and savers of cash for a variety of reasons, including saving up for their medical expenses as they age. China, like most of East Asia, resists the idea and concept of a welfare state.

The two tech giants stand out in this cashless payment economy are Alibaba and Tencent. Alibaba is an online retailer that is China's answer to Amazon.com while Tencent is a social messaging service that runs WeChat (China's answer to Facebook and Whatsapp). Alibaba's Youku Tudou video sites feature electronic advertisements based on individual behavioural data analytics, much like the individually tailored ads that appear on Google and Gmail platforms. In these ways, Alibaba and Tencent have more accurate profiles of their customers than traditional brick and mortar banks. As a social messaging service, Tencent can create groups of followers to trail consumption news, accessing information and news about the latest products from certain companies and even enjoy loyalty discounts. According to the latest statistics, China is outstripping the US in this field. While the US chalked up US$112 billion of smartphone payments in 2016 (Forrester Research data), the same figure for China in the same year was US$9 trillion (Chinese firm iResearch Consulting Group estimates).[1]

Alibaba created incentives for consumers to shop online by offering products that are only sold online through their platform and also seasonal discounts during online fairs and bazaars hosted by the company. When there were no traditional festivals like Lunar New Year (LNY) or Zhongqiujie Mid-Autumn Festival (also known as Mooncake or Lantern Festival), Alibaba would invent festival and special days to create excuses to consume. Tencent latched onto the traditional Lunar New Year festivities and created an electronic version of the *hongbao (ang pows* as they are known in Singapore or "red packets" when translated into English) for distribution to friends and families. Tencent allows users to insert a sum of monetary credits for this purpose.

Playing on human instincts for competitiveness, Tencent made it a rule that anyone who opened the Hongbao first can get a larger portion of a pool of electronic money allocated for the *hongbaos*. Millions signed up Tencent's WeChat system to get a shot at getting the *hongbao* red packets. Cashless mechanisms have literally created marketing machines out of the tech giants. While Alibaba and Tencent are earning interests charged on electronic transactions, they are also accumulating incredible amounts of data. Both companies publicly say they do not sell the data to third parties.

[1] Abkowitz, Alyssa, "The Cashless Society Has Arrived—Only It's in China" dated 4 January 2018 in the *Wall Street Journal (WSJ)* [downloaded on 4 January 2018], available at https://www.wsj.com/articles/chinas-mobile-payment-boom-changes-how-people-shop-borrow-even-panhandle-1515000570.

The Last Holdout in China

One of the last holdouts on electronic cashless payments in China is found mainly in Hong Kong where just 70% of Hong Kongers would use e-payment apps compared to 86% on the Chinese mainland.[2] Nicholas Gordon, a cash advocate and researcher for the Global Institute for Tomorrow (a Hong Kong-based think tank), argued that exchanging cash payment attracts no transaction charges, its physical form means cash cannot be electronically hacked, cash is easily available at ATM-dense cities like HK, HK enjoys high trustworthiness in its financial sector compared to China.[3] Hong Kong already has a cashless mechanism but not in the form of mobile payments. While mobile payments are behind mainland China, the Chief Executive of the Hong Kong Monetary Authority Norman Chan Tak-lam released the statistic that there are 14 million Octopus transactions every day.[4] Octopus cards are Hong Kong's cashless payment mechanism minus the smartphone. Introduced two decades ago in 1997, the iconic Octopus card is usable for payment everywhere in Hong Kong, it is easier to use than mobile payments (requiring no downloads and smartphone hardware) and has the potential to be expanded further for use at more commercial outlets.

Political-Economic Implications

Given the disproportionate amount of data the Chinese tech giants can accumulate, it is not surprising the authorities are moving in to regulate or control their data platforms. Cashless payment mechanisms have the potential to weaken the People's Bank of China (PBOC, Chinese equivalence of the central bank)'s hold on currency movements and flows. The PBOC instituted a new payment platform that makes smartphone payments more transparent and for the state to have a better grip of transaction data. The People's Bank of China created an electronic platform for this purpose, known as the Nets Union Clearing Corp.

All transactions, therefore, between consumers and retailers/service providers will now go through this central processing mechanism or platform. A small fee will be charged by Net Union Clearing Corp for processing these transactions. Eventually, electronic payment mechanisms will be regulated like

[2] Gordon, Nicholas, "Despite 'Falling Behind' Scare Stories HK Is Already Cashless" dated 8 November 2017 in China Daily [downloaded on 8 November 2017], available at https://www.chinadailyhk.com/articles/71/1/46/1510112118680.html.

[3] Gordon, Nicholas, "Despite 'Falling Behind' Scare Stories HK Is Already Cashless" dated 8 November 2017 in *China Daily* [downloaded on 8 November 2017], available at https://www.chinadailyhk.com/articles/71/1/46/1510112118680.html.

[4] Gordon, Nicholas, "Despite 'Falling Behind' Scare Stories HK Is Already Cashless" dated 8 November 2017 in *China Daily* [downloaded on 8 November 2017], available at https://www.chinadailyhk.com/articles/71/1/46/1510112118680.html.

finance and banking institutions. The Chinese regulators may have relaxed its hold on the tech giants for them to develop electronic mobile payment mechanisms to shake up the financial transaction sectors and spur them on for economic reforms. But after that is achieved, and as the two tech giants of Tencent and Alibaba dominate the sector and accumulate data, the state is stepping in to put the house in order and re-assert control.

To restrict fraud cases, the state regulator has imposed limits on the number of transactions that can be carried out via QR codes starting from December 2017. This effectively constrains Tencent and Alibaba from introducing expensive products on their electronic retail platforms eligible for QR coded purchases. It prevents conspicuous consumption at a time when anti-corruption campaigns under Core Leader President Xi Jinping's administration continues to enjoy wide public support. Same goes for microfinancing. The state regulator has stepped in to restrict the interest rates charged by Tencent and Alibaba on microloans. It is only a matter of time before the state regulator comes in to manage data collected by these companies.

Besides leadership appointments, the milestone 19th Party Congress appears to show Chinese state determination to control rampant consumption, runaway debts and opulence are borne out of fear of social unrest arising from debts. Social stability is the top priority of the Chinese government as the Chinese Communist Party (CCP) heads towards its 100th year anniversary. Lessons are learnt from recent financial crises that were triggered off by uncontrollable debt situations like the 1997 Asian Financial Crisis and the 2008 Lehman Shocks. China does not have the same resilience and number of pressure valves to let off steam from angry members of the public if a devastating economic crisis hits the country, compared to a liberal democracy with its democratic vote, a free press and freedom for public gatherings. China prefers to manage social tensions rather than a public display of citizen discontent.

The moves to restrict QR code purchases and institute the Nets Union Clearing Corp platform are probably the first of other forms of enhanced scrutiny and rollbacks by the Chinese state on e-payment mechanisms. This is certainly a change in policy orientation. Up till the recent past, the Chinese government was not proactive in managing or controlling this sector. But, with the vast accumulation of data by Tencent and Alibaba, the state has been alerted and the CCP is traditionally nervous and watchful of any non-party organizations that are accumulating power. In the contemporary situation, data are the new oil, accumulation of data is equated with accumulation of commodities like oil by monopolies of the past.

On the flipside, as the Chinese state play a more active role in regulating electronic transactions and payments, there are concerns that the state would have access to such data for social engineering and control purposes. Such data can be linked to the social credit system that can eventually determine if individuals who score badly on such systems are able to have access to public service jobs, purchase train and plane tickets or travel overseas. Critics of data breaches and misuse by the state point towards Chinese use of big data in Xinjiang to silence critics, select candidates for re-education and clamp down on dissent.

Such concerns may obstruct Chinese acquisition of foreign companies, including US financial firms, due to fears of US data exposure to Chinese state-owned enterprises (SOEs), state-linked companies and/or Chinese companies that are heavily regulated or compliant to Chinese data requirements. In general, Western companies tend to practise higher standards of legal protection of personal data compared to their Chinese counterparts. Foreign entities are not the only ones worried about data misuse. Chinese conglomerate (which also owns Volvo) Geely's owner was cited in local press for saying that Tencent is monitoring daily WeChat transactions and conversations on a daily basis and this prompted Tencent to issue a public statement that they do not archive Chinese chat histories and meta data trails.[5]

INTERNATIONAL/REGIONAL RELATIONS DIMENSIONS AND POLITICAL ECONOMIC IMPLICATIONS

There is also an international dimension to the cashless system. Visa and Mastercard have found it challenging to establish their presence[6] and compete with mobile payments and their proprietary systems. Chinese digitization has led to challenges by foreign consumers and companies in accessing the Chinese market. Regulation is a powerful tool and the international business community is monitoring the situation to see if they can gain access to the lucrative market of mobile payments in China. Looming in the background is the potential US–China trade war over the question of access. There are worries that the digital realm (e.g. e-commerce) would be the next cause of trade imbalance between the two countries and its potential to be politically classified as a non-tariff barrier (NTB) centred upon the issue of access. This could potentially lead to negotiations to open up electronic/online/virtual trade and services access and add it on to the already complicated negotiations of real world commodities and materials like aluminium, iron, steel, soy beans, beef and cars that are already a cause of economic and trade concerns between the two countries.

Global consumers who are used to credit cards are finding the use of mobile payments foreign. American and foreign consumers may be able to register for WeChat but may find it difficult to connect that registered account with their own bank accounts. Plastic is still the preferred mode of payment in the US and cheques remain popular. These factors have motivated

[5]Wang, Yue, "China Tightens Regulation Over Mobile Payment Apps—What's Next for Tencent and Ant Financial?" dated 3 January 2018 in *Forbes* [downloaded on 3 January 2018], available at https://www.forbes.com/sites/ywang/2018/01/03/china-tightens-regulation-over-mobile-payment-apps-whats-next-for-tencent-and-ant-financial/#526f66467f1d.

[6]Abkowitz, Alyssa, "The Cashless Society Has Arrived—Only It's in China" dated 4 January 2018 in the *Wall Street Journal (WSJ)* [downloaded on 4 January 2018], available at https://www.wsj.com/articles/chinas-mobile-payment-boom-changes-how-people-shop-borrow-even-panhandle-1515000570.

Alipay to offer options that accept foreign credit card payments. But the Chinese cashless payment system is expanding regionally, with usability in Bangkok and the cabs of Singapore and in developmental phases (especially in the area of microfinancing and microloans) in India, Pakistan and some Europeans countries. In fact, Singapore considers the Chinese cashless payment system a reference model for catch-up purposes. Singapore has ambitions to go both card-less and cheque-less.

Alibaba and its affiliate Ant Financial have already made its presence felt in Southeast Asia. For example, in the Philippines, Alibaba is building financial technology solutions to strengthen the country's e-commerce capabilities, establish new marketplaces and streamlining logistical procedures while Ant Financial Group will bring down remittance costs for 10 million Filipino expatriate workers based overseas, Alibaba Business School will educate Filipino officials to better manage the company's digital technologies.[7] Cashless payment mechanisms have the potential to help the Philippines track money laundering and control corruption while creating new jobs for the economy. A successful cashless payment system in ASEAN (Association of Southeast Asian Nations) would serve as a demonstrative showcase piece for other ASEAN countries interested in acquiring such systems.

US credit card companies are also ramping up their mobile payments and making it safer by adding security features. Korean company Samsung is also joining such ventures. But they are not yet catching up with their Chinese peers. Tencent and Alibaba are also trying to establish their presence in the US by linking up with individual retailers to offer Alipay or WeChat pay services. But the promise of cashless payment need not result in competition and conflicts. US Mastercard and Visa have combined strengths and resources with China's Union Pay (whose business has been affected by Tencent WeChat Pay and Alipay) to enhance electronic payment transactions between credit card firms and banks through the use of the ubiquitous QR code.

In this sense, the credit card firms and banks are fighting back against their mobile payment counterparts. Such cooperation mitigate political tensions and concerns against the global backdrop of anti-globalization and free trade resistance trends. For now, the cashless payment mechanism is hailed by consumers as a platform of great convenience. Convenience and ease of payment currently appear to overcome concerns about privacy, confidentiality and state control. The politics of control, when resolved, may even facilitate the state's acceptance of cryptocurrencies or Initial Coin Offerings (ICOs) eventually. The PBOC has already formed a research institute to look into this aspect, perhaps this move is a preview of things to come.

---

[7]ASEAN Today, "Alibaba Steers the Philippines Towards a Cashless Revolution" dated 12 February 2018 in ASEAN Today [downloaded on 12 February 2018], available at https://www.aseantoday.com/2018/02/alibaba-steers-the-philippines-towards-a-cashless-revolution/.

BIBLIOGRAPHY

Abkowitz, Alyssa, "The Cashless Society Has Arrived—Only It's in China" dated 4 January 2018 in the *Wall Street Journal (WSJ)* [downloaded on 4 January 2018]. Available at https://www.wsj.com/articles/chinas-mobile-payment-boom-changes-how-people-shop-borrow-even-panhandle-1515000570.

ASEAN Today, "Alibaba Steers the Philippines Towards a Cashless Revolution" dated 12 February 2018 in ASEAN Today [downloaded on 12 February 2018]. Available at https://www.aseantoday.com/2018/02/alibaba-steers-the-philippines-towards-a-cashless-revolution/.

Gordon, Nicholas, "Despite 'Falling Behind' Scare Stories HK Is Already Cashless" dated 8 November 2017 in *China Daily* [downloaded on 8 November 2017]. Available at https://www.chinadailyhk.com/articles/71/1/46/1510112118680.html.

Wang, Yue, "China Tightens Regulation Over Mobile Payment Apps—What's Next for Tencent and Ant Financial?" dated 3 January 2018 in *Forbes* [downloaded on 3 January 2018]. Available at https://www.forbes.com/sites/ywang/2018/01/03/china-tightens-regulation-over-mobile-payment-apps-whats-next-for-tencent-and-ant-financial/#526f66467f1d.

CHAPTER 11

Case Study 6: A Traditional SME (Small and Medium Enterprise) in Singapore Turns to Digital Technologies for Boosting Retail Business

The Gohs have been in the porcelain making and retail businesses for four generations. The family progenitor hailed from the Chinese region of Chaozhou (Teochew in Wades Giles Romanization). The Teochews (Chaozhouren) were well-known among the overseas Chinese communities in several ways. First, they were seafarers, travelling in large numbers to Southeast Asian countries like Thailand and also to Hong Kong when it was a British colony. In Singapore, they are the second largest dialect group amongst the Chinese. Second, they were frugal and well known for entrepreneurial spirit. Urban legend has it that they like to eat porridge (Teochew *muay*) that was affordable with simple non-opulent steamed dishes that was also healthy. Urban legend also has it that Chaozhou women did not bind their feet during Qing dynasty as they wanted to retain mobility and work in the fields and other capacities to derive income for the family. Third, the Teochews were well known for their work ethics embodied in a stereotypical slogan that says they can succeed if they persevere and this slogan has even become the theme of a modern pop song sung at karaoke sessions.

The family business probably dates back to the late Qing to Republican period and it started in the town of Chaoan in Chaozhou. As with many traditional Chinese family businesses, they were regionalized with a branch in Hong Kong and one in Swatow. The father of the current Elder Goh Yong Chiang's owner started a porcelain company in Singapore and named it Thye Nam and Co. Tow Huat Heng Kee Importers and Exporters (T.N. for short). The trademarks "T.N." and "TN and Co." were stamped at the bottom of the wares made and sold or distributed by Thye Nam. It was located at 247 South Bridge Road (this was a subsequent location, not the initial shop address). Besides import and export businesses, it also sold porcelain antiques. The company also manufactured porcelain under its own

© The Author(s) 2019
T. W. Lim, *Industrial Revolution 4.0, Tech Giants, and Digitized Societies,*
https://doi.org/10.1007/978-981-13-7470-8_11

branding T.N. (Tainan in Hanyu Pinyin). The T.N. manufacturing arm of the business was active from the 1960s to the 1970s (and in limited quantities in the 1980s). Elder Goh still has some samples of T.N. products in his current shop.

According to business elder Goh Yong Chiang, his ancestral hometown lays in between two other town districts. One of which was the ancestral hometown of probably the most famous Teochew individual in East Asia, Superman Li or Li Ka-shing, the Hong Kong-based richest man in Asia who finally retired in 2018. His ancestral district traditionally gave rise to the literati and local area officialdom, the local scholar-gentry. (In fact, Li Ka-Shing's plastic floral shop was a few shops away from Thye Nam and Co. in Hong Kong Street in the 1950s.) The other town district was the ancestral village to a prominent businessman in Singapore and it was originally an agricultural district. Sandwiched in between the two districts (one literati and the other agricultural), Goh's hometown traditionally made pottery and porcelain wares at least from late Qing dynasty onwards. The superficial divisions among these three districts disappeared with Deng Xiaoping's economic reforms and modernization which saw the emergence of multi-storey towering blocks in place of farmlands and traditional villages.

The progenitor Goh and his family in Chaoan specialized in making flower pots for consumers. The current patriarch of the family business Elder Goh Yong Chiang and his brothers all continued with the porcelain businesses as first generation Singaporeans. One of Elder Goh's brother was a dealer in antique porcelains (Mingboy was run by Elder Goh's younger brother) while the other used to run a gallery in Outram Park (circa 1967, address was: Outram Park Red Pond #01-85). Their father who had since passed away operated a porcelain retail and wholesale distributor shop in Chinatown. According to Elder Goh, his father was once offered ownership of that shophouse for S$50,000 in the 1970s but he turned it down. This later became a source of regret for Elder Goh Yong Chiang as he had to rent a shophouse to carry on with his business at much higher prices. His current shop is a literal stone's throw away from progenitor Goh's original Chinatown shophouse store.

By the 1970s, the Gohs were distributing Swatow-made kitchenware, including household products like spoons, plates and bowls. They also distributed Swatow-made clay teapots that were popular for consumption of *tieguanyin* tea (a Teochew variety of oolong tea) with Teochew-style clear soup Bak Kut Teh. Elder Goh set up his retail business at Tanjong Pagar town centre when it opened up before moving to his current rental address at a shophouse at Chinatown (circa 1973, address was Tanjong Pagar Blk 1 #01-22). According to Elder Goh, the rent in Chinatown from his father's days had gone up exponentially from S$50 a month to tens of thousands of dollars today. A fact that reflected phenomenal growth in Singapore's economy under the visionary leadership of its post-independence government and its founding father.

The Goh family's traditional business in making flower pots in China was one factor that probably influenced the elder Goh Yong Chiang (now in his 80s) to become interested in bonsai cultivation and promoting sales of potted bonsai to Singaporeans from the 1960s to the 1980s. He had access to the bonsai pots which his family mass manufactured in large quantities. Elder Goh was a fantastic organizer and mobilizer with acute business savvy. He held and organized bonsai and porcelain exhibitions and shows in Gay World, New World and Great World as well as Outram Park retail districts in Singapore. Gay World, New World and Great World were among some of Singapore's premium entertainment districts while Outram Park was the first integrated public housing project that had a self-contained shopping/retail section featuring well-known emporiums like Chancellor and locally-known tailors. Elder Goh's bonsai plants on display would meander around the concrete resting areas that surrounded ponds and atriums in the housing project.

Elder Goh's event organization modus operandi was effective and efficient. He rounded up volunteers including fellow Teochew folks and mobilized them into shifts round the clock to do the logistics and manual work for the shows. He did not pay them salaries but made deals with the nearby *tzu char* (Hokkien and Teochew mixed rice and dishes dinner menu) stalls to cook rounds of foods for the volunteers. Each dinner round cost him S$15, a princely sum in the 1960s. Elder Goh recalled his father used to scold him for being too generous with the dinner treats. When Elder Goh had used up his capital, any profits left over from the sales was then divided into modest shares of S$3–5 as a form of individual stipend for the volunteers. That was how Elder Goh moved his goods logistically and sold his wares to customers.

Elder Goh also managed transnational business operations with his immediate family members coordinated with hometown folks. From the 1930s and 1940s, in his recollection, his family started to diversify into other products. They would, for example, receive shipments from Chaozhou-based Hakka potters and then retail/distribute them to the Nanyang (Southeast Asian) region like Singapore, Malaysia and Indonesia. They would also work with Czech industries to make enamel ware for sale to the same region. Elder Goh only has a few pieces of his enamel wares left in the current shop, including some Czech-made teapots and spittoons. The family business was briefly interrupted by WWII. During the wartime interregnum, Elder Goh's sister escaped to Singapore and took shelter during WWII.

In the post-war years, Elder Goh and his family members globalized their business further and worked with English pottery makers (like J&G Meakin) to manufacture feldspar-laced soft paste porcelain wares with paper transfer designs. They also worked with Japanese porcelain manufacturers when the Japanese were keen to earn foreign reserve currencies to hasten post-war recovery before they emerged as the world's second-largest economy (a global ranking that stayed on until 2010 when China took over that position). As costs of doing business went up, the

Gohs also worked with other manufacturers in neighbouring Malaysia, Goh Ban Huat Diamond brand pottery in Kuala Lumpur. Elder Goh and his sister also expanded the production lines in their family-owned kilns. They started making fine white porcelain Guanyin (Goddess of Mercy) idols similar in texture, feel and aesthetics as Dehua (Tehwa, also known as Blanc de Chine in French) porcelain in Fujian (Hokkien or Fukien in Wades Giles spelling) China. These were popular with Taoists and Buddhist worshippers. Both religions have among the largest numbers of devotees in Singapore.

The Gohs also expanded their family's export base and made "Swatow bowls" (thick porcelain bowls with a wide body and medium depth with stylized hand-drawn designs of flowers or chickens with banana plants) and exported them in large numbers to Malaysia and Indonesia. Elder Goh recalled each order for such bowls ran into tens of thousands of dollars (sometimes 50,000 per run) and they were supplied in large numbers to restaurants. These bowls were often replaced when they were chipped, cracked or broken, thus generating endless demand for their supplies. Elder Goh's wife also recalled the Swatow bowls were supplied in large numbers to hawker stalls as well. She recollected from memory that many of these bowls were used for serving porridge (including Teochew porridge).

It was a roaring business in the good old times, as he recalled. Elder Goh said the recipe to his success at this historical juncture was the ability to attract large orders and sell his wares quickly in rapid turnovers. He could also get credit from the banks at low-interest rates and many services such as cheque book services were inexpensive. He recalled business was so good in the pre-Chinese Deng reform era (pre-1978–1979) that he sometimes got payment from customers even before the goods were delivered and he was willing to take credits from customers up to one month, delivering his goods without the need to ask for immediate payments from his customers. During this heyday period, Goh's shop and its products were featured in local newspapers, newspapers written in foreign language for local communities (e.g. Japanese newsletters), etc.

An interesting point about the Gohs' wholesale supply business is that they managed to capture all socioeconomic classes of consumers interested in hawker fares served in cruder thicker porcelain wares that had simple stylized drawings to high-end fine porcelain wares (Jingdezhen ceramics) that had symmetrical patterns and delicate porcelain body. They provided porcelain wares for all socioeconomic classes of people, serving an important social bridging function between all groups and their specific needs as well as budgets. This situation no longer applies today as Elder Goh noted that even crude wares made in the past are now worth their weight in gold as antiques as these ceramic products are no longer in production and are now valued for their antiquity value and aesthetics by collectors.

China's economic reforms compelled the family business to rethink their business model. During the time of Cold War-era economic embargo by the US and China's socialist isolationism after the Sino-Soviet Split (1959 after the Ussuri River incident), the Gohs were able to find their niche as an overseas Chinese family business intermediary between mainland Chinese hometown manufacturers and Southeast Asian customers. They were an important middleman when China did not enjoy diplomatic relations with Southeast Asian states at the height of the Cold War. But, once Chinese paramount leader Deng Xiaoping opened up the Chinese economy to the rest of the world after the Sino-US rapprochement, the Gohs lost their special access to the porcelain manufacturers in Chaoan, Swatow (Shantou), Chaozhou or even China's porcelain manufacturers as a whole. Malaysian and Indonesian retailers started going directly to China to purchase their wares without having to go through middlemen like the Gohs. This was the beginning of a long slide in their business when it comes to distributorship.

From then on, the wholesale distributor model of business was not possible and they became a shop front brick and mortar retailer. Initially, Elder Goh recalled business in his current Chinatown address was good and he survived well retailing porcelain goods but purchases made by tourists visiting Chinatown appears to have declined as well. The biggest buyers of his products today are Chinese tourists visiting Singapore and they tend to prefer high-quality wares at affordable prices. Elder Goh sometimes finds it challenging to sell the goods due to sentimentality and nostalgia for these antique porcelain goods. Enters Goh Seng Ngee (Goh Jr.), a young and energetic man who is learning the ropes to take over the Chan Ngee (Lee Kee) Trading Company which is the contemporary successor to Thye Nam and Co. Goh Jr. is well-versed in digital technology and started devising new ways to market and retail the traditional family business products. (During the business start-up stage of Chan Ngee (Lee Kee) Trading Co., the addendum "(Lee Kee) 利记" was added because of trademark issues as the same name could be found in another company in the Registrar of Companies (ROC).

Goh Seng Ngee (hitherto known as "Goh Jr." in this writing) helped in the family business and started selling on eBay in 1997. The online service was very popular and business was good at the beginning of digital age (in the era of the so-called "IT boom"). At that point of time, trust was the key component of Goh Jr. outfit's success and many US-based customers preferred to pay in cash for their purchases. Goh Jr. eventually stopped selling on eBay due to intense competition from Chinese retailers and the prevalence of fraud as well as the high commission-based charges of eBay and PayPal. Goh Jr. now markets his family businesses' wares online, using social media tools like Facebook to inform his customer base of the newest products available at the shop and new items he has taken out of the family business' warehouse. Goh Jr. and Elder Goh also rents out the second floor of their shophouse space to auctioneers and exhibitors to run their own activities, collecting rentals as collateral income for the business. Goh Jr. also uses social media to inform his clients about such events (auctions and shows) and takes photos to feature some of the products for the collectors' community. Digital technologies suddenly gave a lease of life for the Goh family business and the possibilities are endless with a larger reach of global audiences, consumers and collectors. It is a good example of micro-national-ization (a play on the word to signify the SME version of multinational) of the traditional family business.

Goh Jr. delivers products worldwide through the postal mailing and courier services. He also posts latest updates and information in the porcelain collectors' world. In other words, Goh Jr. is mirroring his father's business activities in the past like shows and exhibitions in public area but hosts them online in cyberspace instead. Instead of organizing exhibitions in New, Gay and Great Worlds as well as Outram Park. Goh Jr. now organizes such shows online with photographs, descriptions and snippets of interesting news in the auction industry. Goh Jr. was also able to maximize publicity for his company when he was able to take photos with local notables like artists, retired public figures and even pop superstar Seal when they visit his shop or Chinatown.

Posting news about his meeting with Seal the pop superstar (former husband of German supermodel Heidi Klum, now celebrity talk show host and fashionista) in Chinatown lends a popular cultural shine to Goh's Jr. local area knowledge. In the past, his father Elder Goh's nearest equivalent would have been Songnian Fashi (Master Songnian), a well-known calligrapher monk whose writings are snapped up by collectors at exorbitant prices, according to Elder Goh who was very excited when he came to this part in the interview. The big difference between Elder Goh's meeting with public figures and Goh's Jr. coincidental chance meeting with Seal is that followers of Goh's Jr. social media contents were able to learn about the chance encounter almost immediately. This gave social media followers a "live" feel in participating in and feeling resonance with Goh's Jr. excitement about meeting a global superstar. Content provision and refreshing ensure online audiences are glued to his social media account for the latest information on the business, industry and collectors' preferences.

Goh Jr. himself has updated his own knowledge of antique auction news so that he can share interesting nuggets of information online in his Facebook account. He also uses Whatsapp to inform collectors and clients of the latest items on sale, including those he is offering at discounted or special prices. In the brick and mortar shop front, Goh Jr. has also tapped into digital technologies by asking visitors (including tourists visiting Singapore's Chinatown area) to vote and provide feedback for their shop in Tripadvisor. Leaving a positive review on Tripadvisor helps with enhancing the company's branding and reputation. It is effective for tourists who come to the shophouse to purchase products or attend shows. Goh Jr. also posts information about Grab taxis (Grab has taken over Uber in Singapore at the point of this writing) inside his shop to facilitate visitors' travels to and from his shophouse to other locations. Goh Jr. has also tapped on cultural groups, Chinese associations, auctioneers to utilize his second floor shophouse space while optimizing publicity for those events through social media.

Goh Jr. enjoys many other advantages brought about by technology. Unlike his father, he need not keep a large stock of pamphlets for marketing purposes. It saves company budget on printing leaflets, pamphlets and mailing them to clients. Elder Goh even had to get calligraphers to manually write out couplets to give as free gifts and takeaways for visitors to the exhibition. Goh Jr's push out of latest news and updates are instantaneous and did not require postal time like in the days of Elder Goh. Goh's Jr. inventory is also much leaner and rationalized. He did not need to keep a large inventory or store like his father. Sometimes, Goh Jr. needs only to act as a middleman to connect suppliers who bring antiquities and goods to his shophouse with the collectors and customers who are interested in purchasing them. He does not need to spend money to acquire the goods or keep them in warehousing and inventories. In this sense, he has become the online version of the intermediary role that Elder Goh used to play between the Chinese Chaozhou potters and Southeast Asia-based Nanyang customers in the pre-Chinese reform era (before 1979–1978).

PART III

Section on Quizzes

CHAPTER 12

Quiz 1: Tech Giants, Digitized Workplaces and Societies Quiz

1. Binary systems use a series of 1s and 0s to create instructions to run a program. Is this statement true or false?

   A. True
   B. False

2. Most digital tech giant companies in the forefront of Industrial Revolution 4.0 originate from which two countries?

   A. China and US
   B. China and ASEAN
   C. US and Norway
   D. None of the above

3. Which of the following argument is utilized by tech giants to argue they are net job creators and not destroyers? Choose the most appropriate response.

   A. They replace mum-and-pop shops in the locations targeted for an expansion of presence.
   B. They support a whole ecology of workers, entrepreneurs, employees and part-timers through the companies they deal with. In this way, the tech giants behave like the industrial giants before them, except nimbler and with more efficient logistical chains.
   C. They replace traditional logistical companies with more efficient robots and A.I. technologies.
   D. None of the above.

© The Author(s) 2019
T. W. Lim, *Industrial Revolution 4.0, Tech Giants, and Digitized Societies*,
https://doi.org/10.1007/978-981-13-7470-8_12

4. China is also building communication networks and infrastructure under the Belt and Road Initiative (BRI, formerly known as One Belt One Road or OBOR), and the main participants in such projects are the state-owned construction and telecommunications companies (or SOEs, State-Owned Enterprises). Which two countries have already signed up for integration into the Beidou satellite (global positioning) project?

   A. North Korea and South Korea
   B. Myanmar and Cambodia
   C. Pakistan and Thailand
   D. None of the above

5. In Japan, due to rising labour costs and surging demand during its economic high growth period, industrial robots were utilized in the manufacturing sector to meet heightened demand for its consumer products in its economic boom decades and robots would eventually be used to replace human labour resulting from an ageing population in that country. When were industrial robots first used in Japan?

   A. 2000s
   B. 21st century
   C. 1990s
   D. late 1960s to 1970s

6. Which of the following factors did NOT deter the expansion of robot use in Industrial Revolution 2.0? Choose the most appropriate answer.

   A. Robots were still prohibitively expensive and represented long-term investments.
   B. Their installation faced the wrath of trade unions so their numbers were mitigated and curtailed based on the price factor and social conditions.
   C. They ran virtually on A.I. so not too many robots were needed.
   D. None of the above.

7. During the phase of Industrial Revolution 2.0, which of the following statements does NOT reflect the situation on the ground related to robotic technologies?

   A. Most robots were also programmed by humans and were incapable of making autonomous decisions.
   B. Most robots were not self-thinking and most did not have self-learning capabilities that can emulate and clone human actions or decisions.

C. Most robots did not have Artificial Intelligence (A.I.) capabilities, the robots did exactly what they were programmed to do.

D. Most robots were already androids that resembled human appearance.

8. In Globalization 2.0, Information and Communication Technologies (ICT) shrunk the world even faster. Which of the following technologies was not related to this phenomenon?

A. The invention of the fastest transportation technologies, including jet engines that can now fly faster than the speed of sound.

B. Communication and interactions became instantaneous in this era. Message boards, emails, chatrooms and BBS emerged for people to communicate with each other globally.

C. The invention of an internet protocol that enabled computers to become communication devices that linked up each other, even across different computer brands and makes.

D. The ability to teleport, disassembling atomic and sub-atomic particles and then re-assembling them again in a vacuum.

9. The Internet was originally designed to survive a nuclear war and keep communications going among the US alliance network. Is this statement true or false?

A. True

B. False

10. Which of the following are Industry 4.0 technologies? Choose the most appropriate answer.

A. Artificial Intelligence (A.I.)

B. Autonomous vehicles

C. Algorithm-controlled machines

D. All of the above

11. Which of the following are Industry 4.0 technologies? Choose the most appropriate answer.

A. Autonomous weapons systems

B. Algorithm-based predictive behaviour software/apps

C. Social media connected with IoT

D. All of the above

12. Which of the following features describe Facebook accurately? Choose the most appropriate answer.

   A. Facebook was created for users who were interested to put their personal data online in the form of comments, photos, emoticons and textual information and then share it with other members of their network or/and with the public in general.
   B. Facebook was meant to be a free platform that allows people to share information easily and even do their own publicity stunts and self-marketing.
   C. Facebook was a democratic platform where people could post things easily without much technical knowledge needed.
   D. All of the above.

13. Through Facebook, people could also fact-check their governments' materials and debunk propaganda. Is this a possible use of Facebook capabilities?

   A. Yes
   B. No

14. Facebook facilitated revolutions like Arab Spring when incidents of abuse and inequity provoked the masses to topple an authoritarian government. Because Facebook could round up and connect friends, family and like-minded individuals together, ideas could be disseminated quickly to a target audience. Is this statement true or false?

   A. True
   B. False

15. What are some of the drawbacks of using Facebook? Choose the most appropriate response.

   A. Organizations and agencies other than Facebook could also hack into the database and/or data was sold by Facebook to paying parties legally.
   B. Spreading of fake news.
   C. Making people getting jealous and emotional at each other's posts.
   D. All of the above.

16. There are advantages in using Facebook. Which of the following is NOT one of them?

    A. Facebook offers convenience for most users when tapping into their services.
    B. Facebook sharing motivates online friendships, greater intercultural/inter-religious understanding between societies and a smaller, more interdependent world.
    C. Some users upload racist/misogynistic posts.
    D. Facebook reminds us of our friends' birthdays and helps us keep in touch with our circle of friends.

17. Fake news was cited for influencing governments and elections, something made possible by the fact that a large number of people now obtain their news feed from social media. Is this statement true or false?

    A. True
    B. False

18. Data generation is made possible by the convergence of a large number of electronic devices, apps and software through online link-ups and smartphone use. Is this statement true or false?

    A. True
    B. False

19. When individual routines are repeated over a sufficient period of time, it shows certain characteristics, inclinations, personality traits, consumption preferences and other patterns over time. _____ then becomes possible and eventually these machines, algorithms and apps will start prescribing choices for the individual users based on recorded or predicted preferences. Fill in the blank.

    A. Predictive analyses
    B. Teleportation
    C. Deep Space exploration in worm holes
    D. Time travel

20. When data are collected from a large population, the analysis at the macro level becomes more accurate (that is why India and China are ideal labs for data collection). What is the terminology for describing this sort of data collection?

    A. Datacrunchers
    B. Big data
    C. Megadata
    D. Huge Data

21. Which of the following is NOT a positive use of Big Data?

    A. Tracking and predicting earthquakes.
    B. Tracking and predicting diseases spread and infections.
    C. Tracking logistical/transportation movements.
    D. Using personal data for ransoming victims to warn them about the dangers of lax cybersecurity.

22. Tech giants and titans can now collect and scan data from entire societies, countries, organizations and cities. Is this statement true or false?

    A. True
    B. False

Answer Bank

1. Correct answer is A.
2. Correct answer is A.
3. Correct answer is B.
4. Correct answer is C.
5. Correct answer is D.
6. Correct answer is C.
7. Correct answer is D.
8. Correct answer is D.
9. Correct answer is A.
10. Correct answer is D.
11. Correct answer is D.
12. Correct answer is D.
13. Correct answer is A.
14. Correct answer is A.
15. Correct answer is D.
16. Correct answer is C.
17. Correct answer is A.
18. Correct answer is A.
19. Correct answer is A.
20. Correct answer is B.
21. Correct answer is D.
22. Correct answer is A.

CHAPTER 13

Quiz 1: Digital Disruptions and the Workplace Quiz

1. What are two examples of populist resistance to globalization?

   A. California-zation and technocratization
   B. Glocalization and Dub Step
   C. Brexit and American First policies
   D. None of the above

2. What is not a typical coping mechanism for easing unemployment caused by technological disruptions?

   A. The governments of developed economies have had to help ease the transition for these workers to be reskilled to get new jobs.
   B. Governments may consider providing welfare support for workers replace by machines till they are able to find jobs.
   C. Social welfare and safety nets will need to be tweaked to help individuals who are unable to find jobs or are retrenched due to outsourced jobs, jobs replaced by automation and other economic changes.
   D. Carry out wholesale destruction of industrial machines to stop them from taking over human jobs.

3. Which of the following is generally NOT a soft skill favoured by companies and organizations today when hiring humans? Choose the most appropriate answer.

   A. Skills and aptitude to work in a team.
   B. Able to communicate and interact with others and are on time for their appointments and assignments.
   C. Humans displaying empathy.
   D. Beat Box Robotic skills.

© The Author(s) 2019   163
T. W. Lim, *Industrial Revolution 4.0, Tech Giants, and Digitized Societies*,
https://doi.org/10.1007/978-981-13-7470-8_13

4. Which of the following is generally NOT a soft skill favoured by companies and organizations today when hiring humans? Choose the most appropriate answer.

    A. Human persuasion skills.
    B. Problem-solving solutions for problems faced by humans.
    C. Decision-making processes in situational dynamics.
    D. Dub steps in robotic sequence.

5. What does STEM stand for?

    A. Science, Technology, Engineering and Mathematics
    B. Science, Technology, Engineering and Mastication
    C. Science, Technology, Electronics and Mathematics
    D. Science, Techniques, Engineering and Mathematics

6. In 2017, the UAE (United Arab Emirates) came up with the post "Minister for Artificial Intelligence" (globally the first country to do so), coinciding this appointment with skills training to whip citizens into shape employability. Is this statement true or false?

    A. True
    B. False

7. Which of the following option is not a way to manage data to prevent breaches and hacking to the system. Please choose the most appropriate strategy.

    A. In high-security environments, some companies and organizations may choose to use only intranet for security of data and use only a few select stand-alone terminals for external connections to the Internet at the digital workplace.
    B. Some have stored all data stored in the cloud protected by cybersecurity.
    C. Companies typically opt for a specialized department to take care of cybersecurity or set up a committee to oversee the security of data.
    D. Adopt a laissez-faire attitude and leave it to online netizens to police the net for eliminating hackers.

8. For companies (and civil service departments) that rely on both intranet and internet external connection. Some ground rules setting may be useful for employees who use the intranet. Training is provided for the employees to remind them not to use intranet facilities for personal messages. Is using intranet an option to prevent breaches from external parties?

   A. No. It is absolutely out of the question and technically unachievable.
   B. Yes. It is suitable for some organizations with high-security needs and a practical way to prevent breaches.

9. "This is based on the belief that the moment individuals graduate from universities and high schools, their skills will be obsolete due to rapid changes in technologies and management knowhow. Therefore, the philosophy behind lifelong learning is that education does not end with a degree, individuals need to take responsibility to continually upgrade their knowledge, take refresher courses or retrain if existing skills are obsolete." Are these statements a good way to describe the concept of lifelong learning?

   A. Yes
   B. No

10. Which of the following option is NOT a good way to cope with disruptions brought about by technologies?

    A. Governments and societies need to extend more help to the disenfranchised and for those left out of the digital revolution.
    B. There is advocacy and attention paid to augmenting provision of social services and encouraging volunteerism within society to take care of those individuals who have fallen behind in preparing and tapping into the digital economy.
    C. It is better to opt for a zero sum game and let free competition weed out individuals unarmed with digital skills so that society can be stronger by emphasizing survival of the fittest.
    D. Disciplines like service learning and social work are highlighted as career choices for caring about others, showing empathy to the needy and taking care of the less fortunate.

11. "Parasitic singles" is a Japanese anthropological term used to describe those who live off their parents without paying rent and lead a carefree, sometimes high-consumption lifestyle, many of whom are part-timers.

    A. False
    B. True

12. Which of the following items is not a robotic category that can contribute to alleviating the elderly care challenge in aging societies? Choose the most appropriate answer.

   A. Assistive robots
   B. Therapeutic robots
   C. Killer robots for reducing population size
   D. None of the above

13. Which of the following explanations is applicable to differentiating between assignments and jobs?

   A. Assignments are one-off projects that can be accomplished easily by robots when they are programmed for certain tasks. But jobs require human skills that are part and parcel of daily activities at the workplace.
   B. Assignments are secret missions that you can choose to take up or not when they are issued by IMF. Jobs are for regular people.
   C. Assignments are reserved only for humans but jobs are applicable only to robots.
   D. Assignments are tasks carried out by military personnel while jobs are meant for civilians only.

14. Learning will become a lifelong journey because _____. Complete the sentence.

   A. once you graduate, you are set for life and a degree is all it takes.
   B. skills need constant refreshment and upgrading.
   C. they will invent ways to achieve immortality.
   D. cryogenics helps to preserve parts of the human bodies for future sciences to re-activate life in them.

15. In what way are robots NOT replacing humans, disrupting jobs/industries or making lives easier for human workers?

   A. E-commerce starting wiping out brick and mortar shops starting from the IT boom in the 1990s.
   B. Automated bank tellers began to perform the same tasks as counter service staffs in financial institutions.
   C. Barcodes also make logistical delivery easier as deliverers, recipients and parcel senders are able to track the progress of the delivery online.
   D. Robots will be designed as terminators and killer robots so that they can put humans to rest permanently.

16. Eventually, even automated tellers will disappear as all cash transactions become electronic and the world truly becomes a _____ society. Fill in the blank by choosing the most appropriate answer.

A. cashless
B. spiritual
C. animistic
D. harmonious

17. Robots are suitable to perform tasks that are 3Ds jobs. what are 3Ds jobs?

A. dangerous, dirty and demanding
B. dainty, ditzy, doughy
C. downright-foolish, dehumanizing, deeply-spiritual
D. dopey, deceitful, deepthroaty

18. Is the following an appropriate and possible way of explaining the uncanny valley theory? "As robots still do not resemble human beings sufficiently, they are immediately differentiated from humankind cognitively and emotionally by humans. One can tell clearly they are machines and may lack the kind of human emotional bond needed by human nurses, caregivers, team colleagues, human leaders/managers, emotionally distressed patients, babies, children and the handicapped/disabled humans."

A. Yes
B. No

19. Prof. Hiroshi Ishiguro from Osaka University is widely acknowledged as the father of Japanese android development. Is this statement true or false?

A. False
B. True

20. An example of a therapeutic robot seal invented by the Japanese for providing companionship to elderly patients who are lonely, suffering from Alzheimer's is _____. Fill in the blank.

A. Gundam
B. Terminator
C. Paro
D. Astroboy

21. Which of the following choice is an explanation to explain Japanese people's acceptance of robotic technologies.

    A. Japanese children are exposed to benign images of robots since young through animation series with robotic heroes portraying a positive co-existence between humans and robots.
    B. Most Japanese are androids anyway and therefore they react better to machines.
    C. Japanese are part of a digital collective and are in constant touch with each other. Man and machine.
    D. Japan has successfully integrated A.I. into every household.

22. Dual-use technologies. These technologies are potentially usable in both civilian and military applications. True or false?

    A. True
    B. False

Answer Bank

1. Answer is C.
2. Answer is D.
3. Answer is D.
4. Answer is D.
5. Answer is A.
6. Answer is A.
7. Answer is D.
8. Answer is B.
9. Answer is B.
10. Answer is C.
11. Answer is B.
12. Answer is C.
13. Answer is A.
14. Answer is B.
15. Answer is D.
16. Answer is A.
17. Answer is A.
18. Answer is A.
19. Answer is B.
20. Answer is C.
21. Answer is A.
22. Answer is A.

CHAPTER 14

Quiz 1: IoT

1. The two greatest technologies that enable users to detach themselves from desktops and go mobile are _____ and _____. Which are the two Industry 4.0 technologies in the blanks?

    A. smartphones and cloud
    B. steam engine and gas pumps
    C. teleportation devices and time portal
    D. flux incapacitor and infinity gauntlet

2. The invention of smartphones, pioneered by _____, means that humans can now carry a small portable phone with microprocessors and computer chips as powerful as their personal computers (PCs) with them 24 hours a day.

    A. Blueberry
    B. Apple
    C. Huawei
    D. Vtec

3. Which of the following statements does not apply to the Internet of Things (IoT)?

    A. The Internet of Things is an aggregator of data and information coming from all sides and is the conduit to pass on the signals to their end destination devices.

© The Author(s) 2019
T. W. Lim, *Industrial Revolution 4.0, Tech Giants, and Digitized Societies*,
https://doi.org/10.1007/978-981-13-7470-8_14

B. The IoT is also analogized as physical objects expressed as digital information and, using the latter, the IoT can manipulate physical objects, turn them on or off, activate them or operate them using remote control.
C. The IoT manages the forcefield in space to prevent asteroids from entering the atmosphere.

4. Machines that cannot operate autonomously of human actions/inputs and/or receive data are considered "dumb". Is this statement true or false?

A. True
B. False

5. Which of the following statement applies to the terminology of a "smart city"?

A. A city where scores for standardized tests remain high and where there is a clustering of creative talents.
B. A city where hipster looks prevail and individuals look smart.
C. Referring specifically only to Silicon valley.
D. A city in which these sensors and readings are constantly taking readings while human decision-makers are processing the information and taking steps to run the city functions more efficiently is sometimes known as a "smart city".

6. What does "CCTV" stand for in the context of a smart city?

A. Closed Circuit Telegraphic Vision
B. Circuit Centered TeleVision
C. Closed Circuit TeleVision
D. Closed Circuit Telegram

7. _____ devices/apps can help to recognize/identify the faces of individuals using a database. Fill in the blank.

A. Emotive Cognition
B. Emoticons Driven
C. Facial Recognition
D. Morse code

8. The constant collection of health-related readings taken down by medical tracking devices belong to a class of technologies known as _____. Their functions are specialized in the field of measuring and quantifying.

   A. biometric sensors
   B. mimetic sensors
   C. prosthetic sensors
   D. hybrid assistive limb

9. To fully benefit from the availability of data, which one of the following actions is probably not helpful for companies with access to data?

   A. Companies need to groom a strong analytics department to analyse the data sets and translate them into practical use.
   B. Companies would also need to train a strong cybersecurity team to prevent the data from being hacked and/or stolen.
   C. For companies, data collected from customers over a period of time can also contribute to calibrating the maintenance, servicing and parts replacement intervals and durations, so that these functions can be systematized.
   D. Do away with cybersecurity measures completely and hackers test the integrity of the system.

10. What does "IoT" stand for in Industry 4.0?

    A. Internet of Technical Innovation
    B. Internet of Technologies
    C. Internet of Time
    D. Internet of Things

11. Which of the following is a typical virus that can affect digital systems?

    A. Malware
    B. Hepitatis B
    C. Flu virus
    D. Agent Smith

12. Unlike the US which has a laissez-faire economy that has an inbuilt creative destruction process for innovation, China's state-led system has a masterplan for guiding its net lap of economic development. The authorities have put in place a "Made in China 2025" blueprint and one of the features of this scheme is to integrate IoT with China's manufacturing sector. Is this statement true or false?

A. False
B. True

13. China is ambitiously building 500 smart cities all across its country. Is this statement true or false?

A. True
B. False

14. Data about Singapore is publicly available in the website Singstat.

A. False
B. True

15. Singapore opts for an open and transparent platform with global normative standards in building its own access to the IoT. Singapore is against the idea of silo-ed approach erected by tech giants and dominant players. Is this statement true or false?

A. True
B. False

16. In the sector of cybersecurity, adopting any IoT-enabled required corresponding acquisition and installation of relevant security measures to protect the integrity of those devices. This is also to protect the data contained within them. Is this statement true or false?

A. False
B. True

17. What does GovTech agency in Singapore stand for?

A. Singapore's Government Technology Agency (GovTech)
B. Government Technologists (GovTech)
C. Government Technical assistance (GovTech)
D. None of the above

18. Wifi stands for:

    A. Wireless internet access systems
    B. Why Find out systems
    C. Winner Fire All systems
    D. Wireless Fintech

19. Machine to machine communication is not entirely new, it has occurred in the manufacturing sector. They are mostly performing the function of breakdown alerts and maintenance indicators. They warn humans or other machines about the near end of life phases of smart devices and such pre-emptive measures can help to nip defective devices in the bud before they can do real damage to human users/consumers. Are these statements true or false?

    A. False
    B. True

20. The 1990s was an era of irrational exuberance on how the Internet represented freedom and democracy. But it soon dawned on users that the same tools to advocate convenience and openness can also be used to monitor individuals. Is this true or false?

    A. True
    B. False

Answer Bank

1. Answer is A.
2. Answer is B.
3. Answer is C.
4. Answer is A.
5. Answer is D.
6. Answer is C.
7. Answer is C.
8. Answer is A.
9. Answer is D.
10. Answer is D.
11. Answer is A.
12. Answer is B.
13. Answer is A.
14. Answer is B.
15. Answer is A.
16. Answer is B.
17. Answer is A.
18. Answer is A.
19. Answer is B.
20. Answer is A.

CHAPTER 15

Quiz 1: Rise of Smart Cities

1. In constructing smart cities, it may be useful for the technocratic planners to bear in mind that each city is unique and different. Therefore, any solution designed for urban problems must take into consideration the unique characteristics of every city. Is this statement true or false?

   A. True
   B. False

2. Which following item does not accurately describe Singapore's smart city strategy?

   A. A smart nation as well where people have "meaningful and fulfilled lives".
   B. Singapore's approach is inclusive and involves all stakeholders from the government to the private sector and the individuals.
   C. Singapore's philosophy in building smart cities is not sharing an iota of data with anyone else outside Singapore.
   D. Singapore's approach is known as the "whole of nation" approach.

3. What does "AV" stand for in the context of Industry 4.0 technologies?

   A. AVatar
   B. Autonomous Vehicles
   C. AVex Tracks
   D. AViator

© The Author(s) 2019
177
T. W. Lim, *Industrial Revolution 4.0, Tech Giants, and Digitized Societies,*
https://doi.org/10.1007/978-981-13-7470-8_15

4. In constructing smart cities, it may be useful for the technocratic planners to bear in mind that each city is unique and different. Therefore, any solution designed for urban problems must take into consideration the unique characteristics of every city. Is this useful advice dispensed for the construction of smart cities?

   A. Yes, for most parts.
   B. No, in absolute terms.

5. Singapore's approach in building smart cities is _____ and involves all stakeholders from the government to the private sector and the individuals, otherwise known as the "whole of nation" approach.

   A. exclusive
   B. closed door
   C. inclusive
   D. isolationist

6. In Singapore, all smart city stakeholders want to ensure e-payments are _____ and _____. Fill in the blanks.

   A. safe and secure
   B. unsafe and criminalized
   C. safe and insecure
   D. open and unsecured

7. In its smart city strategy, Singapore is not keen to follow the data-centric approach but rather prefer to make their data as usable and accessible to local communities and residents as far as possible. Is this statement true or false?

   A. True
   B. False

8. Singapore, as the ASEAN Chair in 2018, is proposing linking up smart cities within ASEAN. This was proposed in the 32nd ASEAN Summit meeting. Is this statement true or false?

   A. False
   B. True

9. Innovative solutions may empower SMEs to expand their business reach, in the context of Industry 4.0 and smart cities. What does "SMEs" stand for?

    A. SMall Enterprises
    B. Susceptible and Medium Sized Enterprises
    C. Small and Manned Enterprises
    D. Small and Medium Sized Enterprises

10. Cloud computing has become a popular option for companies as it facilitates access to data from all locations but placing large volumes of data in the cloud exposes those data to security issues. Staff members should also be trained in _____ so that their lines of communications and the contents of communications are safe and secure. Fill in the blank.

    A. non-traditional security
    B. unarmed combat
    C. cybersecurity
    D. futures and securities

11. Hong Kong is also keen to tap into technology to support its ageing population and _____ narrative. In mid-2017, Hong Kong started looking into the idea of "gerontechnology". Fill in the blank.

    A. euthanasia
    B. immortality
    C. proactive ageing
    D. active ageing

12. Human characteristics like _____ are now emphasized in human resource (HR) hiring. Which of the following options is not applicable?

    A. empathy
    B. creativity
    C. binary on–off switches
    D. leadership

13. Human characteristics like _____ are now emphasized in human resource (HR) hiring. Which of the following options is not applicable?

    A. listening
    B. moralizing
    C. soft communication skills
    D. absolute rationality with no emotive elements

14. Human characteristics like _____ are now emphasized in human resource (HR) hiring. Which of the following options is not applicable?

    A. teamwork and collaboration
    B. QR-coded facial recognition capabilities
    C. ethical thinking
    D. socializing

15. Human characteristics like _____ are now emphasized in human resource (HR) hiring. Which of the following options is not applicable?

    A. EQ or emotional quotient and intelligence
    B. problem-solving for other humans
    C. empathy
    D. direct interface with the internet without machines

16. In the age of Industry 4.0, learning will become a _____ journey as skills need constant refreshment and upgrading. Fill in the blank.

    A. lifelong
    B. one-off
    C. spiritual
    D. make-belief

17. Jobs reserved for humans will also become increasingly _____ and have less physical work in the long run. Fill in the blank.

    A. knowledge-based
    B. Tayloristic
    C. stop motion-based
    D. nasty, brutish and short

18. What does e-commerce stand for?

    A. Electricity based commerce
    B. Electronic commerce
    C. Empowerment commerce
    D. Entertainment commerce

19. _____ makes logistical delivery easier as deliverers, recipients and parcel senders are able to track the progress of the delivery online. Fill in the blank.

    A. Hot wave stamps
    B. Barcodes
    C. Hot iron stenciling
    D. Flux incapacitor

20. The advent of digital technologies has also created a _____ economy whereby large multinational companies (MNCs) have greater capabilities in implementing digital technologies while the small and medium sized sectors face greater difficulties. Fill in the blank.

    A. never the twain
    B. multilateral
    C. black market
    D. dual track

21. _____ programmes in Singapore may offer some form of training in this area and all individuals can spot courses on the menu that enhances their ability to tap into globalization. Fill in the blank.

    A. The Future of A.I.
    B. The Great Leap Forward
    C. Boston of the East
    D. SkillsFuture

22. The most pressing need in the developing economies is to provide digital infrastructure facilities for the population so that they are empowered to have access to the internet. Which of the following are considered some of the most vulnerable groups in this aspect? Choose the most appropriate response.

    A. minorities
    B. women
    C. physically disabled
    D. all of the above

23. The most pressing need in the developing economies is to provide digital infrastructure facilities for the population so that they are empowered to have access to the internet. Which of the following is not considered one of the most vulnerable groups in this aspect? Choose the most appropriate response.

   A. rural folks
   B. the poor
   C. minorities
   D. the super rich

24. In the UK, _____ is often cited as an example of British middle-class frustration with the European Union (EU) and migrants from former Eastern European states from taking their jobs, which is considered one of the most important British motivations to leave the European Union.

   A. Millenarian Revolt
   B. Brexit
   C. Boxer Rebellion
   D. Great Proletariat Cultural Revolution

25. In North America, the election of President Donald J. Trump, who is extremely popular with some elements of the US middle class (with the following typical profile: divorced, non-college educated white voters), was voted into power with an _____ policy. His administration plans to stem the flow of Mexican migrants to the US (even building a wall to carry this out) and encourage offshore American companies to return back to the homeland again. Fill in the blank.

   A. American Express
   B. Authoritarian First
   C. America First
   D. None of the above

26. Frustrations with globalization have encouraged the emergence of political _____ in the US and this trend is visible in the European Union (EU) as well. Fill in the blank.

   A. homogeneity
   B. uniformity
   C. obedience
   D. populism

27. The Chinese government has set up _____ to censor incoming information from the outside world and also to track and monitor messages sent and received within China itself. Fill in the blank.

    A. Great Firewall
    B. Invisible Forcefield
    C. Skynet
    D. Ellipsis

28. VPNs that can bypass the Firewall are banned in China, so are Google, Gmail, Facebook while WhatsApp was facing some intermittent blocking by the authorities. What are VPNs?

    A. Virtual Private Networks
    B. Very Personal Networks
    C. Vindictive Projection Networks
    D. Virtual Personal Networks

29. How many smart cities are being designed and planned for construction by the Indian national government?

    A. 150
    B. 100
    C. 10
    D. 1000

30. How many smart cities are found in China's vision for development?

    A. 600
    B. 1000
    C. 350
    D. 500

Answer Bank

1. The Answer is A.
2. The Answer is C.
3. The Answer is B.
4. The Answer is A.
5. The Answer is C.
6. The Answer is A.
7. The Answer is A.
8. The Answer is B.
9. The Answer is D.
10. The Answer is C.
11. The Answer is C.
12. The Answer is C.
13. The Answer is D.
14. The Answer is B.
15. The Answer is D.
16. The Answer is A.
17. The Answer is A.
18. The Answer is B.
19. The Answer is B.
20. The Answer is D.
21. The Answer is D.
22. The Answer is D.
23. The Answer is D.
24. The Answer is B.
25. The Answer is C.
26. The Answer is D.
27. The Answer is A.
28. The Answer is A.
29. The Answer is B.
30. The Answer is D.

CHAPTER 16

Quiz 1

Section A: Drawn from Chapter 5 (Conclusion)

1. Historically, one of the manufacturing jobs/functions in the US auto-making industry that was first replaced by robots was the vehicle body-painting assembly line. Is this statement true or false?

   A. True
   B. False

2. No job is considered sacred and many monotonous, standardized, repetitive or/and mechanical tasks can be replaced by machines. Automation will also exert pressure on workers' salaries, particularly the lower skilled jobs. Is this statement true or false?

   A. False
   B. True

3. Today's tech giants like Alibaba are even functioning like banks offering microloans. Tencent founded China's first WeBank on 18 January 2015 while, in the same year, Alibaba launched MYbank which offers financial services for customers in the rural areas. Is this true or false?

   A. True
   B. False

© The Author(s) 2019
T. W. Lim, *Industrial Revolution 4.0, Tech Giants, and Digitized Societies*,
https://doi.org/10.1007/978-981-13-7470-8_16

4. The platforms offered by US-based social media companies and other digital tech giants have extended the reach of small and medium sized enterprises (SMEs) globally. Social media platforms allow these businesses to market their products and services to a much wider global audience and consumer base. This wider reach has inspired some observers to nickname SMEs _____. Fill in the blank.

A. minitechs
B. small fries
C. micronationals
D. none of the above

5. ASEAN is trying to set up a network of smart cities. What does ASEAN stand for?

A. Alliance of South Asian Nations
B. Alliance of Southeast Asian Nations
C. Association of South Asian Nations
D. Association of Southeast Asian Nations

Section B: Drawn from Chapter 6
(Case Study 1 Japan Robotics)

6. According to the Ministry of Economy Trade and Industry (METI), the information technology (IT) industry in Japan is aggressively trying to hire more foreigners (including those from South Asia/India) as the industry is constrained by a deficit of 200,000 IT engineers, likely to expand four times to 800,000 by 2030. Is this statement true or false?

A. True
B. False

7. While Japanese population is ageing and shrinking, robot production is going up, with 340,000 as at 2017 and eventually growing to more than 3 million robots by 2025. Is this true or false?

A. True
B. False

8. The (HAL) and other robot exoskeletons help the elderly, women, farmers, caregivers and other jobs that need physical strength enhancement to do heavy lifting. What does HAL stand for?

   A. Handy Assistive Limb
   B. Hybrid Association Limb
   C. Hybrid Assistive Limb
   D. None of the above

9. The Hybrid Assistive Limb (HAL) and other robot exoskeletons help _____. Which of the following statement is NOT applicable to fill up the blank.

   A. the elderly, women, farmers, caregivers, and other jobs that need physical strength enhancement to do heavy lifting.
   B. alleviates pressure to the backbone and overall physical conditions.
   C. keep more elderly people in the job market by enhancing their strengths.
   D. to eliminate carbon-based lifeforms to make way for more powerful organisms.

10. Which of the following is NOT a typical use of robotic exoskeletons?

   A. Occupations like caregiver, farmers, logistics deliveries, nurses, and other strength-intensive jobs can make use of robotic exoskeletons to enhance human capabilities.
   B. Robotic exoskeletons can stave off retirement for a large number of silver generation citizens.
   C. Robotic exoskeletons keep elderly farmers working in the fields, making up for the hollowing out of Japan's rural areas due to younger Japanese migrating to the cities and prevent overdependence on imported food supplies. Elderly farmers and women can benefit from backbreaking work in Japan's agricultural areas and rice growing regions.
   D. Robotic exoskeletons can arm squadrons of human defenders fight against breaches in their hulls from invading armies sent by machine city.

11. Therapeutic robots like _____ which are built like infant seals can keep company with elderly and dementia patients and such robots help to replace human caregivers that are in short supply in Japan. Which of the following is the name of a popular therapeutic robot, that can fill in the blank?

    A. Paro
    B. Taro
    C. Cairo
    D. Kato

12. Which of the following function cannot be performed by Paro the therapeutic robot?

    A. Therapeutic robots like Paro which are built like infant seals can keep company with elderly and dementia patients and such robots help to replace human caregivers that are in short supply in Japan.
    B. Paro interacts with its human partners using seal-like cries and, when it is out of power, the robot seal is recharged with a contraption shaped like a baby pacifier.
    C. The design concept behind Paro is kawaii which is part of the cute industry in Japan, and such cute things can help regulate stress, anxiousness, pain/suffering and down mental states, according to the studies done by the team behind Paro.
    D. Paro can be hybridized with carbon-based living seal parts, making them part cyborg with living and non-living parts, so that they can be more lifelike in their interactions with humans.

13. What is the name of a more popular commercialized social robot from Japan?

    A. Sugar
    B. Pepper
    C. Salt
    D. Spices

14. Human–robot coexistence is easily implemented in Japan as the nativist religion Shinto attributes a soul to every object in the world, both living and non-living things. Therefore, even non-living things like robots are believed to possess a soul of their own. Is this statement true or false?

    A. True
    B. False

15. _____ is a well-known android scientist in Japan. He has created robotic clones of real people, including his own likeness, his daughter, a journalist with Eurasian heritage, etc. Fill in the blank with the name of a person who is generally regarded as the father or godfather (or at the very least a great figure) of android development in Japan.

    A. Dr. Hiroshi Ishiguro
    B. Dr. Tanaka Ishiguro
    C. Dr. Hiro Sato
    D. Dr. Hiro Tanaka

SECTION C: DRAWN FROM CHAPTER 7 (CASE STUDY 2)

16. For those left out of the digital revolution, there is advocacy and attention paid to augmenting provision of social services and encouraging volunteerism within society to take care of those individuals who have fallen behind in preparing and tapping into the digital economy. Disciplines like _____ and _____ are highlighted as career choices for caring about others, showing empathy to the needy and taking care of the less fortunate. Fill in the blanks.

    A. service learning and social work
    B. euthanasia and genetic selection of humans
    C. black ops and covert operations
    D. germalogical warfare and chemical warfare units

SECTION D: DRAWN FROM CHAPTER 8 (CASE STUDY 3)

17. Reputable international consulting company Deloitte reported that, out of 1000 smart cities projects underway globally, China makes up approximately 500 of them. Is this statement true or false?

    A. False
    B. True

18. What are some of the advantages in having local companies develop solutions for smart cities in China? Choose the most appropriate response.

    A. Local companies that are originally located in the smart cities are most well-placed to recognize local features and develop solutions for them. There is a sense of embedded-ness when local companies are heavily involved in the projects.

B. When the local companies are successful in one Chinese city, they can effectively market their track record and past achievements to other Chinese cities, given that China is such a large market and represent the largest national network of smart cities in the world.

C. With strong relationships forged in a particular smart city among its local companies working together to provide solutions to the city's development, these companies may cooperate and export the same jointly developed solutions to other economies.

D. All of the above.

19. Singapore-led aspirations to link up all smart cities in the region. Which region is this?

A. The NAFTA region
B. The SAARC region
C. The ASEAN region
D. The African Union region

20. China has certain pre-existing advantages over other countries with their high mobile penetration, large existing consumer base for Chinese tech giants like _____. Which of the options below is not a suitable one.

A. Tencent (which owns WeChat)
B. Alibaba (including the cashless payment system Alipay)
C. Baidu
D. Facebook

21. _____ appears to be a milestone date in the formation of Chinese smart cities as the country designated the target number of smart cities construction at 500 beginning that year. Fill in the blank.

A. 2015
B. 2016
C. 2017
D. 2018

22. During the 32nd _____ (25 April 2018–26 April 2018), the chair of the summit Singapore initiated the idea of linking up a network of smart cities in Southeast Asia. Fill in the blank.

A. Boao summit
B. ASEAN Summit
C. Trump-Kim Summit
D. Davos

23. China is strong in indigenous technologies when it comes to hardware (after all, it is nicknamed the world's factory) but it is comparatively weaker in software with only 30% of its start-ups software-based compared to 90% in Silicon Valley. Is this statement true or false?

A. True
B. False

Answer Bank

1. The answer is A.
2. The answer is B.
3. The answer is A.
4. The answer is C.
5. The answer is D.
6. The answer is A.
7. The answer is A.
8. The answer is C.
9. The answer is D.
10. The answer is D.
11. The answer is A.
12. The answer is D.
13. The answer is B.
14. The answer is A.
15. The answer is A.
16. The answer is A.
17. The answer is B.
18. The answer is D.
19. The answer is C.
20. The answer is D.
21. The answer is C.
22. The answer is B.
23. The answer is A.

CHAPTER 17

Quiz 1

Section A: Drawn from Chapter 9 (Case Study 4)

1. Japan is leading in terms of robotic technologies to assist with the elderly while Hong Kong is keen to promote lifelong learning even in skills that can augment and enhance the elderly's financial well-being and investment savviness. Is this statement true or false?

   A. True
   B. False

2. In mid-2017, Hong Kong started looking into the idea of "_____" defined as the "use of technology to meet the needs of the elderly". Fill in the blank.

   A. silver surfer
   B. elderly X-men
   C. gerontechnology
   D. net avengers

3. In the world of robotic suits that enhance human strength, the _____ Corporation built Japan's Hybrid Assistive Limb (HAL) robotic exoskeleton. Fill in the blank.

   A. Skynet
   B. Cyberdyne
   C. Starbucks
   D. Umbrella

SECTION B: DRAWN FROM CHAPTER 10 (CASE STUDY 5)

4. What is NOT a possible factor that contributed to China's transition to a cashless society?

   A. China made the transition to a cashless society easily leapfrogging over the credit card phase.
   B. Credit card did not take off in China as the domestic banking system was relatively less developed compared to those of the developed economies. In fact, debit cards are more common than credit cards in China. China's first credit card only arrived in 1985.
   C. As a latecomer to the market-based capitalist system, China's conspicuous consumption was also a relatively recent phenomenon.
   D. China was a pioneer in free market capitalism since the end of WWII. Its financial system is so advanced that it did not require credit cards for payment at all. They developed smartphone-based cashless payment system in the 1960s but were not allowed to export this system overseas.

5. The scanning process is based mainly on a _____ designed by Japan's Denso Corp in the 1990s for storing more data than the traditional bar code. _____ was adapted by China's cashless mobile payment systems for electronic transactions. Fill in the blanks.

   A. SR code
   B. QR code
   C. QC code
   D. SD code

6. What does QR code stand for?

   A. Quality Rechecked code
   B. Question for Reasoning code
   C. Quick Response Code
   D. Quality Reassurance code

7. Which of the following has become a payment mechanism of choice in China?

   A. WeChat Pay
   B. Chatting Woai
   C. Fenqing
   D. Chat Paywave

8. Cashless payment mechanisms are much faster than conventional payment schemes. It takes only _____ to swipe and scan codes, much faster than taking out coins and paper notes. Fill in the blank.

   A. seconds
   B. minutes
   C. hours
   D. days

9. Which of the following is NOT a possible reason for the implementation of cashless payments in China?

   A. Convenience. It takes only seconds to swipe and scan codes, much faster than taking out coins and paper notes.
   B. Safety. Carrying vast amounts of cash is somewhat dangerous in case of robbery and/or forgetfulness in leaving the cash at a public space.
   C. Accountability. Electronic cash also means that the state is able to track monetary flows and stop transactions if necessary. This will make it difficult for money laundering or unaccountability of cash inflows to occur. (Cash on the other hand is more difficult to track and accounted for.) These features can assist the Chinese Xi Jinping administration with its campaign to end corruption.
   D. To end the use of money itself and switch to a utopian society where a person is judged by her/his moral merit rather than the amount of money she/he makes.

10. The PayPal system was the first major system to allow Palm Pilot hardware to transfer funds electronically in the 1990s. True or false?

    A. False
    B. True

11. In China, the cashless mobile payment platforms have become de facto banks, giving out small loans and microfinancing to small and medium sized enterprises (SMEs) on top of individuals. Is this true or false?

    A. False
    B. True

12. Alibaba is an online retailer that is China's answer to Amazon.com while Tencent is a social messaging service that runs WeChat (China's answer to Facebook and WhatsApp). Is this true or false?

   A. True
   B. False

13. Alibaba's Youku Tudou video sites feature electronic advertisements based on individual behavioural data analytics, much like the individually tailored ads that appear on Google and Gmail platforms. Is this true or false?

   A. False
   B. True

14. Tencent latched onto the traditional Lunar New Year festivities and created an electronic version of the _____ for distribution to friends and families. Tencent allows users to insert a sum of monetary credits for this purpose.

   A. yashuiqian (ancient copper coins)
   B. cow shells (ancient shells used as currency denomination)
   C. fapiao (communist-era ration tickets)
   D. hongbao (ang pows as they are known in Singapore or "red packets" when translated into English)

15. While mobile payments are behind mainland China, the Chief Executive of the Hong Kong Monetary Authority Norman Chan Tak-lam released the statistic that there are 14 million _____ transactions every day. What is the name of Hong Kong's cashless payment mechanism? Fill in the blank.

   A. Hydra
   B. Decepticon
   C. Octopus
   D. Squid

16. What is the Chinese equivalence of the central bank? This institution monitors currency movements and flows.

   A. People's National Banker (PNB)
   B. People's Financial Institution (PFI)
   C. People's Bank of China (PBOC)
   D. People's Banking Centre (PBC)

17. Cashless payment mechanisms have the potential to help governments track money laundering and control corruption while creating new jobs for the economy. True or false?

   A. False
   B. True

SECTION C: DRAWN FROM CHAPTER 11 (CASE STUDY 6)

18. Multinationals are to MNCs as _____ are to SMEs. Fill in the blank.

   A. mininationals
   B. business federations
   C. trade unions
   D. micronationals

19. TripAdvisor has user-generated content that allows users to provide feedback on the places that they have visited on their overseas and out-of-town trips. Is this true or false?

   A. True
   B. False

20. Uber is an app that facilitates ride-sharing and cab-calling services. True or false?

   A. True
   B. False

Answer Bank

1. The answer is A.
2. The answer is C.
3. The answer is B
4. The answer is D.
5. The answer is B.
6. The answer is C.
7. The answer is A.
8. The answer is A.
9. The answer is D.
10. The answer is B.
11. The answer is B.
12. The answer is A.
13. The answer is B.
14. The answer is D.
15. The answer is C.
16. The answer is C.
17. The answer is B.
18. The answer is D.
19. The answer is A.
20. The answer is A.

INDEX

CPSIA information can be obtained
at www.ICGtesting.com
Printed in the USA
LVHW080100100519
617270LV00002B/64/P